DESIGN THINKING
FOR THE GREATER GOOD

DESIGN THINKING FOR THE GREATER GOOD

Innovation in the Social Sector

JEANNE LIEDTKA, RANDY SALZMAN, AND DAISY AZER

Columbia Business School
Publishing

Columbia University Press
Publishers Since 1893
New York   Chichester, West Sussex
cup.columbia.edu

Source of the LUMA Institute planning tools in chapter 6: *Innovating for People: Human-Centered Design Planning Cards*. Copyright © by LUMA Institute LLC. Reprinted by permission of LUMA Institute LLC.

Library of Congress Cataloging-in-Publication Data
Names: Liedtka, Jeanne, author. | Azer, Daisy, author. | Salzman, Randy, author.
Title: Design thinking for the greater good / Jeanne Liedtka, Daisy Azer, and Randy Salzman.
Description: New York : Columbia University Press, [2017] | Series: Columbia business school publishing | Includes bibliographical references.
Identifiers: LCCN 2017008777 | ISBN 9780231179522 (cloth : alk. paper) | ISBN 9780231545853 (e-book)
Subjects: LCSH: Human services—Management. | Public administration—Decision making. | Management science. | Social responsibility of business.
Classification: LCC HV40 .L49 2017 | DDC 361.0068/4—dc23
LC record available at https://lccn.loc.gov/2017008777

CONTENTS

ACKNOWLEDGMENTS

This book would not have been possible without the assistance and support of the people who shared their stories with us, and we deeply appreciate their generosity and candor. Their honest recounting of their experiences, complete with the ups and downs involved in tackling tough problems, is just more evidence of the courage we saw them exhibit throughout their stories.

Despite heavy workloads, they took significant amounts of time to give us detailed accounts of their work, shared their project artifacts, and contributed the rich detail found in the stories in this book—all so that they could offer examples so that others could follow in their footsteps. Research projects like the one just completed can span years, and we are grateful for those who stuck with us until the end and to those who picked up where others left off.

It is also impossible to thank the dozens of thinkers we spoke with about stories that did not end up in this book, for various reasons. Their insights and thoughts both led us to other sources and impacted the direction of the writing. Their efforts to utilize design thinking to address society's problems were often just as inspiring as the stories we chose to include in this limited volume.

Our deepest thanks also go out to Stephen Wesley and Myles Thompson at Columbia, and to our editor Karin Horler, whose wise advice and editing make us sound so much better than we deserve. And we thank the Darden School of Business and the Batten Institute for Entrepreneurship and Innovation, without whose support this book, and the research behind it, would never have happened.

Finally, we thank all of you who practice collaborative creativity in the social sector. You are making our world better, and we appreciate it immensely.

From Jeanne

First, a profound thank-you to my coauthors, Salz (my partner and chief inspiration in life as well as design thinking) and Daisy, both wonderful colleagues who participated from the earliest stages of the research. To my wonderful children and their wonderful children and partners and all my beloved Loudkas, who bring such joy to my life every single day. To my colleagues at Darden who have been a source of inspiration, learning, and encouragement for the past twenty-five years, most especially the LOCAs. I consider myself blessed to have found a home at such an extraordinary place, amid such extraordinary people. And I thank my parents, who always believed in me and who taught me to believe in myself. Finally, I want to thank my private design posse—the wonderful cast of characters who know so much more about design and innovation than I and who have taught me everything I know and have opened doors that made this work possible—Rachel Brozenske, Ed Hess, Karen Hold, Josh Marcuse, Arianne Miller, and Tim Ogilvie.

From Daisy

Collaborating across distance and time is neither simple nor straightforward, but it is easier and significantly more enjoyable with the right partners! Humor, of course, helped; it is always a balm.

To Jeanne, for the tremendous opportunity to work on this book and in design thinking. It has been educational and inspirational above and beyond design thinking, and I am immeasurably grateful. To Salz, for always being forthright, an admirable quality, particularly as it comes with a charming Southern accent. There is nothing better than an unvarnished opinion with a view to making things better, and a willingness to see differently. To all those who are practicing design thinking and engaging in the conversation it sparks, thank you for sharing your experiences, wisdom, and questions—and for making the world a better place, and me a better design thinker. I dedicate the work to my father, Samir, a businessman who was *both* kindhearted *and* prescient with his innovative ideas and business models, and my mother, Nadia, who has spent her entire life fighting for the greater good.

From Salz

While I, Randy Salzman, will always be grateful for the love of my children and family, I must single out the driving force in both my life and this book—Jeanne Liedtka. She, primarily, devised the splendid four-question, fifteen-step model of design thinking that makes teaching collaborative creativity effective, and she is, and I hope will continue to be, an inspiration to many, especially me, because she is a "George" who has successfully taught herself to be a "Geoffrey." I must also thank my other coauthor, Daisy Azer, whose calm demeanor on several occasions, and persistent questioning on others, drove rational thinking back into the occasionally irrational reality of three people—two of them married and both too headstrong for their own good—attempting to write three hundred coherent pages. Daisy also deserves thanks for the extreme effort she put into ensuring the illustrations, graphics, and photographs are readable and effective, not to mention legal. Thank you both.

PART I

Why Design Thinking?

CHAPTER ONE

Catalyzing a Conversation for Change

The Case of the Smoking Cucumber Water

The article in the *Washington Post* seemed innocuous. It described high hopes for the 2012 opening of the new innovation lab at the US Office of Personnel Management (OPM), the agency charged with overseeing the education and development of all federal employees. Located in the subbasement of OPM's DC headquarters, the Lab@OPM was hardly sumptuous, occupying just three thousand square feet. Renovation costs barely topped $1 million (not enough to even register as a decimal point of OPM's $2 billion budget that year), and almost half of that was to remove the asbestos in the ceiling. Total headcount was six employees.

But the article's passing reference to a pitcher of cucumber water apparently attracted the unwanted attention of the House of Representatives' Committee on Oversight and Government Reform, which formally requested that the Government Accountability Office (GAO) conduct a full audit of the year-old lab. For the next nine months, lab staff spent much of their time talking to auditors rather than encouraging innovation. Eventually, the GAO audit produced a largely favorable review of the work of the lab, but the only widely publicized finding was the GAO's criticism that the lab had failed to implement a "rigorous evaluation framework" in its less than eighteen months of existence. The *Post*'s "Federal Insider" columnist reported this while ridiculing the "Silicon Valley buzzwords" behind the vision of the "so-called innovation lab."

Amid the hoopla, it was overlooked that a lab staff member had, in fact, purchased that cucumber with his own money at Safeway and had cut it up himself to add to the tap water in the pitcher. And in the background was general frustration with the OPM in other areas, like retirement claims processing and security clearances. "It gave them their shot at us," one lab staffer commented ruefully.

Doesn't that just say it all about the challenges of doing innovation work in the social sector, of trying to design for the greater good?

Good work by dedicated people gets caught in the cross fire of politics and media, the right intentions and their complex reality sidelined by a combination of circumstances that few in the business sector would ever deal with.

The cucumber water story has a surprisingly happy ending. The GAO accountants in charge of the audit quickly grasped the challenging nature of the Lab@OPM's work and were impressed. The extraordinarily resilient lab staff soldiered on to make significant contributions to the state of innovation in the federal government, which they continue today.

But when you talk to government innovators in DC, you can still sense a kind of posttraumatic stress syndrome, traceable back to that cucumber water, just below the surface. We have no way to know how many potential innovations in Washington have been lost to the fear of audits or public criticism.

We live in a world of increasingly *wicked* problems. Nowhere are they more evident than in the social sector. Whether we look at private or public efforts, across sectors like health care, education, and transportation, at the global or local level, organizations of all sizes and stripes struggle with thorny issues:

- stakeholders who can't even agree on the problem, much less the solution;
- employees who are reluctant to change behaviors and take risks, who are often rewarded for compliance rather than performance;
- decision makers who have too much data, but little of the kind they need;
- leaders who are more likely to have short tenures and whose every move is scrutinized by funders, politicians, bureaucrats, and the media; and
- users of their services—students, patients, customers, citizens—whose expectations are sometimes rising as fast as resources to meet them are declining.

And to face this scenario, would-be innovators are armed with an outmoded tool kit premised on predictability and control, optimized for solving tame problems, in a world that offers fewer and fewer of them. Our goal in this book is to offer a new set of tools—ones better suited to the complexity and messiness of the challenges that social sector innovators face. Standing still is no more an option in the social sector than it is in the for-profit world. Innovation is an imperative.

THE LAB@OPM

The Lab@OPM has gone on to become a driving force behind innovation in the US federal government. We think of it as patient one in the viral spread of design thinking in DC—it is where innovators caught the fever for human-centered work. Scratch the surface of almost any interesting innovation success story across a wide variety of government agencies in Washington and you'll find the lab's guiding hand. The seed for the lab was planted in 2009, when President Obama appointed John Berry as director of the OPM and gave him the mandate to "make government cool again." As the government's chief "people person," Berry was responsible for recruiting and developing almost 2 million federal employees. Berry brought a young Stanford grad, Matt Collier, on board to help in this effort.

In 2010, they took a tour of Silicon Valley, visiting the usual haunts—Google, Facebook, IDEO, and Kaiser Permanente's Garfield Innovation Center. All of these companies had carefully architected their work spaces to support and encourage collaboration. "They were the kind of places that made you want to come to work," Matt observed. When the OPM team thought about what they wanted to bring back to the East Coast, the notion of space and the IDEO-inspired design thinking approach were at the top of their list. As he explained:

> We didn't want to create just another meeting space. It was more about what we wanted to do in the space—to try to build a design thinking practice, to build a little IDEO inside of government, to bring that capability in-house. It was set up like a teaching hospital: we will do some teaching, but we will also do some application.

The lab staff selected LUMA Institute as their partner. They were drawn to LUMA's reputation as an education company whose goal was to build capacity in human-centered design for individuals, teams, and organizations.

The lab has survived—in fact thrived—despite the GAO audit during its infancy and the change of senior leaders at OPM. Matt has a theory why:

> It began as a political appointee–driven initiative that was rightly and appropriately embedded into the bureaucracy. The reins were handed over to the senior career leadership—not in a burdensome way but in a way where they wanted those reins. And everyday employees within the lab's orbit were equipped and, indeed, expected to apply design thinking in service of their work and that of their colleagues. Because of that, the lab has survived. That was a huge success. Had we not given leadership over to career executives, the lab and all of the design thinking activities that went along with it could have easily gone by the wayside.

In facing challenges both obviously large (fighting hunger and poverty, encouraging sustainability) and seemingly smaller (getting invoices paid on time, increasing blood donations, decreasing hospital patient stays), social sector innovators are deciding that design thinking has the potential to bring something new to the conversation. They are bringing together people who want to solve a tough problem—not hold another meeting—in a world where forming a committee can be seen to count as action.

Design thinking is being used today in organizations as diverse as charitable foundations, social innovation start-ups, global corporations, national governments, and elementary schools. It has been adopted by entrepreneurs, corporate executives, city managers, and kindergarten teachers alike. In just a small sample of the stories we will discuss in this book, we see it helping impoverished farmers adopt new practices in Mexico, keeping at-risk California teenagers in school, reducing the frequency of mental health emergencies in Australia, and helping manufacturers and government regulators in Washington find common ground on medical device standards. Across these vastly different problems and sectors, design thinking provides a common thread. Maybe we could even call it a movement.

The shift under way seems to us, in fact, much like the one that created the quality movement. In the same way that the arrival of Total Quality Management (TQM) revolutionized the way organizations thought about quality, design thinking has the potential to revolutionize the way we think about and practice innovation.

Let's take a quick look at the quality parallel. TQM had a transformational impact and drove a paradigm shift (not a term to be used lightly) about quality, from the old quality assurance mindset (scholars call this Quality I) to a completely different conception of

WHAT IS DESIGN THINKING?

Design thinking is a problem-solving approach with a unique set of qualities: it is human centered, possibility driven, option focused, and iterative.

Human centered is always where we start—with real people, not demographic segments. Design thinking emphasizes the importance of deep exploration into the lives and problems of the people whose lives we want to improve *before* we start generating solutions. It uses market research methodologies that are qualitative and empathetic. It is enthusiastic about the potential to reframe our definition of the problem and engage stakeholders in co-creation.

Design thinking is also *possibility driven*. We ask the question "What if anything were possible?" as we begin to create ideas. We focus on generating *multiple options* and avoid putting all our eggs in one particular solution basket. Because we are guessing about our stakeholders' needs and wants, we also expect to be wrong sometimes. So we want to put multiple irons in the fire and let our stakeholders tell us which work for them. We want to manage a *portfolio* of new ideas.

Finally, the process is *iterative*. It conducts cycles of real-world experiments to refine ideas, rather than running analyses using historical data. We don't expect to get it right the first time—we expect to iterate our way to success.

what quality meant and whose job it was (Quality II). In Quality I, quality was seen as the domain of a small group of experts. In Quality II, quality became everybody's job, and TQM made that possible by providing a language and tool kit for solving quality problems, which everybody could learn. TQM *democratized* quality.

That same kind of revolutionary shift is under way today in innovation. Innovation I, the old paradigm, looks a lot like quality assurance. It is isolated in experts and senior leaders, decoupled from the everyday work of the organization. In Innovation I, innovation is about big breakthroughs done by special people. Design in the Innovation I world is mostly about aesthetics or technology.

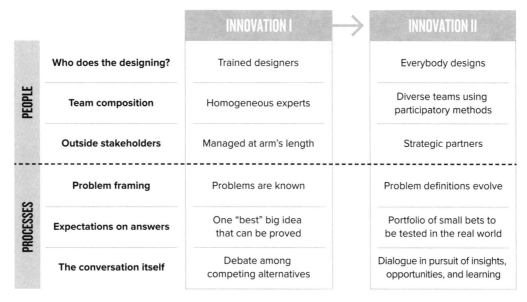

		INNOVATION I	INNOVATION II
PEOPLE	Who does the designing?	Trained designers	Everybody designs
	Team composition	Homogeneous experts	Diverse teams using participatory methods
	Outside stakeholders	Managed at arm's length	Strategic partners
PROCESSES	Problem framing	Problems are known	Problem definitions evolve
	Expectations on answers	One "best" big idea that can be proved	Portfolio of small bets to be tested in the real world
	The conversation itself	Debate among competing alternatives	Dialogue in pursuit of insights, opportunities, and learning

The shift from Innovation I to Innovation II.

We are seeing the emergence of Innovation II, the democratizing of innovation. In this world, we are all responsible for innovation. Even the term itself has a new meaning. Innovation isn't only—or even mostly—about big breakthroughs; it is about improving value for the stakeholders we serve. And everybody in an organization has a role to play. It is not that we no longer care about big, disruptive innovations or that we don't still need expert innovators and designers—it is just that we acknowledge two truths: first, it is often impossible to tell early in the life of an innovation just how big or small it will someday be; and, second, many small things can add up to something big.

As Innovation II emerges, design thinking provides a common language and problem-solving methodology (as TQM did in quality) that everyone can use to help their organization more effectively accomplish key strategic objectives, whether those objectives involve traditional business outcomes like profitability and competitive advantage or social outcomes like reducing poverty or creating jobs. As organizations develop this organization-wide capability for innovation, they will enhance their ability to achieve their objectives by generating more innovative and effective outcomes and processes that create better value for the stakeholders they serve and that make the organizations more effective in meeting their missions.

Design thinking makes Innovation II possible by encouraging distinct shifts in mindsets and behaviors. These shifts impact the individuals, teams, and extended group of stakeholders who do the designing, the way in which they identify problems and seek solutions, and the basic nature of the conversation itself. It also involves changes in the organizational context to facilitate such work at the individual and team levels.

In the remainder of part 1 of this book, we provide an overview of what such a change looks like and how it impacts the behavior of the specific people involved. In part 2, we share ten stories from a broad cross section of organizations, which allows us to look in depth at the different roles design thinking can play. Part 3 contains a detailed, step-by-step walk through our own design thinking methodology, illustrated with a final story about a group of educators attempting their first project, which aims to provide a blueprint of how the complete end-to-end process looks in practice. The book concludes with some thoughts about how to build an organizational infrastructure to better support the democratizing of innovation.

As we get started, we first want to talk at a more strategic level about the differences we observe in Innovation I versus Innovation II organizations and why they matter. In the remainder of the book, we will look at how these new Innovation II mindsets and behaviors play out in innovation projects led by real people in real organizations.

It all starts with who does the innovating.

Who Gets to Innovate? Engaging New Voices

The most obvious marker of the transition to an Innovation II world is the question of *who* is invited to innovate—in other words, who designs? In Innovation I, innovation and design are the domain of experts, policy makers, planners, and senior leaders. Everyone else is expected to step away. This perspective was vividly illustrated by a comment made to us by the chief design officer of a large global corporation, who suggested that encouraging nondesigners to practice design thinking was like encouraging those without a medical license to practice medicine.

In Innovation II, the search for opportunities to innovate is everybody's job, so *everybody* designs. Here, design is not primarily about the design of products or even user experiences; instead, design thinking is seen as a problem-solving process appropriate for use by a wide variety of people. Design tools like *jobs to be done*, *journey mapping*, *visualization*, and *prototyping* become as much a part of the manager's tool kit as Excel spreadsheets, as much a part of a teacher's tool kit as lesson plans, and as much a part of a nurse's tool kit as a stethoscope. Many of the most compelling stories in this book illustrate the power of inviting a broader and more diverse set of people into the design process and demonstrate how design thinking can be used to provide a common language, method, and tool kit to make such widespread participation efficient and scalable.

But the role of individuals isn't the only thing that changes in the evolution from Innovation I to Innovation II. The composition of the teams driving innovation changes as well. When a group of faculty meets in isolation to design a new curriculum, you are witnessing the Innovation I end of design. These homogeneous teams of "experts" consist of people who share the same functional experience and outlook and, as a result, the same mental models. This homogeneity has the advantage of reducing friction and speeding decision making, but often at the cost of more creative solutions.

As we move toward Innovation II, a more diverse set of voices is included. In the early stages, this inclusion often takes the form of ethnographic research rather than actual participation. Even if the room is still full of engineers, teachers, or health care professionals, they are now bringing data in from people with different perspectives.

The role of external stakeholders also starts to shift in the path from Innovation I to Innovation II. Echoing how suppliers were treated in Quality I, in the world of Innovation I, knowledge is proprietary and relationships are instrumental: citizens are segmented by how they vote, students are vessels to be taught, patients are bodies to be healed, and subcontractors are members of the supply chain—all elements of an organization's ecosystem that must be *managed*, kept at arm's length, and informed on a need-to-know basis.

Relationships differ in Innovation II, and co-creation and open innovation play an important role. Trusted partners are engaged. The Innovation II organization seeks strategic allies outside of its normal orbit. It seeks partners with similar intentions, who bring missing competencies to achieve a shared vision. In these partners, it seeks interests that align and capabilities that are complementary. Such external partners represent new possibilities of inventing together, rather than constraints to be managed.

How Do They Innovate? Changing the Conversation

As the capability for innovation spreads across the organization and its ecosystem, *how* the organization designs changes as well. The nature of the innovation *conversation* itself begins to shift, influencing both the definition of problems and opportunities at the outset and the differing expectations for the kinds of answers that emerge at the end of the process.

We first notice the difference in the conversation around framing the problem. In Innovation I, defining the problem is rarely seen as part of the challenge, nor is the obvious definition questioned as a starting point. Problems are treated as given, as *known*. The focus moves quickly to the more relevant, action-oriented issue: how to solve them.

But, much as the search for root cause became central in Quality II, attention to careful definition of a problem is seen as critical in Innovation II. Decision makers begin the process with less confidence in the correctness of their initial problem definition. The definition of the problem is a hypothesis to be tested, as are its solutions. And for effective problem framing, local intelligence is almost always critical. We will see, in many of the stories that follow, that breakthroughs come with the redefinition of the problem itself.

As we turn to the solution space, it too will look different in Innovation II. We employ design thinking in the first place because we want better answers to our problems. But the changes we observe in the answers in Innovation II organizations go well beyond enhanced creativity. Perhaps most striking is the belief about *how many* answers we need to work with. In the Innovation I world, decision makers really do believe that one "best" answer exists. In traditional economics, that would be the equilibrium point, the magical intersection of supply and demand. Decision makers in Innovation I even believe that they can "prove" that the answer is the correct one right at the start of the process.

But even economists (the last academics on record who truly believe people are rational actors) are abandoning the notion that one best equilibrium point exists in today's complex social systems, where the interactions are too complicated to predict cause and effect and where even small changes in initial conditions can yield massive changes in outcomes (the famous butterfly effect). Accordingly, in Innovation II, the search is for "better" rather than "best." Solutions are seen as man-made inventions rather than eternal truths. Attempts to demonstrate the superiority of any single solution before its implementation give way to a preference for optionality. Multiple solutions are moved into testing because decision makers distrust their ability to predict success and believe that numerous answers are possible—and desirable. We really won't know what works until we try it. In our stories, success results from the energy that implementers bring to particular solutions that emerge during the process. It is expected to take multiple iterations of testing and refining and to be more a result of learning than of getting it right the first time.

In the absence of confidence in the ability to predict winners and losers, the size and scope of the ideas considered worth pursuing change as well. We have entered the land of "small bets" and "fail fast," terms we often hear these days. But these are more than just Silicon Valley platitudes; they reflect the reality of designing effectively and efficiently in complex environments with high uncertainty. Instead of big ideas scaled quickly, basic logic tells us to start small and defer scaling any one solution until its underlying assumptions have been thoroughly vetted. It is not that Innovation II–minded organizations want ideas to *stay* small; they just believe in *starting* small.

But nowhere is the shift between Innovation I and Innovation II in the organizations we have studied more striking than in the innovation conversation itself. In Innovation I, innovation usually *begins* with solution identification, as we talked about earlier. The problem with beginning here, in a complex world with diverse stakeholders, is far more serious than just missing a few creative alternatives. It colors the entire dynamic of how members of the conversation interact with each other. Because participants tend to bring solutions from their own worldviews into the conversations, it sets up immediate debates among alternatives, with advocates for competing ideas each marshaling their own supporting evidence. The definition of the problem to start with, the alignment on assumptions, and even the generation of the ideas themselves are taken almost for granted. The emphasis is on evaluation and selection. And if participants bring the kind of diversity to the conversation that we have said leads to more creativity in *theory*, this same diversity of worldviews often will drag them down a path of conflict in *reality*.

In Innovation II, the focus is on developing previously unseen *possibilities* rather than starting with existing identifiable options. A significant investment is made in the exploration of existing conditions as a precondition to the generation of ideas; the extensive use of ethnography is meant to make the idea generation process more user driven and data driven. In the design thinking methodology, the pursuit of *insights* precedes the pursuit of solutions. Insights about the needs of those we are designing for— and the subsequent design criteria these insights spawn—are the heart of user-driven idea generation.

The only way to turn theoretical diversity into actual creativity is to change the nature of the conversation itself to incorporate an increasing role for dialogue as well as debate, for inquiry as well as advocacy. We need to learn to listen to understand rather than to argue, to listen for possibilities rather than for weaknesses. Design thinking's tools for collaborative problem solving can assist in the search for higher-order solutions by offering a structured process in which that dialogue and inquiry occurs, and where divergent views are surfaced and explored, rather than relying solely on the skills of the leader of the conversation.

Where Do They Innovate? Changing the Organization

To move from Innovation I to II, it is not only people and processes that have to change. Organizations will need to create a context in which doing things differently makes sense and feels safe. They will need to acknowledge the reality of messy problems, cultivate variance rather than driving it out, and help people choose action over inaction.

Acknowledging the Reality of Messy Problems

Among the qualities of Innovation I organizations that stymie the shift to Innovation II, none is more obvious in our research than discomfort with ambiguity and messiness. Innovation II requires a willingness to wallow in the data—to struggle with ambiguous problem definitions, search for better insights, and sometimes get it wrong. Design thinking offers a structured process and tools that acknowledge this reality. In fact, a prime source of design thinking's distinctive contribution, under conditions of uncertainty, is its refusal to presume that clarity exists when ambiguity is tangible, to tidy up when

CREATING A BIAS FOR ACTION

David Edinger, the city of Denver's chief performance officer, works with the support of Mayor Michael Hancock to battle the "cost of hesitation," as he calls it: the tendency of staff to fall back onto what they are used to, "their habit of compliance, not performance." The city of Denver launched its Peak Academy, an initiative to create an action bias at every level of the organization, in 2011. The academy offers training in innovation and Lean methodologies for interested employees, asking in return only that they identify and actually try something specific to improve performance in their work areas. Peak is not asking for ideas; it is *requiring action.* Denver's assurance that no employee will lose a job over efficiency gains provides staff with the emotional security to risk creativity.

After seeing the successful results in Human Services—food stamp processing time decreased from sixteen days to overnight, with no layoffs involved—other employees began to take notice. "We never advise employees to slow down," David says. "We measure success by the number of innovations that occur, even saving nine cents in paper clips. But each team has to begin iterating *something*." Reviews at thirty, sixty, and ninety days lead to better performance or to abandonment of the new concept. Either outcome is acceptable. At any point, the employees who designed the innovation are completely free to veto their own project.

"We want the employee to take a chance, and we don't care if it results in anything, or even if it's very small," David explained. "Just doing what I did yesterday has a very strong gravitational pull to it. Unless there's someone near them, to inspire, it's very easy to fall back into daily work mode and never actually make the jump to continuous improvement. We reinforce the notion that everyone is capable of innovating."

messiness is what reality offers, or to pursue an illusory efficiency based on measures of things easily counted. Design thinking insists on recognizing the likelihood of failure, which can only be reduced, not eliminated. Many design thinking tools and steps, we have noted, address how to manage and minimize risk. Challenging organizational norms can be unsettling in mature organizations that expect perfection and fear chaos. The need for clarity and closure is embedded in most organizations, but to move toward an Innovation II operation, they must reward the courage to step into messiness, and give people the tools to do so intelligently.

Cultivating Variance

Mature organizations are designed for control and predictability; their aim is usually to standardize and drive out variance. Yet innovation requires willingly inducing variance and tolerating the ambiguity, lack of control, and seeming inefficiency that result. Variance may be the mother of waste, as W. Edwards Deming noted, but it is also the mother of invention. Cultivating variance on the design *team* helps us bring a more creative perspective to problem definition, get more insights out of our research, and uncover solid design criteria. Cultivating variance in our design *solutions* fosters experimentation and gives staff the ability to place small bets fast and to iterate from the resulting learning. This level of ambiguity—and the attendant fear of the chaos of too many opinions—can be profoundly unsettling in traditional bureaucratic settings.

Design thinking's role is to reduce this discomfort and create confidence that increasing diversity in the discussion will translate into better solutions.

Helping Staff Choose Action

This need for order and predictability is not just organizational; it is also deeply embedded in many human individual psyches. Psychologists have demonstrated that many of the choices we make are driven primarily by a fear of making mistakes; thus, we prefer inaction to action when any choice risks failure (more on this in chapter 2). In the face of this normal human response, significant psychological safety is necessary to encourage individuals to choose action over inaction. Making it safe to take action in the face of uncertainty requires senior leaders' support. Even in organizations where senior leadership is committed to creating a culture that tolerates mistakes and learns through iteration, many employees will find the change difficult.

As the appetite for the design thinking tool kit and methodology spreads, the challenge for the organization shifts from encouraging and enabling people to try it to *scaling* it. In order for everyone to design, everyone needs to achieve literacy in design thinking, a significant challenge for people raised in an analytic world. But scaling involves more than providing training. It requires the development of other structures and resources: decision autonomy to conduct experiments, access to stakeholders for study and co-creation, and a culture willing to manage risk instead of avoiding it. It also involves the creation of an infrastructure to guide the process, and a willingness to rethink what we measure and how.

What Is in the Way?

It is easy for us to say that "everybody designs," but we know from our research that the reality of successfully democratizing design will be harder than it sounds. A series of things must happen for it to work.

First, we have to successfully *engage a broader, more diverse set of stakeholders* in the innovation conversation. A wealth of academic research testifies that *difference* provides the fuel for innovation. In interacting with and learning from people who are different from ourselves, we come to see new possibilities. But the same difference that fuels innovation also breeds conflict and mistrust. Tapping into the potential contribution that diversity represents can be especially difficult in the social sector, where differences can run deep and come with embedded values attached. Difference can quickly feel personal and threatening.

We have all been in conversations that made a situation worse instead of better because people with strong opinions disagreed. How do we ensure that our conversations don't descend into arguments that push us farther apart instead of closer together in agreeing on solutions to critical problems? Even more elemental, how do we decide who to invite into the conversation in the first place? The answer is not "Everybody" for all issues—it is the *right* set of people for that particular issue. Even when we succeed in identifying the appropriate stakeholders, how do we encourage them to join the conversation? What if they have difficulty participating or communicating their needs—if they are disabled, poor, or sick, for instance? Or what if they are reluctant or fearful to join in? In part 2, we'll look at the variety of ways social sector organizations are successfully addressing these questions.

Then, assuming we can get the right parties into the conversation, how do we keep their different worldviews from paralyzing progress? How do we help people escape the prison of their own perspective? As we think about generating solutions, how do we avoid focusing on the wrong problems or issues? How do we see together what none of us see separately? With so many options, how do we drill down to what really matters? Increasingly the big challenges we face in the social sector happen at the systems level. How do we get the parts of the system to talk to each other? How do we avoid a "build it and they will come" mentality?

As we move from designing to implementing, we face another intimidating set of challenges. What if the people we need to impact are afraid of change? Or what if we lack the organizational capabilities to successfully implement the new idea in practice?

All of these challenges to doing work that achieves a greater good—engaging a broader group of voices, achieving alignment and consensus, finding workable solutions that people will actually adopt—must be surmounted to make a reality of the idea that we are all innovators at heart.

That's why we wrote this book.

Our path into the world of design thinking came entirely through the for-profit world. For almost a decade now, we have been studying design thinking as a methodology for improving business innovation and growth, examining its successful use in global corporations like IBM, Toyota, and 3M. Then we noticed that the most inspiring stories of all were coming from the social sector—from government, health care, education, charitable foundations, and the like. We realized that the fundamental reason design thinking worked so well in business—the ability to create better value for customers served—was even more urgently needed in the social sector. There, the problems were bigger and messier—and solving them mattered even more. We became fascinated by the ability of design to make the world a better, not just more profitable, place. As researchers and teachers, we wanted to know more details. Exactly what did these efforts look like in practice? Where and why were they working—or why not? What could we learn from them?

Our intention was to identify organizations outside the traditional, for-profit business sector—in areas such as health care, education, the arts, the environment, government policy, transportation, and social services—using design thinking approaches and methods to improve the quality of what they delivered, utilize their resources more efficiently, and create enhanced experiences for those they served. We wanted to codify and disseminate the kinds of opportunities they were pursuing and the kinds of practices they used in ways that would benefit other organizations and their leaders. As part of this exploration, we wanted to convene a conversation in which those involved in bringing the design thinking approach to the social sector could find a forum to share challenges and opportunities and to support and coach each other.

We had already seen evidence of the increasing interest in design thinking on the part of social sector organizations. Many participants in Darden's massive open online course, on the Coursera platform, came from outside of traditional business and wanted not-for-profit examples of success. Design thinking consultancies such as IDEO and LUMA Institute were placing increasing focus on the sector, and even traditional strategy consulting boutiques like McKinsey and Boston Consulting Group were expanding their public sector offerings. IDEO offered an online course on human-centered design for social innovation, and various governments and nonprofits were opening innovation labs. Governments in Denmark, New Zealand, and Singapore were leading the way.

Much of the excitement around this topic within universities is being led by a new generation of students with heightened interest in social innovation. Even at traditional business schools like Darden, student interest in innovation in general is growing, and interest in social innovation and entrepreneurship is exploding. At one end of the demographic, young social entrepreneurs, like Blake Mycoskie of TOMS Shoes, create businesses that aim at doing good and making money simultaneously; at the other end, a growing number of highly successful individuals, like Bill Gates and Steve Case, want

DESIGN THINKING IN NEW ZEALAND

How does design thinking help a government when what it is doing is working and also not working?

That's the case in New Zealand, where, in one example, the Ministry of Transportation is living with the aftermath of its very successful stiffening of driver's licensing examinations in 2003. Aiming to reduce one of the world's highest mortality rates among teenage drivers, they created a graduated driver's licensing system that is credited with significant increases in safety, decreasing the death rate of teenagers in automobile accidents by an impressive 66 percent.

But the law of unintended consequences has shown up with a vengeance.

The new system requires a series of tests, 120 hours of practice, and an almost two-year-long process to officially learn to drive, which is causing more lower-income, rural, and Maori and Asian youths to not even try to get a license and, instead, to drive without legal sanction.

And not getting a license, it turns out, is a kind of "gateway drug" for creating future personal and societal problems. A simple ticket for rolling a stop sign becomes driving without a license and carries a stiff fine; failure to pay these fines compounds the problem. In some marginalized communities, like the suburbs of South Auckland, only one in six drivers under the age of twenty-four has a license. Since about seven in ten jobs in New Zealand require a driver's license for identification and security, the failure of Kiwi youths to obtain licenses has repercussions throughout New Zealand's social, economic, and political realities. New Zealand, it seems, must choose its poison: road safety and youth alienation or high mortality rates.

Enter design thinking, and a commitment by the New Zealand government to a new, more human-centered mission: "making smart choices easier." This government-wide initiative focuses on first understanding what motivates citizens to follow or not to follow any particular regulation, and then on helping these people to make better choices in future actions. Figuring out the "why" causes each agency to seek out the unarticulated needs, desires, and problems of those they serve and has led to changes in regulations and, in almost all cases, to better compliance with laws.

In the case of the graduated license, it involved using design thinking to understand, and to iterate toward, ways that maximize the safety benefit of the driver's licensing program, without inhibiting the ability to get a license. This work has spawned new initiatives, like the Community Mentoring program, in which the government partners with local organizations like the Salvation Army in Christchurch, a sporting trust in Auckland, and the mayor's office in Gisborne. The program identifies and addresses the prime practical issues holding back youths at the local level by providing community volunteers to act as driving partners, with cars provided by corporate partner Hyundai and fuel by Chevron.

Reports from the mentoring program indicate that 95 percent of mentored youths pass the licensing tests on their first try (almost double the national rate among middle- to upper-income kids), but the benefits go far beyond that. In Gisborne, Community Mentoring is under the auspices of the mayor, and police are given hours on the clock to sit in the passenger's seat while at-risk teenagers learn behind the wheel. This program is producing unanticipated benefits, shifting the dynamic between law enforcement and at-risk youths from negative toward positive. Hours together in the front seat have led to deepening relationships and to mentors' attendance at high school soccer and rugby games, addressing issues created by low-income kids' traditional first—and almost always negative—interaction with police, as part of a traffic stop or arrest.

It turns out that the law of unintended consequences sometimes has an upside.

to leave a legacy, realizing that, without change, their children and grandchildren face ever worsening problems. All are looking for concrete examples of innovations that work in the social sector, stories that go beyond hype and accurately capture the learning process in action and the complexity and challenges inherent in these environments.

So we reached out and asked people to tell us their stories—and did they ever! We were astonished at the scope and diversity of the efforts in progress all over the world.

We saw people tackling problems both large and small. In Peru, a country with one of the lowest blood donation rates in Latin America, a group of MBA students worked with the Red Cross to figure out why and what to do about it. In Cape Town, South Africa, city managers teamed with designers to address the challenges of refugee camps. In Istanbul, Turkey, a young manager who worked in vendor invoice processing for the city—inspired by a college class she was taking and a professor who encouraged his students to be agents of change—tackled bureaucracy and inertia to improve the process. And those are just a few of the stories that didn't make it into this book!

Catalyzing a Conversation for Change across Difference

One discovery we made as we listened to these stories was the way in which design thinking was creating improved outcomes by *providing the tools and process to foster a better conversation across difference*. Sometimes those differences were within organizations themselves—across functional silos or different levels. Other times they were across different types of organizations, like government regulators and businesses, or were about differing stakeholder needs and trade-offs. They often turned out to be about local versus global, and even sometimes about science versus traditional values.

Design thinking's greatest gift, we came away believing, was to provide a *social technology* that channeled conversations into more productive arenas and provided guardrails that made it feel safe for the individuals involved to talk about and work across their differences. It helped them find higher-order solutions that were better than what anyone brought into the room in the first place, solutions that made a difference in their stakeholders' lives.

In part 2 of this book, we will look at a collection of stories that examine in depth how design thinking accomplishes this and addresses exactly those challenges to the greater good that we described earlier: engaging a broader group of voices, achieving alignment and consensus, and finding workable solutions that people will actually adopt.

At the US Department of Health and Human Services, the Ignite Accelerator program is democratizing innovation by inviting frontline employees throughout the country to tackle opportunities for innovation that they see in their own backyards, and building their creative confidence that they can succeed.

At the Kingwood Trust in the United Kingdom, we'll find an organization that has succeeded in bringing new voices into the conversation by reworking traditional design tools to include in the innovation process the adults with autism they serve, along with their support staff.

The medical staff at Monash Medical Centre will show us how they have brought together clinicians from across specialties and helped them align their differing views to achieve consensus on changes both small (increasing hand washing) and large (redesigning their outpatient psychiatric clinic).

In Washington, DC, the US Food and Drug Administration will offer an example of how to use design thinking to turn adversarial debates into dialogues.

In Ireland, we will observe a community beset by economic problems and depopulation that is using design thinking tools to have a community-wide conversation about solutions, not just problems, aiming to strengthen the economy on the Ring of Kerry and provide opportunities for young people to stay.

At United Cerebral Palsy, we will drop in on a series of traveling innovation labs that aim to create a supply chain connecting entrepreneurs with engineers, people with cerebral palsy and their caregivers, and design students, to search for opportunities to improve the lives of people with a range of disabilities.

At the Community Transportation Association of America, we see the power of localized decision making that uses design thinking as a backbone to foster grassroots problem identification and solving to address the transportation difficulties faced by low-income workers.

In Mexico, indigent farmers and scientists come together to improve crop yields and income, using design thinking methods to both honor tradition and encourage adoption of advances in farming practice.

The Transportation Security Administration demonstrates how technology can make us more human and, in the most risk-averse of circumstances, advance innovation and trust.

Finally, Children's Health System of Texas takes a deep look at the challenges of achieving population health and wellness in Dallas and teaches us how to enlist uncommon partners to assess and build the capabilities to meet the needs that design thinking has surfaced.

In part 3, we focus on what it takes to make design thinking a reality in organizations today. In this part, we take a deep dive into our own methodology, which focuses on asking four simple but critical questions as we enter the innovation space: **What *is*?**, **What *if*?**, **What *wows*?**, and **What *works*?** We illustrate the process in step-by-step detail by accompanying a group of educators at Gateway College and Career Academy in Riverside, California, as they use design thinking to reduce the dropout rate of at-risk teenagers.

We conclude the book with a look at how organizations can work to foster and spread the capacity for innovation beyond individual projects and teams. Though our research focus was to dig deeply into the actual approaches and experiences of social sector innovators—to be able to talk in detail about the specifics of *how* and *why* they incorporated design thinking into their work, the challenges they faced, and the successes (and sometimes failures) they experienced—we also, along the way, gained some insights into a higher-level *how*: how the organizations they worked within were facilitating—or stymieing—their efforts. We saw no one-size-fits-all approach being followed as they reached toward Innovation II mindsets and behaviors. Each organization seemed to follow its own path. This diversity of roadmaps is itself consistent with design thinking—responding to the particular personalities, preferences, and needs of its leadership and the nature of the challenges they face. And though we don't advocate any "right" path or model, some general insights did emerge around the value of creating an organizational infrastructure for team formation, capability development and coaching, access to stakeholders, and resources for experimentation. We will see evidence of these in our stories in part 2.

Another higher-level observation emerged about the direction from which these changes emanated. In most of our stories, innovation activities do have a single starting point, but they do not align with the normal juxtaposition of "top down" versus "bottom up." Instead, they underline the important role each person can play in the reality of diffusing a design thinking capability throughout an organization. We observe small experiments at the front line, unleashing employee resourcefulness, while additions to organizational structure such as innovation labs and tournaments illustrate management's commitment and provide cover and resources for grassroots efforts by employees interested in trying something new.

We see the combination of a loosely linked, almost viral movement by frontline and middle management innovation champions, supported by training and programmatic resources provided by senior leadership, as a highly effective approach. The government of New Zealand offers a case in point. Strong senior leadership there created infrastructural supports, like laying out a common set of national ambitions that required out-of-the-box thinking and enhanced collaboration across agency partners, partnering with innovation consultancies like ThinkPlace, and creating the Auckland Co-Design Lab. But the heart of the frontline progress in areas like driver's licensing was driven at the local level. Arianne Miller, managing director of the Lab@OPM today, captured this interplay between top-down and grassroots movements when she reflected on the importance, but also the limitations, of top-down management:

> It's like a garden: somebody has to plant it—prepare the ground and scatter the seeds. But if you only look at what happens aboveground, you miss the point. The health of a garden is about the strength of the root system. Sure, you can stick a vase of beautifully blooming flowers in the ground and it looks great for a while, and then you wonder why it dies.

Throughout this book, we will meet a wide variety of social sector innovators—hard at work both above- and belowground—who have inspired us. We hope they inspire you!

CHAPTER TWO

How Do We Get There from Here? A Tale of Two Managers

It was the best of times, it was the worst of times.

Charles Dickens, *A Tale of Two Cities* (1859)

It is easy to talk in theory about the shift from an Innovation I world to Innovation II, but what does it feel like to live through it? In chapter 1, we talked what that transition looks like at an organizational level. Now we'll consider what it means to the behavior of real people in real time. We'll drop in on George and Geoffrey, two managers trying to actually accomplish innovation in their organizations. Both are intelligent and dedicated, but they see life—and work—from two entirely different perspectives. We'll look at the obstacles they face as innovators and how design thinking can help. After that, we will consider the simple methodology that we talked about in chapter 1, focusing on the four questions we've found to be invaluable to would-be design thinkers all over the world, seeking to uncover the innovation magic inside all of us.

We argue that all of us possess a latent ability to find and pursue innovation, and that organizations need to tap into this capability if we hope to solve the wicked problems that surround the social sector. But let's be honest: some of us need more help than others. A world where everybody designs can be a mixed bag—the best of times for some, the worst of times for others. For some, the invitation to innovate is a glorious opportunity; for others, it is a source of anxiety and confusion. Particularly for those of us who have worked in the large, bureaucratic organizations often found in the social sector, innovation can be intimidating; we may need to "unlearn" thinking styles and behaviors before we can tap into our creative capabilities. To do this, we need enabling tools to structure and guide our efforts. That is a role design thinking can play: helping to democratize innovation by giving everyone in the organization the confidence and capabilities to act.

To understand what this dynamic looks like in action, let's contemplate the experiences of George and Geoffrey—both highly capable and committed, both working in large, bureaucratic social sector organizations. Developed through years of studying managers faced with innovation challenges, George and Geoffrey are archetypes, representing two markedly different behavior patterns we've observed in our research. One struggles, one succeeds at innovation. Why?

Let's first meet Geoffrey. When our research team encountered him, he had just joined a large health care organization. He arrived there from a well-known innovation strategy firm, bringing with him experience in different businesses and functions. Having started up two new marketing ventures and been involved in change management at a previous employer, Geoffrey arrived at his new employer with a mandate to lead innovation. He also brought with him some beliefs from past experiences: (1) that innovation should begin with a deep understanding of stakeholders' everyday existences and an ambition to make those lives better, (2) that innovation is a *discipline* that can be learned, and (3) that success rarely comes on the first try.

Our second manager, George, has a track record of success at his organization, a charitable foundation, yet finds himself struggling with new expectations around delivering innovation. His background is different from Geoffrey's but equally impressive. An engineering major in college, George obtained an MBA and joined a well-run foundation known for its solid management and careful attention to process. George has done well and has not been interested in "jumping around" (as he describes it) to various functions or other employers. He has focused on developing a depth of experience and detailed knowledge about the foundation's operations. George is respected as the go-to person for any technical question.

As Geoffrey was taking on his new role at the health care firm, George got an offer to lead a large but struggling department within his foundation. George was more apprehensive than Geoffrey about accepting the new challenge—it was clear that meeting this department's goals represented a stretch. Expectations for improvements in the department's performance were beyond what George thought realistic, given the staff and their capabilities, and George hated to fail. The challenge of managing a contentious group of stakeholders, including funders, applicants for funds, employees, and special interest groups, seemed daunting. Regardless, when it became clear to George that continued advancement in his career required him to tackle this challenge, he accepted the job.

George immediately asked his staff to pull together all the data the organization could find on its stakeholders and their perspectives. After weeks of detailed study, he was confident there was not much about the dealings between these groups and the foundation that he didn't know.

Geoffrey, meanwhile, not content with existing research, decided he required more hands-on exposure to what his new organization's stakeholders really wanted and needed. He assembled a diverse team from across departments, including clinicians, administrators, and patient representatives, to engage patients and their families, with the aim of understanding how health care interactions impacted all aspects of their lives. The team interviewed and observed, searching for emergent patterns. Throughout, Geoffrey focused his team on one question: "What could we be doing for our patients that would really make their lives better?"

Soon they recognized what he called "something so fundamental it makes you want to cry." They observed that almost every service the organization offered had been designed with its own needs in mind, not the patient's. Geoffrey and his team set a goal of imagining what one or two key services would look like if they started with the patients' preferred journeys in mind. Team members tried a few experiments that didn't produce hoped-for results, but finally, after several attempts, more detailed work with clinicians, and a few new insights, they scored their first "win" with a service redesign that simultaneously improved patient satisfaction and reduced the cost of delivery.

On the basis of their early interviews with stakeholders and a successful pilot, Geoffrey and his team quickly explored improvement opportunities for other key services. As word of their successful approach got around, they started to get calls from interested colleagues with problems that they thought might benefit from the new approach. The team identified a set of outside groups (insurers and community leaders) as critical to the successful adoption of many promising opportunities, so they started sounding those possible partners on their needs and wants.

Geoffrey suspected that respected outsiders would be critical for internal buy-in—achieving necessary support and alignment across his organization's many departments was not going to be easy or quick. Geoffrey also believed that offering theoretical arguments, both internally and to insurers, for the viability of his team's ideas would produce long, unproductive debates. Geoffrey especially believed in the need for speed:

> I think one of the things that most people don't get—and this is the big challenge in the innovation journey—is this notion of *speed*. An entrepreneur doesn't have the luxury of time or lots of resources. And that's why I think a lot of entrepreneurs are better at innovation than those who work in large organizations.

All in all, attempting a large rollout would likely be slow and painful, he concluded. So Geoffrey elected to affiliate quickly with a few selected insurers to prototype new concepts and conduct small-scale experiments, carefully monitoring results. A critical aspect was observing and interviewing patients and clinicians as they experienced any new service, and learning from these insights. Geoffrey's team was especially interested in testing assumptions in areas such as how the flow of the new service would impact both patient satisfaction and speed of delivery.

Meanwhile, George and his team were struggling to find the "big idea." George shared Geoffrey's commitment to making people's lives better; he was just not sure how to do it. His team had been given ambitious strategic targets to hit but couldn't find a substantive strategy for achieving them. Senior leadership had been clear that they expected a big impact, but uncovering that kind of opportunity wasn't proving easy. Despite abundant data and significant analysis, and even after hiring some expensive consultants, the "big win" remained elusive. Nothing seemed big—or sure—enough. So George and his team kept looking.

Finally, George's team located an idea they thought could be the big win. It involved entering a field that the foundation had not previously supported. The need for the foundation's work was certainly there, and it looked like a solid opportunity on paper, but it involved bringing on board expensive specialized talent and building visibility with a new group of partners. The team had no hard data on how the organizations that needed funding in this new segment would react to the foundation's entry into the field, or whether the foundation would have the capability to make good decisions, especially in comparison with foundations already well versed in that area. Months of debate ensued.

Eventually, George's team got the go-ahead. As he moved forward, George was careful to protect the foundation's reputation. He was wary of talking too much to outsiders about the new offering. Most of the data was internally generated or obtained from consultants' reports. Planning to make a major pronouncement that would "take the field by storm," George wanted to be sure there were no leaks in advance of the announcement.

But George's people were growing increasingly worried. The news coming in as the initiative began to roll out was not reassuring. Potential donors in the field didn't seem to grasp the many additional benefits that George's foundation brought to the table. Potential recipients of the funds also seemed uninterested, and George's staff was getting discouraged. Everybody knew that George's prospects were riding on the success of the big rollout—he was in no mood to hear bad news. "Failure is not an option," he repeatedly reminded his staff. "Do whatever it takes" was his response when they raised concerns.

Back in Geoffrey's world, results looked promising. The success demonstrated in the early field experiments quickly persuaded other insurers to support the new designs. And in the face of such demonstrated demand, Geoffrey's team was finally able to work through territorial challenges within his own organization. Working with insurers early in the development process not only had cemented their interest in the new approach but also had convinced Geoffrey's senior leadership, who responded to insurers' enthusiasm with increasing support.

For George, however, things were not working out as well. After substantial investment but with little sign of interest from donors or recipients, his boss pulled the plug on George's big idea. New employees dedicated to the initiative had to be let go, and George's reputation and career took a hit. In retrospect, he wondered where he, a manager with a strong track record of success, could have gone so wrong. Was it just bad luck? Or was the answer in the unknowable "black box" of the innovation process itself?

From our research, we know that neither bad luck nor the inherent uncertainty of the innovation process accounts for the different outcomes that George and Geoffrey experienced. Geoffrey's behaviors are simply better suited to an Innovation II world. His life experiences have equipped him with both a mindset and a tool kit that help him succeed in the face of uncertainty and conflicting demands. For Geoffrey, life (and success) is all about *learning*, an orientation that has followed him throughout his life. Because learning is sparked by stepping away from the familiar, Geoffrey accepts the uncertainty that inevitably accompanies any new experience and, as a result, he has actively sought new opportunities and built a diverse set of career experiences.

Contrast this with George's outlook (probably acquired as a young child and reinforced by a lifetime of experiences in Innovation I organizations), which is that the world is a test in which the object is to not get answers wrong. George lives his life trying to avoid mistakes. Because moving into uncertainty leads logically to more mistakes, George avoids that, too, and therefore has tended to shun the new experiences that would have given him a broader perspective for identifying possible opportunities. By the time we meet Geoffrey, in midcareer, his broad repertoire of experiences that span functions and organizations has prepared him to see opportunity. At midcareer, George's repertoire is significantly narrower than Geoffrey's, not because he is any less intelligent, well educated, committed, or capable than Geoffrey but because he has had less exposure to other ways of doing things. George may have an expert's repertoire, valuable during stable times, but it is narrow and specialized. It does not set him up for success in innovation.

These early differences in mindset and repertoire set the stage for two very different self-sustaining cycles. For George, despite the fact that his attitude and skills have helped him achieve success in a stable environment, when the world becomes more uncertain as innovation becomes the goal, his behaviors often trap him in a pattern with a high likelihood of failure. He relies exclusively on quantitative data, places one big bet, spends a lot of time trying to "prove" his idea in advance, and then ignores disconfirming data as it emerges. For Geoffrey, the cycle more often leads to success in innovation. He invests in gaining new insights about his stakeholders' needs before testing ideas, manages multiple options, and reduces risk by keeping his bets small and enlisting outside partners.

The consequences of their differences continue to accumulate as each works through his specific innovation challenge. Geoffrey has a deep and personal interest in his stakeholders as people rather than as data. His focus is on offering services within the context of their lives, in ways that improve them. This deeper "knowing," when combined with his broad repertoire of experiences, helps Geoffrey identify opportunities that others miss.

George, on the other hand, is somewhat detached from his stakeholders—he "knows" them through data rather than through firsthand observation or experience. His interactions with them are staged. When this detached view of important stakeholders is combined with a narrow repertoire, it inevitably is harder for George to surface new opportunities for innovation, despite the fact that he, like Geoffrey, truly cares and wants his stakeholders and organization to succeed. But he has few clues as to how to do this, whereas Geoffrey's deep knowledge of his stakeholders' needs helps him focus on the larger jobs they are trying to accomplish, giving him a much clearer, qualitatively data-driven path for harnessing his organization's skills toward helping them.

Even having both *seen* an opportunity, each chooses a different response to move it forward. While seeing opportunity, Geoffrey *expects* to make mistakes, so he never puts all his eggs in one basket. He adopts an experimental approach, conducting multiple small trials to test the ideas in action. He reduces his risk whenever possible and increases his learning by partnering with outsiders, such as his insurers.

George, on the other hand, pushed to find innovation despite his narrower repertoire and stakeholder understanding, continues to search for the one right answer and puts all his eggs in that basket when he thinks he has found it. His (and his organization's) expectation is that all projects should succeed, that he should look only for big wins at the outset, and that he should be able to *prove* the value of his idea before moving forward. These beliefs are fatally flawed in the context of the uncertainty surrounding innovation.

Geoffrey knows that there are no single right answers—there are only experiments—and does not attribute failed experiments to his personal failings. Instead, he recognizes that the inability to predict is a property of the uncertainty surrounding any new idea.

George continues to rely on analysis in his search to "prove" that the opportunity is good and to calm his own anxiety in the face of uncertainty. Though it is logically impossible to use historical data to definitively demonstrate the value of a future project, this is what George has been taught to do and what intelligent individuals like him still try to do. The outcome is often gridlock: the Georges of the world end up spending much time in meetings, debating and defending the value of their proposed ideas. Yet learning only occurs when they *try* something new. Tragically, George's approach actually unnecessarily *increases* risk, rather than reducing it as he intends. When he limits his options to one "big idea" and avoids seeking input from outside stakeholders, he ends up placing bets that are bigger and less informed by the reality of actual stakeholder needs. Worse still, he places them slowly, because of his ongoing search for "proof" before action. He ignores disconfirming data, his anxiety making it hard for him to listen to bad news. Hence, his colleagues stop bringing it to his attention, and his chance to cut his losses early evaporates.

Geoffrey pursues an alternative course. He conducts small, inexpensive experiments that give him positive results to promote—or, if the results are negative, allow him to table projects before upper management starts looking. In the end—to the surprise of no one—it is Geoffrey who generally succeeds. And even when he fails (as some of his experiments surely do), these failures often pass under the radar. Each manager is locked in a self-sustaining cycle, but in conditions of uncertainty, one cycle encourages success and the other, failure.

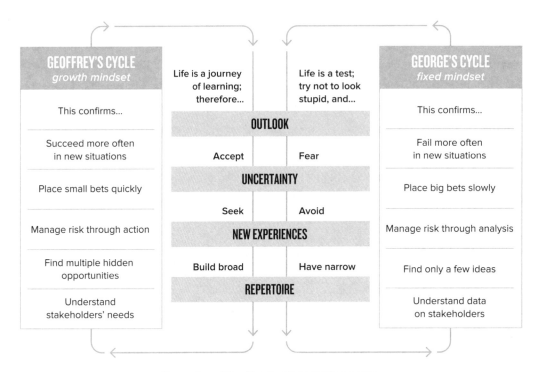

GEOFFREY'S CYCLE *growth mindset*	Life is a journey of learning; therefore...	Life is a test; try not to look stupid, and...	GEORGE'S CYCLE *fixed mindset*
This confirms...	**OUTLOOK**		This confirms...
Succeed more often in new situations	Accept	Fear	Fail more often in new situations
Place small bets quickly	**UNCERTAINTY**		Place big bets slowly
Manage risk through action	Seek	Avoid	Manage risk through analysis
Find multiple hidden opportunities	**NEW EXPERIENCES**		Find only a few ideas
Understand stakeholders' needs	Build broad	Have narrow	Understand data on stakeholders
	REPERTOIRE		

George's and Geoffrey's self-sustaining cycles.

George's is a sad story: the same tools and approaches that he learned in an Innovation I world, which drove his past success, now thwart his attempts to innovate. Geoffrey, on the other hand, behaves as though he lives in an Innovation II world, even though his organization may still have an Innovation I mentality.

Most of us find ourselves somewhere on a continuum between George and Geoffrey, depending on circumstances. Perhaps we are naturally more like Geoffrey, an optimistic blue-sky thinker open to possibilities. We see ourselves as well suited to an Innovation II world but are constantly frustrated by colleagues who always seem to slow down our action with their endless questions and demands for more "proof" that our ideas will work. Or perhaps we are more like George, a grounded, skeptical thinker, and have taken on behaviors that succeeded in Innovation I, when innovation was someone else's job, but have no idea where to start when it becomes ours.

So, what does this tale of two managers mean in a world where everyone designs?

In working with leaders charged with accelerating innovation in their organizations, we find that those who identify with Geoffrey are tempted to write off the innovation capacities of the Georges of the world. Let them worry about keeping the existing organization running, they suggest, and find more Geoffreys to provide innovation. We think this strategy is fatally flawed, for a number of reasons:

1. Generally, there aren't many Geoffreys working in the big bureaucracies that characterize many areas of the social sector, like government, education, and health care. If they join such mature organizations at all, they don't last long before frustration with the slow pace of change and the levels of permission needed to act send them to greener pastures.

2. Even if bureaucracies *could* find enough innovation-driven Geoffreys, their ability to drive significant innovation is likely small—because George is usually the boss (large organizations tend to promote based on George's solid, predictable competencies) and he will find their efforts risky and questionable. End-running the boss is never easy.

3. What the Geoffreys of the world do best, perhaps, is create social innovation start-ups. Why not let them, instead of larger organizations, be the drivers of innovation? Certainly, much good work is being produced by entrepreneurially minded Geoffreys focused on making the world a better place by starting up new organizations. But is it realistic to think that social innovation start-ups can do the heavy lifting to solve the social sector's wicked problems? We think not. Big organizations must participate as well, and their potential for impact is too large to ignore, given their clout and capabilities and the magnitude of the challenges we face.

But achieving change in large bureaucracies, whether in business or in the social sector, comes with special challenges. Most are still firmly ensconced in an Innovation I worldview and are slow, siloed, risk averse, and data obsessed, all qualities that are anathema to successful innovation. You simply can't succeed against these obstacles with all the Georges on the sidelines. The potential innovation capacity lost in writing off George is tremendous—and unnecessary. To accomplish the creativity we need in the social sector, George must be invited into the innovation conversation. He can make a valuable contribution. But how? How do we move innovation forward in a world where Geoffrey and George are often at odds? In ten years of teaching, we have almost always found an innovator hiding within George, waiting to be invited out. George has the commitment, the discipline, and the good intentions, but he needs support, direction, and new mindsets and tools. And Geoffrey needs help too—but of a different kind.

We see an opportunity to enhance the skills of each—to help George envision more creative futures and to help Geoffrey better navigate the bureaucracy. The point is not that we need George to *become* Geoffrey. The task is much simpler: we need to reduce George's anxiety in the face of uncertainty and teach him some new tools to help him navigate the innovation process.

Cue design thinking.

What Geoffrey enjoys intuitively—a learning mindset, empathetic understanding of stakeholders, an experimental approach to solving problems—is what design thinking's methodology and tool kit are all about. Design thinking can help George comfortably emulate the innovation-oriented behaviors that make Geoffrey effective, and Geoffrey can learn how to better utilize George's analytical and testing skills.

Improving the dialogue between George and Geoffrey is essential, so that they can work together and bring their individual strengths to innovation conversations rather than regard each other with suspicion and create gridlock. The merger of ideas and everyday realities in successful innovation requires both the expansive thinking of Geoffrey and the hard-eyed critical analysis of George. George's gift is his ability to see clearly the constraints limiting any idea's feasibility. Trouble is, his timing is often wrong. He rushes to point out constraints as soon as an idea surfaces. This kind of skepticism prevents initial concepts from being developed into something better and casts a pall on the enthusiasm of the idea generation process itself. Innovation, in its earliest stages, is fragile. A gust of negativity will often kill it. The key for George and Geoffrey is to learn respect for what the other brings, so that

George's analytical approach is introduced at the right time—during idea testing, not idea generation. Design thinking offers a method for taking this inherent tension and turning a seeming negative into a positive.

We wrote this book mostly for the George in all of us. Design thinking's human-centered front end will build his creative confidence and transform his ability to see new, more innovative possibilities. But we also wrote this book to help Geoffrey deal effectively with George and recognize that analysis can minimize his mistakes, not just limit his freedom to explore. The experimental orientation at the back end of design thinking makes this possible, not by giving Geoffrey carte blanche and ignoring George's desire for data but by transforming George's *veto* into carefully constructed *experiments* that address his concerns. Taking this hypothesis-testing approach breaks the debates that lead to gridlock in conference rooms and moves ideas into action—but in the form of inexpensive assumption tests that George helps construct, rather than costly pilots he grudgingly OKs.

How is design thinking going to do this? By giving George and Geoffrey the tools to work together to answer a simple series of questions: **What *is*?**, **What *if*?**, **What *wows*?**, and **What *works*?**

In previous books, such as *Designing for Growth* and *The Designing for Growth Field Book*, we laid out our four-question tool kit and approach. In part 3, we will review that process in detail and illustrate each step. For now, we just want to provide a brief overview of the process as a foundation for the stories in part 2.

The first of the four questions—**What *is*?**—explores current reality.

All successful innovation begins with an accurate assessment of what is going on today. Starting by developing a deep understanding of the present situation is a hallmark of design thinking and is at the core of design's information-intensive and user-driven approach. With only statistical data in hand, efficiency-minded would-be innovators frequently want to run immediately to the future, to start the innovation process by brainstorming new options and ideas. They are impatient to get to what feels like action: generating solutions. They often forget the human element. Consequently, using ethnographic research to develop a deeper understanding of current experiences and unmet needs of stakeholders is critical. It helps to broaden and perhaps even change completely the definition of the problem itself. Otherwise, we can unwittingly throw away all kinds of opportunities for innovation.

This attention to the present as it is experienced by stakeholders, not statisticians, helps to uncover unarticulated needs, the secret sauce for producing innovative solutions that stakeholders value. Exploring **What *is*** saves George from having to rely on his imagination as he moves into idea development. It gives him new insights—built from empathy and a view of his stakeholders as real people rather than spreadsheet numbers—into what they truly want and need, reducing the risk of a new idea's failure.

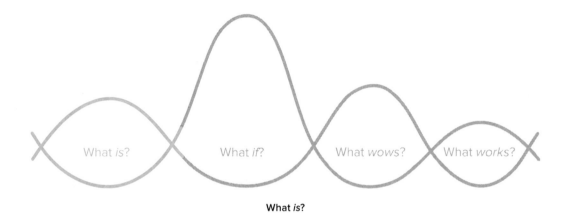

What *is*?

During the **What *is*** stage, you gather information from the stakeholders you are interested in creating value for, using time-tested ethnographic research tools like open-ended interviewing, jobs-to-be-done analysis, and journey mapping, while always paying attention to the stories and quotes that vividly illustrate your findings. Then you look for patterns in the information you've gathered, with the goal of developing new and deep insights into unmet needs. In the final phase of **What *is***, you translate these insights into design criteria that specify what a great solution will look like, without yet stating the solution itself.

Involving a broad team in the identification of insights and the specification of design criteria is critical. Remember who designs in an Innovation II world? Diverse groups from inside and often outside the organization. It is difficult to look deeper into data on our own—we need others who see things differently to push us to think outside our normal mindsets. The bigger, hidden payoff of this inclusion, however, goes beyond pushing you to think more creatively; it also aligns colleagues' views of the current reality, creating a common mind. This alignment pays dividends throughout the remainder of the design thinking process, as we will see in our part 2 stories.

Now, armed with the criteria that any good solution should meet, you are ready to ask our second question—**What *if*?**—and to begin to generate ideas. In **What *is***, you examined the data that you gathered, identified patterns and insights, and translated them into specific design criteria. Now you will use those criteria to focus on identifying new possibilities. *What if anything were possible?* is one of the most powerful questions anyone can ask. Too often we get trapped into starting with George's constraints rather than Geoffrey's possibilities, and then the future ends up looking a lot like the present. Design thinking insists that we start with possibilities and address constraints later.

This is where brainstorming occurs—a process that many Georges don't enjoy. But in design thinking, brainstorming is a disciplined, repeatable process. Successful brainstorming helps you create many possible alternatives, from which you'll select only a few for further development. But rather than relying entirely on imagination during the idea generation process, a team will use the insights and criteria generated during data gathering in **What *is*** to pose a series of questions that guide creative idea generation.

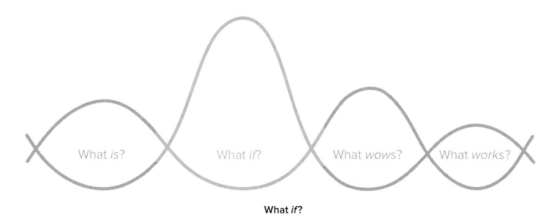

What *is*?   What *if*?   What *wows*?   What *works*?

What *if*?

Think of each of the ideas generated during brainstorming as a single toy Lego block. After brainstorming, you combine them (the way kids do with Lego pieces) in different ways to produce different creations. These are your concepts, or coherent clusters of ideas, organized around themes. You want to develop *multiple* concepts so that you can offer a choice to your stakeholders. You want a portfolio of concepts because you are going to let the stakeholders tell you which ones best satisfy their needs. Whereas brainstorming is best done by a diverse group that includes people outside the innovation project, concept development works best with a dedicated core team because outsiders often lack the context of the project and the time it takes to perform concept development. Again, design thinking offers the best of both worlds: it invites others into brainstorming to share their diverse insights and ideas, but it relies on a small, dedicated team to do the heavy lifting of concept development and to maintain momentum.

Now that you have a set of concepts, you are ready to move into the first stage of testing by asking the third question: **What *wows*?** In this stage, you consider each of the concepts a hypothesis and begin to think systematically about evaluating them against your design criteria. You will usually find that you have too many interesting concepts to move them all forward, so you have to make some hard decisions. Here, George excels. As you winnow the field of concepts to a manageable number, you are looking for those that hit the sweet spot where the chance of a significant upside for your stakeholders matches your organizational resources and capabilities and your ability to sustainably deliver the new concept. This is the "wow zone." Making this assessment involves surfacing and testing the assumptions about why you believe each of the concepts is a good idea. The concepts that wow are good candidates for turning into experiments to be conducted with actual stakeholders.

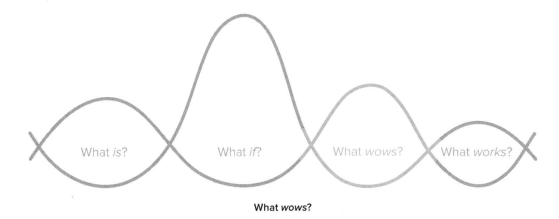

What *is*?   What *if*?   What *wows*?   What *works*?

What *wows*?

In a traditional analytic approach, this is where you would start *asking* people whether they like the new idea. You might convene a focus group or send out an online survey, with a description of the new idea, and ask them to tell you what they liked and disliked and whether they would use or want the new offering. But that approach, we know from many years of academic research, is high risk, because most people don't know what they want until they see it—and sometimes not even then. Decades of research in psychology affirm what most of us already recognize—we often are unable to accurately describe our own *current* behavior, much less make reliable predictions.

Through a number of methods, design thinking addresses this problem. One happens during the **What *is*** stage: ethnographic tools like journey mapping and jobs-to-be-done analysis ask users to describe what they are trying to accomplish and to walk through an actual experience, describing their thoughts, reactions, and satisfaction at each step, to get at needs that they can't articulate—instead of asking them what they want.

In **What *wows*** we will look at another powerful solution to this problem: prototyping. Prototyping helps to elicit effective feedback by creating a more vivid experience of the new future. Psychologists have found that helping people to "pre-experience" something novel can be an effective proxy for the real thing and significantly improves the accuracy of forecasting. New evidence emerging from neuropsychological research shows that human reactions to imaginary events activate many of the same neurological pathways that the actual events later will.

So prototyping is really about creating a pre-experience by providing a concrete and tangible artifact that allows your potential users to imagine the future more vividly. Whether in the form of storyboards, journey maps, user scenarios, or concept illustrations, the low-fidelity and often two-dimensional prototypes used during **What *wows*** and **What *works*** offer specific tools to make new ideas more tangible and allow you to solicit more accurate feedback.

When many of us hear the word *prototyping*, we think of fully featured versions almost ready for prime time. Design thinking prototypes start off much simpler. The goal of prototyping is not perfection, or even getting it right; it is to bring concepts to life in others' minds in order to reduce the risk of innovation failure by learning from and adapting to the best feedback we can get. We seek the bad news, the disconfirming data, while providing as much space as possible for humans to fill with their own realities. Psychologically, it is easier for people to co-create with a penciled drawing than with a polished PowerPoint.

Prototypes in hand, you are ready to learn from the real world by asking the fourth question—**What *works*?**—and trying out a low-fidelity prototype with actual stakeholders. Your early tests will be one-on-one conversations with selected stakeholders, a process that designers call co-creation. If stakeholders like it and give useful feedback, then you refine the prototype and move it into a more realistic set of experiments that we call a "learning launch." Always testing your assumptions, always seeking additional data, you continue iterating in this way until you feel confident about the value of the new idea. As you move through **What** *works*, you work in fast feedback cycles and minimize the cost of conducting experiments.

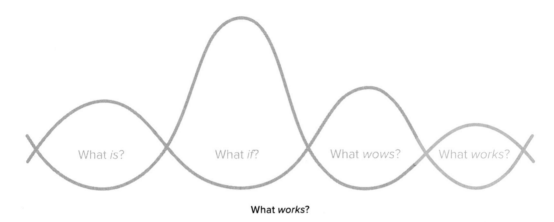

What *works***?**

These testing activities—the surfacing of assumptions in **What** **wows** and the design of learning launches in **What** **works**—demonstrate the power of bringing George's natural skepticism into the innovation conversation, but in the productive form of designing good experiments. Geoffrey's optimism helps him to see opportunity and develop concepts, but it often blinds him to the key assumptions embedded in them. George's more analytical bent requires human-centered design insights to fuel his imagination in the idea generation process, but it renders him an outstanding designer of experiments.

And there you have it. Four questions that build bridges to more innovative solutions, that help George find the innovator inside and help Geoffrey put his best ideas into action. We like to think of it as a systematic, data-driven approach to creativity. This might sound like an oxymoron, but we don't believe it is. By breaking the process into four questions, potential design thinkers can explore the "how to" in a way that feels safe and structured to George, and that allows him and Geoffrey to work together in powerful ways.

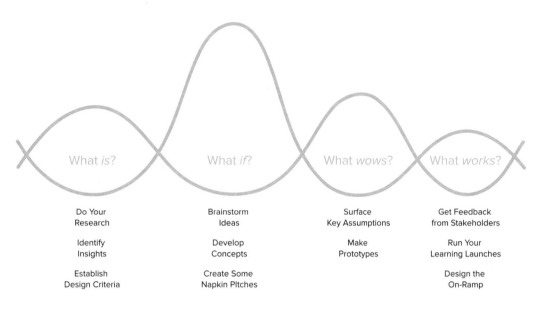

The four-question design thinking approach.

   In the remainder of this book, we will look at design thinking tools in action. The ten stories in part 2 highlight the use of different design tools and approaches in different social sector organizations. Some of the stories involve all four questions, others only one or two. We'll meet a lot of people solving a lot of problems. Some of them will remind you of Geoffrey, others of George. All of them, we believe, have something to teach us about how to succeed at innovation amid the uncertainty and complexity of life in the social sector.

PART II

The Stories

CHAPTER THREE

Igniting Creative Confidence at US Health and Human Services

THE CHALLENGE TO THE GREATER GOOD

The idea that everyone in an organization is invited to innovate may be intimidating, rather than empowering, to those who don't think they have the capabilities or permission to succeed at it. How do we encourage and support people to join design conversations, to step into uncertainty and ambiguity—especially staffers who don't believe themselves capable? The Georges among us, especially, schooled in bureaucracy and anxious to avoid error, may have ideas and enthusiasm but not know where to begin.

DESIGN THINKING'S CONTRIBUTION

Having worked with thousands of people new to design, at every level, in all kinds of organizations, we believe inspiring creative confidence is one of design thinking's greatest gifts. In every organization, employees are waiting for the invitation to use their knowledge to generate better value for those they serve. Using design thinking's structured processes to empower frontline staff—to give employees permission to act and the tools to act wisely at the local level—is the mission of the Ignite Accelerator program at the US Department of Health and Human Services (HHS). Ignite offers decision makers training in design thinking and Lean tools, along with mentoring, financial support, and visibility, to build the creative confidence of all employees in the agency and enable them to tackle opportunities for innovation that upper management simply cannot see.

Despite widespread skepticism about the ability of the US government—arguably one of the world's most intimidating bureaucracies—to innovate, exciting work is under way in Washington, DC, that is making a difference in citizens' lives. At the US Department of Health and Human Services, one of the largest agencies of the US government, the Ignite Accelerator, a program of HHS's Innovation, Design, Entrepreneurship, and Action (IDEA) Lab, is bringing design thinking and Lean Startup methodologies to employees across the United States.

HHS's Ignite Accelerator offers education and encouragement, with a small funding stipend, to boost projects that offer the hope of addressing agency problems, both large and small, with innovative approaches. The three-month Ignite Accelerator program helps HHS staff improve the way their offices carry out the agency's mission by supporting and testing creative ideas in meaningful ways. Many of these projects aren't the big, messy, wicked problems we are so often told that design is about. In fact, we love the smallness and nonwickedness of what Ignite encourages employees to tackle.

Read Holman, program director of Ignite, described the rationale behind the HHS Ignite approach:

> Policies, rules, and cultural norms—once tools to standardize processes and drive efficiencies within the organization—eventually become forces that resist new ideas, that innately de-emphasize organizational innovations. It's not necessarily that anyone out there is proactively blocking progress. Rather, it's just that new ideas are disruptive to the social fabric and thus can be uncomfortable. Thus, experimenting with new concepts doesn't become a priority. And the

DO ALL PROBLEMS NEED TO BE WICKED?

Mention the term *design thinking* and the idea of "wicked" problems—those famously messy multistakeholder challenges for which design thinking is famous—almost immediately shows up. But design thinking works for other kinds of problems as well. When we democratize design, we invite people to use it on problems that fall within their own jurisdiction, that lie in what Stephen Covey called each person's circles of influence and control. Sometimes these problems are seemingly small and their solutions don't seem to be all that novel; we see this work dismissed as not "disruptive" enough to constitute real innovation. But these problems matter a lot to the people who have them, and solving them creates real value. That is innovation enough, in our view. As Matt Collier, from the Lab@OPM story in chapter 1, told us:

> We sometimes get stuck thinking that innovation means big change that is revolutionary. We can do that from time to time, but let's not let the search for game-changers get in the way of the incremental innovations that we can do today in the course of our daily work. In the government space, particularly, small changes to policy or process, when played out at scale, can have an outsize impact on everything from agency budgets to citizen experiences.

implementation of change gets back-burnered . . . We provide concentrated opportunity for experimentation. We provide a safe space where new ideas, cultivated by people, can grow. We take project ideas at all stages of development, from the nascent to the tested, and help them demonstrate value and get woven back into the organization so as to generate real impact.

Inspiring projects have already developed out of HHS's Ignite Accelerator. One that especially intrigued us came to the IDEA Lab from a Native American reservation in Arizona, where HHS employee Marliza Rivera stepped up to the plate to make her hospital a more welcoming place for Native American elders. Marliza is in charge of performance improvement at Whiteriver Indian Hospital. Her story demonstrates the power of a program like Ignite, showing what a simple invitation reaching out to would-be innovators at all organizational levels and locations can spark.

The Whiteriver Hospital Story

In late 2013, Whiteriver Hospital on the Fort Apache Indian Reservation faced a serious situation: close to 25 percent of emergency department visitors were leaving without being seen, a problem attributed to long wait times. The patients leaving were rarely in crisis, but treatable minor and semiurgent complaints were turning into major, expensive issues because of the lack of medical attention. Fort Apache covers 1.6 million acres and has a population of seventeen thousand, mostly Native Americans. Whiteriver Hospital has forty inpatient beds, serving a significantly higher population per bed than the national average. Last renovated in 2006, Whiteriver's emergency department is the reservation's prime stop for health care, regardless of acuity level.

Like patients in many sparsely populated areas, members of the White Mountain Apache tribe used the Whiteriver emergency room for most treatment needs, including prescription refills. On any given day, two-thirds of the emergency room visitors were not seeking crisis treatment. Nonemergency patients consistently got delayed as staff addressed true emergencies, sometimes waiting as long as six hours before being seen. Whiteriver's history was clear: when potential patients left the emergency room (which they did at a rate twenty times the national average), midlevel problems worsened. Often, when their problems finally became true emergencies, patients needed to be helicoptered off the reservation for more-expensive care. The Whiteriver story mirrors that of hospitals across America. Experts believe that almost one in three patients who leave without being seen require emergency treatment within two days.

Marliza, a member of the Kiowa tribe of Oklahoma, was raised in Chicago after her parents were displaced due to the Indian Relocation Act of 1956. She first worked as a director and administrative officer in home health care. Finding it more rewarding to work with tribes, she accepted the job with Whiteriver.

In 2013, an e-mail landed in Marliza's inbox, detailing information about HHS's Ignite Accelerator program. Sensing an opportunity to receive help dealing with the challenges facing Whiteriver, Marliza—who was new to the performance improvement job—pulled together a team of employees and sought ideas about how to utilize Ignite. Together, the team (Marliza plus emergency department supervisor Alysia Cardona, staff development officer Jose Burgos, and public health nurse Justin Tafoya) submitted seven projects. One, an electronic kiosk to improve the emergency room process and reduce wait times, was selected as an Ignite finalist.

Though the team's Ignite application focused on the Whiteriver situation, they noted that, if successful, the concept might be applied across the four hundred–plus Indian Health Service and tribal health care facilities in the United States.

Marliza had come up with the kiosk idea after reading about its success at Johns Hopkins Hospital in Baltimore. There, a patient electronically signs in upon arrival, and the electronic system informs other parts of the hospital—the pharmacy, specific physicians, testing laboratories—of that patient's potential needs. Saving administrative time, the kiosk also speeds the process of identifying the best medical approach for any particular patient.

Beginning their Ignite journey with both anticipation and nervousness, and with solid approval from hospital leadership, two Whiteriver team members, Marliza and Alysia, headed to Washington, DC, to attend a three-day Ignite boot camp, in early spring 2014. The Whiteriver team entered Ignite with their solution already formulated: an electronic sign-in kiosk would provide information to hold patients in the emergency department until treatment and would speed the process by providing a quick way to triage needs. But through reevaluation and ethnography, the team—like many Ignite finalists—discovered that their original idea wasn't optimal for addressing the actual concerns of those involved.

Though applicants enter the Accelerator contest with a solution in mind, starting with our **What *if*?** question rather than **What *is*,** Read and his team are aware of the risks of starting with solutions in hand. Often, what teams see as the problem, much less its solution, might not address actual stakeholders' needs. The Washington, DC, staff of IDEA Lab therefore seeks to find the right mix of openness and delayed action to help innovators avoid false starts.

The Whiteriver team's initial "aha" moment about the solution they'd brought struck the first morning. The opening thrust of the boot camp experience encouraged participants to reexamine their definition of the problem by questioning the suppositions on which their solution was based.

Marliza and Alysia had arrived in Washington confident they were on the right track. They knew the problem of wait times was significant and thought the kiosk idea best addressed it. Marliza recalled:

> We went there thinking we knew what we were going to do and nobody was going to change our mind, that this is what we need! We had all this research on it, and knew these great places doing it, and it's the best thing ever. One of the first things IDEA Lab taught was "Challenge your assumptions. Challenge them over and over again." And we learned to not be stuck in one place thinking this is the end-all, be-all answer. If you question everything, you're going to probably end up in a better place and with something that is more fitted to what you really need. You've got to be willing to give up the ego and give up the idea that was set in stone, and work through it. You've got to ask the hard questions.

The Ignite approach raises an interesting alternative to our traditional design thinking path, where we begin by asking **What *is*?** and resist moving to solutions too soon. In our model, assumption surfacing occurs later, in the **What *wows*** stage, as we move into testing of ideas. The Ignite process, however, begins with solutions, making it essential to surface assumptions much earlier.

The important question: How would Whiteriver patients respond to a high-tech solution? Marliza thought of her eighty-seven-year-old grandmother's likely reaction to the electronic display. She realized that many of the tribal elders, Whiteriver emergency room's main visitors, would not be comfortable with new technology. Some did not speak or read English. An electronic system, no matter how efficient in Baltimore, might create *more*, not fewer, delays at Whiteriver, they recognized. The

Whiteriver team, in their initial research, had clearly heard patients' frustrations and established the wait-time problem. But their assumed solution—technology—had not come with stakeholders' input.

Hence, after phone calls back to Fort Apache to speak with elderly patients, the team made their first course correction in their innovation journey. The kiosk concept was replaced with a paper form that aimed to discover the acuity of patients' medical issues as soon as they entered the emergency department. Saving time and money at the front end, the simple form literally asked patients whether they needed emergency or nonemergency care, such as a visit with a nurse or a prescription refill. Since anyone in the emergency room could help non-English-speaking patients check boxes on a one-page form, Marliza and Alysia thought that any patient, without being seen by a clinician, could then be routed to the appropriate care.

Returning to Arizona, the team prepared to move into **What *works***, taking the new paper-based concept into testing in the actual hospital. Then the next shoe dropped. IDEA Lab staff connected them with the Centers for Medicare and Medicaid Services, and the team discovered that the Emergency Medical Treatment and Labor Act of 1986 made the use of any pre-examination form illegal. In an effort to prevent emergency rooms from turning away those without insurance, this "no dumping" law stipulates that everyone who comes into an emergency department must be assessed by a medical clinician.

"We were not trying to violate the law—we were trying to help!" Marliza explained. "But HHS legal advisors said, 'No. As long as that door says *Emergency* and they walked in and they've registered, you can't send them anywhere else until they've been evaluated.'"

THE POWER OF ASSUMPTION TESTING

Every idea that fails can be traced back to some assumption we made about the world that proved not to be true. It could be that we assumed our users wanted the new offering and then they didn't, or that our organization could successfully make it happen and then we couldn't. Paying careful attention to what we are *assuming* is true and then challenging that, as Marliza and Alysia did with their kiosk, and looking for ways to test it, is the surest way to reduce the risk of any new idea. We believe that the most efficient and effective place to begin this surfacing and challenging of our assumptions is in how we define the problem in the first place, long before we reach the solutions stage.

Abandoning the paper form, the team circled back to **What *is***, visiting other hospitals and gathering more face-to-face data from patients. Guided by the data, the Whiteriver team moved to their next iteration: a fast-track system that placed medically qualified personnel at the emergency room entrance to quickly—within fifteen minutes—assess each patient's condition and direct appropriate visitors to nonemergency services. Looking for existing data to evaluate their latest solution, Whiteriver turned to other Arizona hospitals that used fast-tracking in their emergency departments, such as Yavapai Regional Medical Center, Mercy Gilbert Medical Center, Summit Healthcare, and Mountain Vista Medical Center. They discovered that less than 2 percent of patients in these facilities left without being seen. Though all these hospitals were significantly larger than Whiteriver and handled proportionately fewer emergency room patients, their fast-track approaches were similar to the team's idea—and seemingly effective.

The Whiteriver team then designed and ran a four-day learning launch, arranging for an experienced physician to greet each emergency room arrival. The results were impressive. The percentage of arrivals abandoning Whiteriver's emergency room without treatment was reduced from 17.75 percent on the control days to 1.25 percent during the experiment. When Marliza and Alysia did a rough calculation of the effects such a reduction would have on hospital finances, they came up with $6 million savings against a cost of $150,000 to do the work required to redesign the emergency department and separate patients with basic medical concerns from those actually needing emergency services.

Starting with the existing performance indicators (in this case, wait times, costs, and lost revenues), the Whiteriver team estimated how these would change with the implementation of the suggested

LEARNING LAUNCH

A learning launch is a small, inexpensive experiment that tests an idea in the real world. In a typical scenario, in an Innovation I world, we might devote significant time to planning and justifying a new idea before we try it out. We'd analyze it in detail. In a learning launch, analysis is replaced by experimentation. You move your idea through one or more small, quick tests, as the Whiteriver team does here, using existing resources (a physician who already works there) and a prototype of the new idea (he or she greets all arrivals) but without actually redesigning the physical space or hiring someone for the new role—things that would involve a significant investment. You just start with a quick and simple mock-up and get it out in front of a small group of real users quickly.

innovation. The team knew that the Indian Health Service was losing money when potential patients left without being seen, but they had to quantify the effect to demonstrate the value of their ideas to administrators. They did their own basic, conservative math. The team's cost analysis included factors that few urban or suburban hospitals will ever consider. Because Whiteriver is so far from major medical centers, most seriously ill patients are flown to Tucson. But since so many emergency room visitors with minor problems leave and then return when they are seriously ill, catching patients in the middle zone, when they can be admitted to Whiteriver, leads to higher bed-use efficiency and more income from the federal government.

Beginning with the unrecovered revenue from the 20 percent of potential patients who left without being seen, the team used the hospital's average daily income of $384 per patient to calculate slightly over $3 million in uncaptured revenue. In addition, basing their calculations on the average patient, they estimated that the eight thousand patients who left would also have needed some $2 million in pharmaceuticals. Finally, the mean cost to transfer patients from Whiteriver to bigger hospitals was $1,700 per patient. Although one thousand patients were flown elsewhere in an average year, the team decided to use a conservative estimate that roughly one-third would still require transfer, which put that cost savings just over $1 million. To simplify the calculation, the team did not include lost lab and testing fees or the cost of having to admit patients to intensive care, deciding that those figures were too tenuous.

When the team presented the figures, Whiteriver Hospital leadership found the fast-track idea compelling. Administrators budgeted $150,000 for emergency room renovation in the next budget cycle. The new design moves the reception staff from behind a glass window to a desk in the middle of the waiting area, where the triage expert (probably an EMT or a medical technician) will quickly analyze

ASSESSING IMPACT

Although design thinking may seem at odds with a bottom-line mentality, thinking creatively about how to assess impact can be as essential as thinking creatively about solutions. Organizations today live in quantitative cultures, so figuring out how to put together a compelling financial case for an idea's potential value is often crucial in finding the support, funding, and other resources needed to launch a creative concept. Such an assessment helps determine whether the concept really "wows" and delivers to the organization and its stakeholders anticipated benefits that justify the investment needed to scale it.

each case and send patients either to true emergency services for further triage or to one of two fast-track rooms for quick response to nonthreatening issues, such as providing prescription refills and setting appointments for specialist visits. Signage will be improved, and two new assessment rooms are being added. In the meantime, a second clinician has been added to allow fast-tracking to continue during peak times, even before the renovation is complete.

A Closer Look at Ignite

Let's take a closer look at the Ignite process in its current form. Read Holman contrasts the Ignite Accelerator with the government's "business as usual" approach (which looks a lot like Innovation I):

> The standard governmental process is—and this is definitely a broad, sweeping stroke but there are definite truths here—put a bunch of experts in a room, usually with a nice big oak table and leather chairs, and have a series of meetings for six months, where they chart out what needs to happen. Then they write a statement of work. Then dollars, typically millions of dollars, are put towards that statement of work, and a contractor comes in to build and launch it. And then it turns out most of these new programs don't work quite like they were supposed to. The Ignite Accelerator is trying to provide a space for testing the idea prior to the point of putting funds towards a contractor.

Two years after the Whiteriver team joined Ignite, HHS announced the fifth round of the accelerator. In the HHS IDEA Lab blog, Read gave these reasons why HHS staff might consider one or both of the programs:

- Because you know that there's got to be a better way to do things.
- Because that annoying operational problem isn't going to fix itself.
- Because you're seeking a professional growth opportunity.
- Because you've been at HHS for under 5 years and you're starting to lose your mind.
- Because you've been at HHS for over 5 years [and] wouldn't mind a spark to (ahem) ignite a significant effort.
- Because you're an example of how wrong the stereotype of the government employee is.
- Because ... Well, why [the] heck not?

Even the tone of the announcement makes it clear that Ignite is far from government as usual.

In selecting its fifth class from among eighty-two ideas and teams from across HHS's dozen agencies, the IDEA Lab worked to ensure rigor and validity, with a twist. Assigning scores based on a project's alignment with both HHS's and the specific agency's mission, their description of the problem and its related systemic issues, and the anticipated merits of any proposed solution, HHS used twenty-five reviewers, in panels of five, to ensure that each team's idea was analyzed thoroughly. If any review panel unanimously voted to advance an idea—even if it didn't produce a top score—that team also made the finals. And then, outside of all scoring, IDEA Lab staff pulled another sixteen wild card teams into the finals. "We believe in rules and algorithms to ensure fairness, but we also hesitate to over-rely on them at the risk of losing the touch of human judgment," Read explained.

Finalists were introduced to human-centered innovation tools and techniques and received mentoring from former Ignite program winners. Each finalist team completed at least ten interviews to ensure that their ideas were in line with their stakeholders' reality. In this discovery phase, the finalist teams became acquainted with the ethnography to address the **What *is*?** question. They then produced a five-minute pitch for a handful of Read's staff and faced thirty minutes of questioning in hopes of becoming one of twenty teams to advance to the full Ignite Accelerator program. In the full Ignite Accelerator, the twenty winners received intense design thinking training at the three-day boot camp in DC, and a $5,000 stipend.

Winners also had the inside track to compete for venture funding, a post-Ignite extension offering funds to assist innovative teams and ideas in taking their validated concepts to the next phase. Although HHS hopes that the final Ignite teams find money within their agencies to continue piloting any innovative ideas—as Whiteriver Hospital did—they also provide $50,000 to $100,000 grants to innovation as part of a venture fund.

Overall, the HHS approach works to ensure good use of resources. IDEA Lab staff judge the depth of the teams, the strength of their commitments, and the general feasibility of their ideas. They are especially interested in the passion, determination, and curiosity of the applicant teams, more so than the strength of whatever idea they are proposing. The question is whether teams can back off their personal investments in already existing "solutions"—solutions that, after all, got them into the Ignite finals—if and when the data fail to support their assumptions. Fighting the urge for winning teams' original ideas to focus all thinking and drive all research efforts, IDEA Lab staff constantly underline the research, insight, and reasoning underlying any concept, before it is chosen for a learning launch. Staying in the "question space" until the team truly understands a problem and the stakeholders involved with it can seem inefficient to type A "doer" personalities—often the types of people who apply for projects like the Ignite Accelerator—but IDEA Lab constantly works to counterbalance that natural yearning, because a rush to judgment can mask major issues.

Ignite's three-day design thinking and innovation boot camp in Washington, DC, designed to transform the twenty winning teams into innovation champions, is not unusual in today's world. Across government and business, many attempts to spread design thinking use such workshops, which build enthusiasm for new ways of doing things. But we worry that many of the ideas they generate end up on the cutting-room floor when employees return to their day-to-day obligations. Through the entire Ignite process, HHS is working to ensure that this doesn't happen. Besides requiring the teams to commit up front to a three-month program, of which the boot camp is just the kickoff, the IDEA Lab requires supervisors' agreement to provide the teams with time to work on their projects during a full quarter of the fiscal year. In fact, the twenty winning teams are told to expect that 25 to 50 percent of their time in the three months after the boot camp will be spent brainstorming, honing, and reimagining their projects. During that time, they receive consistent mentoring and often find that their original solution missed the problem, as Whiteriver did.

One team in the 2015 Ignite class, for example, entered the Ignite Accelerator process with the intention of redesigning an awkward eleven-page form used in the Centers for Disease Control and Prevention (CDC). Instead, doing ethnography with CDC scientists, team members discovered that, more than anything, the scientists wanted to understand the whole technology transfer system. In the end, rather than simply redesigning the form, the team developed cartoon videos and an electronic tracking document, which were well received by CDC staff. One participant highlighted how the program encouraged a new mindset: "I think about problems differently now and focus on what a user actually needs. Just because we see something as problematic, doesn't mean that's the problem users want us to solve!"

The Ignite process stresses the iterative nature of design thinking, and the IDEA Lab encourages teams to remain open to divergent thinking even into the learning launch and piloting stages of the project. "There's the notion of low-resolution prototyping," Read noted. He explained:

> Instead of automatically putting funds towards a contractor that does the work, we make all teams go through a stage of low-resolution prototyping where they do the prototyping themselves. They use basic paper and pencil to start and then iterate through regular engagements with end users, constantly getting feedback and testing the underlying business assumptions.

Often, as happened at Whiteriver, the discussions with stakeholders and end users can result in the need for substantial change to proposed ideas. For this reason, a thorough up-front analysis of stakeholders can be an efficiency booster as teams select areas of opportunity to explore with design thinking. This includes involving others beyond just the end users that the new service targets. Creating great solutions for problems others don't think they have can frustrate would-be innovators. The "back burner" problem—that is, delays by senior management—often kills innovation because delayed decision making can create timing issues and frustrate potential innovators. Ignite has crafted a solution to this difficulty by using their staffers' clout on behalf of innovators throughout the organization. In addition to webinars and conference calls across all the final teams, mentors reach out to ensure ongoing progress and help the teams by utilizing their own extensive networks within HHS. Innovators without this kind of high-level support need to think carefully in advance about the campaign they need to wage to get such attention on their own.

The Evolution of Ignite Accelerator

The continual reshaping of Ignite itself illustrates learning in action. In its first three years of existence, the Ignite Accelerator evolved with each successive offering as Read and his team gained new insights each time they ran the program. Changes have included shortening Ignite team time from six to three months, reducing stipend funding from $5,000 to $3,000, and working harder to embed creative thinking throughout HHS by means of weekly contact with winning teams. Realizing that more money and longer training do not necessarily lead to better innovation—in fact, often the opposite is true—has led the IDEA Lab to recognize the potential of small, fast bets produced under the agency's political radar.

Building comfort with these new methods involves battling practices that can be deeply entrenched. One of the major changes over the years is that Ignite now offers consistent mentoring from prior IDEA Lab winners, between the boot camp and final presentations. Read says this was the most difficult aspect of putting together the program, because innovators are "super smart people who would make great mentors" but "because they're super smart, they are really, really busy," but it has paid off.

The twenty Ignite teams face IDEA Lab staff and an assembled team of experts in a "shark tank" to hone their final pitches to upper management. In the shark tank, the polished concepts are tested against the realities of funding, team assumptions, and even personality conflicts. "We want to put them in front of the key decision maker within that agency, and it's up to them to make that pitch and sell it, to present what they'd do next if they had further funding and investment," Read explained. "A little more than a third of our teams have actually gotten funding. Only a handful have not gotten anywhere." The original shark tanks, Read explained, were brutal, but the IDEA Lab team has backed off to ensure that good ideas don't get buried, and their proposers discouraged, by negative feedback. Yet again, the IDEA Lab team iterates their own concepts and practices. Indeed, a recent Ignite Accelerator participant commented on the supportiveness of the program:

> Ignite gave me the courage to challenge myself in a safe space: I am not one who enjoys public speaking, but the Ignite environment, mentors, and other teams were all very encouraging so I volunteered a bunch to speak up and even gave our team's final pitch on Demo Day. Last but not least (and this will be cheesy), Ignite really did "ignite" a part of me to help promote innovation.

Reflections on the Process

As Marliza reflected on her Ignite experience, she pointed to several aspects of the IDEA Lab, in addition to the educational component, that made a difference in inspiring her to try creativity, and then continued to engage her throughout the messy process of innovation. One was the simplicity of the tools. She especially found HHS's suggestion of the Business Model Canvas helpful and became deeply interested in the fiscal concepts around innovation. She recalled:

> I thought this was ingenious. Rather than an old-school business plan, the size of a big binder book, that you'd give to investors and bankers, they took us through an easy business model, which we had to work out on butcher-block paper. Who were the customers, what were we trying to do, who might support us, what resources. We had to do a lot of brainstorming on that.

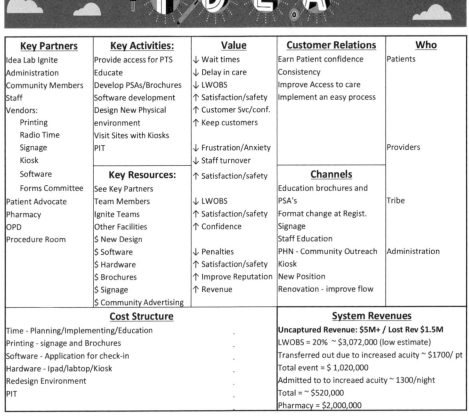

Key Partners	Key Activities:	Value	Customer Relations	Who
Idea Lab Ignite	Provide access for PTS	↓ Wait times	Earn Patient confidence	Patients
Administration	Educate	↓ Delay in care	Consistency	
Community Members	Develop PSAs/Brochures	↓ LWOBS	Improve Access to care	
Staff	Software development	↑ Satisfaction/safety	Implement an easy process	
Vendors:	Design New Physical	↑ Customer Svc/conf.		
Printing	environment	↑ Keep customers		
Radio Time	Visit Sites with Kiosks			
Signage	PIT	↓ Frustration/Anxiety		Providers
Kiosk		↓ Staff turnover		
Software	**Key Resources:**	↑ Satisfaction/safety	**Channels**	
Forms Committee	See Key Partners		Education brochures and	
Patient Advocate	Team Members	↓ LWOBS	PSA's	Tribe
Pharmacy	Ignite Teams	↑ Satisfaction/safety	Format change at Regist.	
OPD	Other Facilities	↑ Confidence	Signage	
Procedure Room	$ New Design		Staff Education	
	$ Software	↓ Penalties	PHN - Community Outreach	Administration
	$ Hardware	↑ Satisfaction/safety	Kiosk	
	$ Brochures	↑ Improve Reputation	New Position	
	$ Signage	↑ Revenue	Renovation - improve flow	
	$ Community Advertising			

Cost Structure		System Revenues
Time - Planning/Implementing/Education		**Uncaptured Revenue: $5M+ / Lost Rev $1.5M**
Printing - signage and Brochures		LWOBS = 20% ~ $3,072,000 (low estimate)
Software - Application for check-in		Transferred out due to increased acuity ~ $1700/ pt
Hardware - Ipad/labtop/Kiosk		Total event = $ 1,020,000
Redesign Environment		Admitted to to increaed acuity ~ 1300/night
PIT		Total = ~ $520,000
		Pharmacy = $2,000,000

Whiteriver's Business Model Canvas. Source: Strategyzer.com.

Even more significant for Marliza was IDEA Lab's continual involvement in the Whiteriver project, primarily through its mentoring program. Mentors constantly asked if there was anybody participants needed help to sell their ideas to. Since the Whiteriver team had strong support from its direct management, the answer was always no, but for others, subtle pressure from the office of the secretary of Health and Human Services—where IDEA Lab is headquartered—nudged management to pay attention to innovative concepts. Again, being able to reach across the network mattered, as Marliza explained:

> They know everybody in DC, and they could get the head person to back you up. When dealing with all these heads of agencies, you could run into some obstacles, and even at a lower level, with your supervisor, your director. IDEA Lab wanted to ensure that, once we started, we had all the support we needed from our own agency. If they needed to intervene, they would. They asked, "Anybody you need us to talk to; anyone we need to get information to; anyone we need to sell to?" They asked over and over again.

Another helpful aspect of Ignite was the internal political "cover" that involvement in the program gave Marliza within Whiteriver Hospital itself as she devoted half of her time to the project, having to exercise extensive prioritization to fulfill her full-time, day-to-day responsibilities. The existence of a formal program and process, with small potential funding grants, made it easier to justify her time and efforts to the Whiteriver leadership. "Once involved, we got very excited, but it was really stressful," Marliza said. "It required a lot of time and resources backing us up. We had to have almost all the employees supporting us when we did our beta test."

A final valued aspect was the camaraderie and networking the other Ignite teams provided. The connections formed at the boot camp were lasting. The teams coached each other, both formally through the conference calls and informally through personal communications. Providing access to this new network was an important element of Ignite. Marliza noted:

> The other teams were extremely supportive. We got to know each other during boot camp as we had to listen to each other's presentations quite a few times. Their stories were compelling and we wanted to support them too. Some of those other agencies—CDC, NIH [National Institutes of Health], places I've never heard of and things I've never imagined—all those little things they were trying to do in background, wow. Later,

when we made the final presentations, everybody was hugely supportive. A lot kept in touch afterwards, and as a result of that, along with the folks in the shark tank, the who's who in business of what you need, we learned so much from their questions. IDEA Lab chose people who knew what we do in patient health and made them part of our shark tank; they were basically the people we had to sell our idea to. What we kept hearing was, "Hey guys, this is a no-brainer." That gave us the confidence that we needed to go to leadership.

Recently, Marliza left her role at Whiteriver to attend law school. She told us:

I thought about how having those credentials could not only help within the Indian Health Service and serving the Indian community, but also my passion with wanting to help the immigrant women and children get out of these for-profit detention centers in Arizona. Law school won't teach me how to think like an innovator, but it will certainly help move my innovative ideas forward.

As this book goes to press, Whiteriver's plans have evolved into a multimillion-dollar construction concept across the hospital, and the new emergency supervisor, Emily Gaffney, is building on the fast-track idea and meeting with architects in preparation for construction. "We are doing fast track right now when we can, even though the space which we have is not ideal," she explained to us. Triaging patients early, even without the best space, has helped to lower Whiteriver's left-without-being-seen rate to 9 percent, about half of what it was in 2014. She believes the new hospital construction, when finished, will drive the number even lower.

CREATIVE CONFIDENCE

What is creative confidence? Popularized by the famous Kelley brothers in a book of that name, creative confidence is defined by a follower of IDEO, a design consultancy, as "having the freedom and courage to fail/take creative risks and the knowledge that all of the ideas you create have value." Sounds like an apt description of Marliza and her team.

Some might argue that what Marliza and her team accomplished is not dramatic enough to be classified as "innovation," but we disagree. What if even a fraction of HHS's eighty thousand employees around the United States were motivated to follow the lead of the Whiteriver team? Imagine the increase in the quality of experience of patients at the many HHS hospitals. Imagine the savings to taxpayers. We'd call those outcomes dramatic. That's the point of Ignite—tapping into even a small percentage of the innovation potential of the agency's vast employee base could make a big difference.

By encouraging and enabling small changes that can accumulate to have a large impact, the Ignite Accelerator demonstrates the power of democratizing innovation. The creation of an infrastructure that offers training, mentoring, and resources like time, supervisor support, and access to the HHS network is fundamental to creating the kind of context in which employees like Marliza, with her passion for improvement, can succeed.

At the end of the day, Ignite certainly seems to have lived up to its name, helping the Whiteriver team to develop the creative confidence that successfully democratizing innovation will require. Marliza's own words capture that best:

> Not being in Washington, not part of a tech environment or an innovative environment, it was intimidating. We're babies, and others are so much more sophisticated, more educated. Were we going to be too far behind them? It was scary. But if that e-mail hadn't come to me, I would have never known that I had the ability to make this happen, that I could step outside our little agency . . . I think my experience with Ignite will definitely help me to be fearless in "disrupting" the status quo and looking for new and innovative ways to find solutions. I also think it gave me confidence to be willing to propose anything and everything without concerning myself with rejection of any new idea.

CHAPTER FOUR

Including New Voices at the Kingwood Trust

THE CHALLENGE TO THE GREATER GOOD

One prominent theme in these stories is the inclusion of more voices—particularly those excluded in the past—in innovation conversations. Traditionally, experts in fields such as health care, education, and government have designed *for* people in need. How can they design *with* them, instead? And what if the stakeholders we want to include are reluctant or have difficulty participating in typical ways?

DESIGN THINKING'S CONTRIBUTION

Design thinking provides opportunities to invite those previously excluded into innovation conversations, even those who have difficulty communicating their needs. In the United Kingdom, the Kingwood Trust is committed to such inclusion, reworking traditional design tools to accomplish it: inviting the adults with autism they support, along with their families and support staff, into the design of their homes, outdoor spaces, and daily activities of life. Beginning by reframing the nature of the opportunity, Kingwood has developed creative ways to allow even those who don't use written or spoken language to participate in creating the designs that impact their lives.

In the world of Innovation I, "experts" do the designing. Especially when the stakeholders involved are disadvantaged—poor, ill, or differently abled—the expert's voice dominates the innovation conversation, often silencing other voices. In Innovation II, we search for value-creating ideas by inviting the stakeholders into the conversation. Design thinking has explicit processes embedded within the four questions to make this inclusion a reality. In the **What *is*** phase, we go deep, using ethnographic tools to try to understand what the world looks like and how it is experienced from the stakeholders' perspectives. In **What *if*,** the stakeholders participate with us in idea generation. In **What *wows*,** we create prototypes that make the new concepts vivid and tangible for them. In **What *works*,** we seek their feedback and incorporate it into our evolving design.

But imagine a setting in which the people whose needs you are trying to meet are unable to communicate with you in the ways you are accustomed to. Engagement might seem difficult to achieve. The story of how the Kingwood Trust engaged the autistic people they support represents some of the most creative and impressive inclusion strategies that we have seen anywhere.

The Kingwood story starts with a determined mother in the United Kingdom, Dame Stephanie Shirley, who decided to ask a different question. Her son, Giles, was diagnosed with autism spectrum disorder, believed to affect about 1 percent of the world's population. As Giles grew to adulthood, he needed care that his parents alone could not provide. This lack of facilities for adults with autism is a global problem. An opinion piece in the *Washington Post* recently noted:

> One of the most urgent . . . needs is more services for adults with autism. Such adults
> are too often treated as if they are invisible. It's the children with autism who tug at
> our heartstrings . . . But those kids grow up . . . Many of them could live with a greater
> degree of independence if there were more funding for affordable housing tailored to
> their needs. Many could have the satisfaction of a productive job if given the necessary
> training and support.

With no alternative available at the time in the United Kingdom, Giles's parents were forced to hospitalize him in an institution, where, in Stephanie's own words, "there were probably zoos in Britain where the quality of the inmates' lives was a higher policy priority." She saw that caregivers had given up all hope of helping patients to lead better lives. Instead, she said, "they were kept alive and physically safe but had been deprived of most of their human rights." But Stephanie saw an opportunity that others did not, and in 1994 she founded the Kingwood Trust, a UK charity dedicated to pioneering best practices to help people with autism and Asperger's syndrome live full and active lives.

From its founding, Kingwood chose to deliberately step away from focusing only on safety and security and to commit to a higher bar—designing with a goal of growth and development. As Colum Lowe, their partner at BEING, a design consultancy, explained to us: "Everything we do is about giving people that Kingwood supports opportunities to express themselves, to develop their interests, and to challenge themselves in a controlled way. That changes everything."

Fast-forward to today, when Kingwood has incorporated design thinking into the core of their strategy. Over the past seven years, they have identified for redesign a series of areas that touch the lives of people with autism—beginning with the design of independent housing, moving on to the design of outdoor green spaces, and then addressing personal tasks of daily living, such as making a sandwich or vacuuming a carpet. Despite the challenge of developing a deep understanding of people who often have limited speech and additional learning disabilities, Kingwood has invited these autistic people, their support staff, and their families into the design process as active participants. In doing so, Kingwood has succeeded in developing new design standards and inclusion practices that have become influential throughout the United Kingdom. The cumulative impact of these initiatives has dramatically improved the ability of those they support to lead more independent lives and, in Kingwood's own words, has helped people with autism "live the lives they choose."

Their design thinking journey began in 2009, when Kingwood CEO Sue Osborn contacted Colum Lowe at BEING. The Kingwood Trust wanted to build new accommodations for its residents but could

REFRAMING THE QUESTION

Regardless of whether we frame our starting point for designing as a question, a challenge, or a problem, successful design really begins with giving careful thought to the space that we want to explore. Our initial framing of the question shapes the boundaries and direction of the entire innovation journey, as is evident in the Kingwood story. Stephanie Shirley, a loving mother, asked a different question than the experts of the time were asking. She was concerned with a much broader, more ambitious challenge than just keeping her son physically safe. Her aspiration was for him to lead as full and active a life as possible. That new framing of the question opened up a completely different innovation conversation.

find no guidelines for designing for adults with autism. Colum was an expert in the design of health care facilities and was commissioned to carry out a review and produce a proposal outlining how Kingwood could develop guidance for the design of residential housing for adults with autism. Colum's proposal included commissioning the Helen Hamlyn Centre for Design at the Royal College of Art to carry out a yearlong project to conduct the research, with input from renowned experts in the worlds of dementia and autism, and to produce the guidance.

Their initial research, conducted by Andrew Brand, suggested four themes to guide the development of the new environments: Growth and Development, Triggers, Robustness, and Support Tools. Growth and Development meant encouraging people with autism to explore their environment in ways that built their confidence and providing spaces for developing interests and skills. Triggers focused on reducing stimuli that might negatively impact the residents, while providing spaces that would meet their sensory needs. Robustness reflected the provision of a safe environment for residents and staff and an environment tolerant of things being used for unintended purposes. Support Tools had a goal of helping staff to allow them to provide their best care.

These themes guided the design of common areas as well as personal spaces. Calming neutral colors were used in common areas, while residents could choose their own preferred colors for private bedrooms. Common spaces (spaces with no prescribed function) were used for a variety of purposes, including dancing and computer work. Sleeping spaces had inset lighting that could be a standard, neutral light color or a range of colors, depending on personal preferences. Sensory preferences guided projects designed to engender growth and development. Underfloor heating and plumbing were used to provide a safe and secure environment.

Shortly thereafter, in 2010, textile designer Katie Gaudion, with a passion both for understanding how people engage with the sensory qualities of the environment and for enriching the lives of people with neurodevelopmental conditions, joined the team at the Helen Hamlyn Centre. Katie brought Kingwood's developmental aspiration to life by putting aside the triad of impairments that often dominates the autism discussion: impairment in social interaction and communication, understanding, and imagination. Instead, she developed a new design framework called the Triad of Strengths, which views autism in a positive and enabling light.

With the Triad of Strengths, Katie sought to maximize the *positive* impact of sensory preferences, special interests, and action capabilities. As before, this reframing of the opportunity itself—moving from prevention of bad events to active encouragement of good ones—set the stage for innovation. With this focus as their guide, the team moved beyond merely removing the "pain points" we talk so much about in design. Instead, they set out to conduct studies aimed at exploring an individual's sensory preferences, special interests, and capabilities, to create points of joy and learning and development.

In the early part of the design thinking process, it can be challenging to engage a broader and more diverse group in the design conversation in a way that facilitates the kind of deep discovery and insight generation required for innovation, and the Kingwood design team faced multiple challenges as they began their research. One challenge was that the researchers could not always *ask* the autistic adults at Kingwood about their experiences, needs, or preferences. Though they knew that many people with autism are highly sensitive to sensory input such as light, sound, and smell, there was little detailed research on how these sensitivities could be accommodated in the design process. Another research challenge related to the autistic participants' sensitivity to their environment—the very presence of a researcher in their midst often disrupted their lives.

As we learned more about the Kingwood story—and eventually read Katie's PhD dissertation, which chronicled the design team's approach and the intensive involvement of key stakeholders in every aspect of the process—the team's data gathering and insight identification in the **What *is*** phase, idea generation in the **What *if*** phase, and testing in **What *wows*** and **What *works*** stood out to us as critical. Accomplishing these steps required the team to adapt existing research tools to their stakeholders' unique ways of experiencing the world. In particular, their extensive use of the design tool visualization—in many forms, ranging from prototyping to storyboarding—not merely in the testing process but

VISUALIZATION

The use of visualization is one of the cornerstones of the design thinking approach. Many of us associate visualization with drawing, but it is really about making our thoughts visible in ways that render them more accessible to others. At its simplest level, visualization is about creating images, stepping away from our reliance on spoken language and text. At a deeper level, it is about seeing with our *mind's* eye—conjuring up vivid depictions of what we are thinking in terms that are clear and compelling to others.

also as an important part of the discovery phase, was critical in helping to surface insights that the autistic participants, support staff, and family members might not have recognized or articulated otherwise.

Exploring What *is*

Even though it is clearly understood that the physical environment has an impact on people, existing research has not focused on the relationship between people with autism and their environment. However, the team found that the relationship of some autistic people with items in the environment might be very different, even with respect to everyday items, such as toasters and washing machines. A washing machine might provide pleasure to a person observing its spinning motion, and a toaster might trigger anxiety because of the toast popping up unexpectedly. What may seem like destructive behavior, such as ripping pages in a magazine or rubbing against a wall, might actually provide pleasure.

With this realization in mind, Katie conducted studies over a period of several years: one for the design of the outdoor space, the other for the everyday activities project. For both projects, Katie created a range of sensory and creative activities and used the tools of mirroring interests, participatory observation, and shadowing as well as traditional interviews with support staff and family. Wherever and however possible, the people that Kingwood supports, all of whom were adults with autism, were invited to participate in the research.

In the design of the outdoor garden space, for example, Katie organized a two-hour garden activity, complete with furniture, props, and activities designed to incorporate sensory experiences based on the autistic participants' interests. Props were designed to reflect sensory properties (for example, touch, sound, sight, smell, or movement) and were used to gain insights about the sensory preferences and action capabilities of the residents. For example, one participant, Pete, enjoyed props that offered resistance through stretching and pulling. This resulted in the design of a prop called fiddle bricks (think of large, soft, malleable Lego pieces), which Pete appeared to very much enjoy during the two-hour garden activity. A trampoline was added for those who enjoyed the movement of jumping.

As the garden was being designed, areas for different sensory experiences were added. For example, one individual might enjoy seeing bubbles, smelling earthy and floral scents, walking barefoot, running, jumping, or touching sand. As Katie explained, "A person's interests can help inform the choice of specific features and activities, which greatly increases the likelihood of active engagement with the garden." In another example of a creative activity, the design team made mobiles with both the autistic participants and their support staff. The team extended their work by creating a guide to making sensory props, and they held co-creation workshops during which support staff made personalized sensory props for the person they supported.

To develop a better understanding of the residents' sensory preferences, Katie took well-established sensory profile questionnaires and adapted them into a set of visual sensory preference cards. For people who had difficulties in communicating likes and dislikes verbally, the cards provided a way to facilitate the communication of their sensory likes and dislikes and to create an overview of their individual sensory profile. The cards enabled the autistic participants to express their preferences by pointing or by initiating eye contact. This process directly involved autistic people.

Example of a sensory card.

For the daily activities project, Katie developed a set of forty-three visual cards called Objects of Everyday Use. These cards, too, were based on an existing questionnaire, the Lawton Instrumental Activities of Daily Living Scale. The photographs of daily activities on the cards provided visual prompts to help participants better understand what activity was being considered. Simple questions that could be answered by checking a box made it easier for the residents to participate in filling out the cards. Again, the focus was to make the process more inclusive for the Kingwood residents and to enable them to express the things they did or didn't like to do around their home.

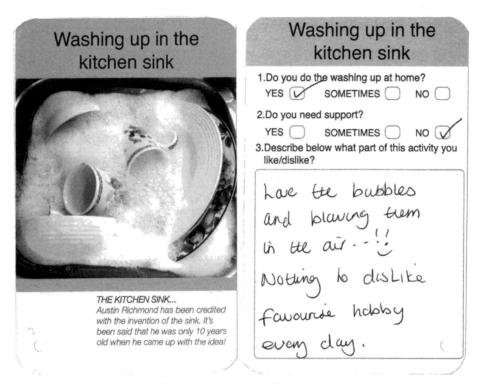

Example of a daily activities card.

Often, in our research, we find that the most important outcome of a design thinking project is not necessarily the new designs that emerge; it is the impact on the people involved. The cards succeeded because they gave the autistic participants a chance to express themselves in ways they had not before—giving them more control and independence to describe likes and dislikes. Likewise, these visual tools help support staff and families summon insights they were previously unable to recognize and learn more about the people they supported, facilitating changes in their daily practices.

Support staff enjoyed working with the cards. As one explained:

> The pictures seem to make what we should be asking more precise, which makes me feel more confident about providing an answer. I also like how the picture cards help towards involving the people we support. It is about them, after all, and it's important to give them the tools to be heard and contribute opinions and input.

With the help of support staff, seventeen adults with autism completed the cards about their daily activities. Katie noted that "the cards enabled research teams to explore patterns and correlations between the most popular and least popular activities, the amount of support required to perform an activity, and the reasons, when possible, why the participants liked or disliked various activities." For instance, an interest in bubbles motivated some participants to wash the dishes because of the sheer pleasure of engaging with the bubbly suds.

"When the people we support would like a cup of tea, it is probably faster for the caregiver to make it for them, but this encourages learned helplessness," Colum told us. "We want to create a program for those we support to start doing things for themselves. Don't make a cup of tea for them; help them make a cup of tea. Help them make a sandwich." The idea was to support them by breaking the task down and, through an understanding of what helped or hindered an individual autistic participant, to redesign the steps by building on the person's sensory preferences and strengths to do just that.

It became clear to the design team that these everyday activities involved a series of steps, each with a potential draw or obstacle. If the obstacle could be understood and removed, or an interest added, the task might become more attractive. "Pinpointing which part of an activity the autistic person finds difficult, and detecting where in an activity a person may need extra prompts and support, helps identify what needs to be adapted or designed differently to complement a person's capabilities," Katie explained. For example, if a person dislikes a toaster because the toast pops up without warning, someone might be able to time the popping to give a warning indicator of when it will happen. A small thing like setting a timer could solve the challenge and facilitate the task.

For the daily activities project, Katie drew on research to create a taxonomy of interests. An illustration of a tree was used to visualize the interests of each autistic participant. Each color-coded branch represented an area of interest. Leaves on each branch reflected a specific individual's interest in that area, such as dancing on the sports branch, music on the creative arts branch, or radio on the machines branch. With some branches covered in leaves and others fairly empty, each tree clearly showed a visual snapshot of that person's specific interests.

A tree representing the interests of an autistic participant. Illustration by Katie Gaudion.

The Kingwood story drives home the power of empathy. For most of us, a washing machine is a machine that we use to wash clothes. We rarely consider it from the perspective of sensory inputs, and if we do, we likely pay little attention to those thoughts and reactions. If a washing machine is noisy, we get annoyed and we move away until the cycle is done. Perhaps the next time we buy a machine, we will purchase a quieter model. But for someone with autism, the sensory inputs from everyday objects and the environment can have a tremendous impact on daily life. As we've seen, a washing machine can potentially be a source of enjoyment as you watch the clothes spinning. A toaster, on the other hand, might cause serious distress. The distant sound of a car engine can be like a gong clashing in the same room.

For a "neurotypical" designer to truly see through the world through the eyes of an autistic person is a significant challenge—even for a designer already committed to empathy. Direct observation can be a powerful design tool.

Katie described one of the moments of insight that came early in her work, as she first observed Pete. The first time Katie visited Pete at home, she saw him involved in a series of seemingly destructive acts—picking at a leather sofa, ripping a magazine, and creating indentations in a wall by rubbing against it. She focused on documenting Pete's behavior and wondered how she could help to design solutions that would prevent it in the future. But, on Katie's second visit to Pete's house, she elected to *mirror* Pete's behavior and discovered, to her surprise, the sense of sensory enjoyment that came from ripping paper, flipping a magazine, picking at the leather on a couch, or holding an ear against a wall. Unable to ask Pete directly what he liked about doing these things, Katie mirrored his actions and experienced it for herself:

> Picking the leather off the sofa was surprisingly satisfying and could be equated to
> the satisfaction one gets from popping bubble wrap. So, instead of a ruined sofa, I now
> perceived Pete's sofa as an object wrapped in fabric that is fun to pick. Pressing my ear

THE DIRECT OBSERVATION TOOL

While ethnographic interviewing is likely to be the most used design tool, direct observation can often yield crucial insights that merely talking to people does not. The responses we get when we ask people about their behavior have biases and limitations. Direct observation helps us learn more about the discrepancy between what people say and what people do, what designers call the "say/do" gap. In ethnographic observation, we step into the "native habitat" of those we want to learn more about and try to capture the full context, without interpretation or judgment. This is not easy to do, as Katie's description of her observation of Pete reflects.

against the wall and feeling the vibrations of the music above, I felt a slight tickle in my ear . . . So, instead of a damaged wall, I perceived it as a pleasant and relaxing experience.

On her first visit to his home, Katie had used her own frame of reference and labeled Pete's acts as negative and destructive. On her second visit, she began to truly empathize with Pete—the sofa, wall, and music revealed vital clues that helped her understand the things Pete liked to do. She explained, "I thought empathy was innate but now realize that it can grow and evolve. For this to happen . . . it requires a perceptual shift in thinking that is open to different ways of being in the world."

Co-Creating What *if*

As the design team moved from exploring **What *is*** to generating new ideas in **What *if***, they kept in mind this understanding of sensory preferences, interests, and capabilities, and they facilitated co-creation workshops to generate design concepts for the garden project. Support staff and family members were invited to imagine what a shared garden space might look like. A paper representation of a rectangular patch of grass and cards that showed possible garden features, such as furniture, flooring, partitions, and activity ideas, were given out. The participants were also given stickers representing the autistic person they support, and they were asked to place them in areas of preference, giving the team an idea of what features might be expected to be popular.

The result was a visual representation of a garden, showing the desired activities in various spots on the patches of grass and a sense of who would likely spend time in the various activity areas. The co-creation workshop quickly gave the team a sense of popular and recurring themes. The exercises were engaging and useful because they tended to allow for spontaneous and revealing conversations. Although the garden was being designed for adults with autism, it became clear that the garden space would be an area for all to enjoy time together, including staff and family members.

The final garden design included seven different activity spaces: escape, exercise, occupation, sensory, social, transition, and wilderness. "Escape" recognized the need for solitude, calm, and quiet, and "sensory" recognized the influence of sensory experience and the effort to use it to positive effect. For example, specific sensory spaces were designed to reflect sight, smell, sound, and touch. In addition, the activity spaces were designed to be separate and compartmentalized, to help the residents transition between these areas of activity. This design would allow for individual preferences and interests and would facilitate change and acclimation. Spaces closer to the house were purposely designed to be more ordered and to be static and unchanging (with plants and trees that do not change with the seasons), for those who do not like change. Areas farther away could include more seasonal change and less order. The garden was designed to provide low sensory input at the entrance and to allow more sensory exploration the farther one went into the garden. This arrangement helped to balance a person's hyper- and hyposensitivities.

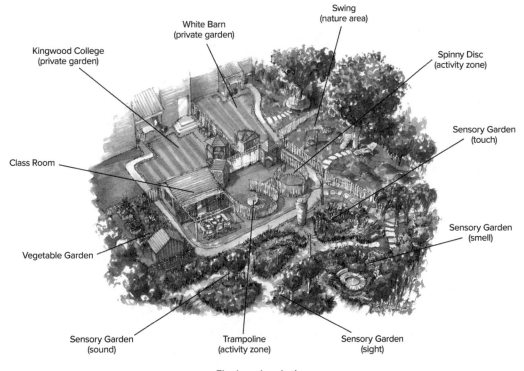

Kingwood College
(private garden)

White Barn
(private garden)

Swing
(nature area)

Spinny Disc
(activity zone)

Sensory Garden
(touch)

Class Room

Sensory Garden
(smell)

Vegetable Garden

Sensory Garden
(sound)

Trampoline
(activity zone)

Sensory Garden
(sight)

Final garden design.

To accommodate those who did not like to get dirty but who might still like to garden, raised planter boxes were designed to allow for gardening activities that are not too messy or challenging. The exercise space was floored with rubber mulch, and foliage lining the fences helped to dampen the noise from other garden areas. The sensory areas were divided to allow for a focus on one sense at a time. Using the sensory preference cards, some residents expressed a preference for jumping, so a trampoline was considered as a potential addition. Escape spaces offered seating with privacy, while the social space included an outdoor classroom in the garden center. These activity spaces, which came out of the co-creation sessions, were used to develop the final concepts.

During co-creation sessions for the daily activities project, a member of the support staff noted that many residents liked bubbles and found using a vacuum cleaner challenging, so one idea offered was to link the enjoyment of bubbles to the task of vacuuming to make it more enjoyable. Katie developed the idea of attaching a spinning disk to a washing machine to enhance the enjoyment of those participants who liked spinning objects. By recognizing strengths rather than deficits, support staff became better able to help the residents do the tasks that played to their strengths and to manage obstacles that might otherwise get in the way. As Katie noted:

> The support staff were really key, because they were the interpreters and the mediators and they hold so much information about the person they support. But they almost did not realize that themselves. So a big part of the design process was creating a platform for them to be able to share and express their ideas with each other—and explore ways in which they themselves can generate new ideas about the person they support, making it less abstract and more concrete and tangible.

Prototyping What *wows*

Hands-on activities were an important part of the Kingwood design process. The team developed "Ready Steady Make" workshops that pushed exploration further through the use of prototyping. In one of these workshops, Kingwood support staff turned cheap and easy-to-find materials into personalized garden props. These sessions allowed staff to consider the people they supported in terms of their sensory likes and dislikes and to share and communicate experiences and ideas. Although these interactive workshops, in which staff are considered experts and learning is facilitated collaboratively and creatively, first met with some cynicism, they became very popular as the staff enjoyed being creative and thinking about the people they supported. The sessions continue to be provided on an ad hoc basis.

For the daily activities project, another Ready Steady Make workshop was created to allow a mix of newer and longer-term support staff at Kingwood to share their ideas and experiences. They first created paper storyboards of the residents' activities (staff drew step-by-step stories on paper, using stick figure drawings with captions) and then expanded them into three-dimensional theater sets (using creative, three-dimensional representations of the activities).

Also in this stage, two different prototypes were made of a bubble-blowing attachment for the Henry vacuum cleaner (appreciated by many residents for its cheerful appearance), to link bubble blowing with the task of vacuuming. One of Katie's learnings was around the particular nature of the prototypes she needed to create:

> I've learned that my prototypes need to be detachable and be destroyable, because sometimes the only way that residents can communicate that they do not like something is to destroy it, to get rid of it. And I am glad that they are able to do that, because that is the clearest indication that they did not like it.

Testing What *works*

An important part of each of the design activities, after idea generation, was evaluation and testing. After the garden was developed, for instance, the team created a visual evaluation form for staff and the person they support to go through, after each use of the garden, to determine how the garden was being used and what the response was. What time of day was the garden used? What was the weather like on that day? What areas were being used? What was the reaction to the space? What did you like and do? Positive and enjoyable got a happy face. Negative and unenjoyable resulted in a frown. The data gave the team a sense of how the garden was being used and how the autistic participants felt after using the new garden.

The challenge of measuring outcomes at Kingwood is perhaps even greater than in other situations—here the users of the design cannot easily express their likes and dislikes. In some ways, the response of the staff has been the clearest sign of impact, as they have moved from skepticism to enthusiasm for using the design tools.

The tools developed at Kingwood have the potential to have an impact on many projects involving people who are neurologically diverse and are being adapted for use with other populations. For example, in Boston and New York, therapists are now experimenting with the use of the sensory preference cards with people who have dementia.

Reflections on the Process

Kate Allen, who succeeded Sue Osborn as chief executive in 2015, reflected on the importance of understanding the *why* behind Kingwood's continued commitment to innovation and the way in which the use of design thinking had invited the entire organization into the process:

> It's our employees who are working with someone with autism on a day-to-day basis—they're the ones that really make the difference. They are the ones that have the power to make so much difference in that individual's life. And so that member of staff needs to understand and be part of Kingwood's passion—they need to understand why we're doing it. They need to see the benefits and they need to know it can positively impact the person that they're working with right now. Initially, it was an effort to get people to come to the design workshops, because they didn't know what the purpose was. They didn't see why Kingwood was doing these crazy things. You have to link your design idea with a real benefit. It has to be real and tangible to the entire organization. Then they will see the benefit of what we're doing, and then they'll buy in. We're now entering our seventh year of research. And ideas move both upward and downward within the organization. We're all listening to each other.

Kingwood shows us the importance of framing new questions, involving new voices despite the challenges of doing so, and adapting tools like cards and props, in creative ways, to make their input meaningful. It is ultimately impossible to put ourselves in the minds and bodies of another person, but we *can* make tremendous strides in engaging others and increasing our understanding of their experience by using design thinking tools. But, as Katie notes, this requires shifting our perception. Making sense of the preferences of others is possible if we reserve judgment, question our assumptions, and allow exploratory research and prototyping to offer new data and understanding. As we see at Kingwood, even with adults with autism who have limited speech and additional learning disabilities, we can develop a valuable understanding of individuals' experiences through ethnographic research that involves them, their families, and support staff, so that we can work with them to achieve a greater good, making their lives more active and fulfilling.

While the Kingwood story highlights one of the most challenging situations for engaging stakeholders in the design process, in reality, most people have limits in their ability to clearly communicate their own needs. Here lies the promise in the difficult act of committing to deep discovery as a prelude to idea generation. The creativity of the Kingwood project team is perhaps most evident not in their eventual solutions but in their ability to surmount obstacles to learning that might have deterred most of us. It demonstrates what is possible when we engage a broader set of voices—when we offer those we design *for* the opportunity to co-create *with* us and participate in the design of their own daily lives in a meaningful way.

CHAPTER FIVE

Scaling Design Thinking at Monash Medical Centre

Challenges in the social sector often live at the systems level. Yet organizations are often collections of siloed specialists who find it difficult to talk across their differences. How do specialists who control different pieces of a system come together to take action on critical problems? Nowhere is this dilemma more apparent than in health care, where the complexities of the system and deep-seated differences can stymie urgently needed organizational reforms.

Imagining a new future together across difference starts with seeing today in a new way. Design thinking brings potent tools to drive this kind of alignment around **What *is*** at a systems level. The medical staff at Australia's Monash Medical Centre demonstrate how human-centered design can help clinical specialists with differing perspectives align on what matters most. As a university medical center in an urban area, Monash faces many woes characteristic of health care institutions today, from the macro—an aging population, lengthening hospital stays, increased reporting requirements—to the micro—the difficulty of getting people to wash their hands. At Monash, these troubles were exacerbated by critical internal challenges around staff engagement, low levels of patient satisfaction, and turnover of the entire senior staff. As part of a multipronged effort that combines design thinking with systems thinking and operations research, clinicians at Monash are mastering design thinking methodologies and working together to make the entire institution more innovative and patient centered.

M onash Medical Centre in Melbourne, Australia, is demonstrating that health care clinicians and staff can lead the way in innovation and bring an entire organization along with
them. There, Dr. Don Campbell, professor of medicine, and Keith Stockman, manager of
operations research, have reached across professional boundaries to mobilize teams of colleagues in
an approach they call "systemic design thinking." The HealthCare InnovationbyDesign initiative they
founded in 2012 is attacking an array of health care challenges as diverse as extended patient stays,
hand hygiene, and mental health. Across projects, they are united around two common beliefs: first,
that new ways of thinking about health care delivery must focus on patients' experiences and their interactions with frontline health care delivery teams; and, second, that these teams must be involved in
any transformation. Change, the Monash team believes, must attend to people, process, and systems,
including the role of human emotions. In particular, an appreciation for the power of the larger system
to drive both intended and unintended behaviors and outcomes is critical.

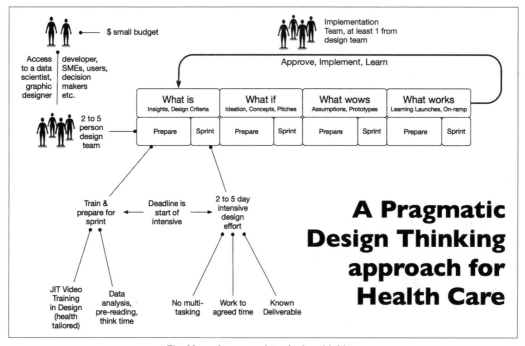

The Monash approach to design thinking.

"I have a three-legged stool model," Don explained. "Clinical management is one leg. Operations research is another leg. Systems thinking is the third leg. And the seat, to bring it all together, is design." Monash has adapted the four-question model to their unique health care environment in powerful ways, thinking deeply about details from the composition of the teams to the pacing of the design conversation. Examining what Monash is accomplishing allows us to consider how design thinking fits into the larger story of system redesign and brings the human voice into operations research. It demonstrates that quantitative and qualitative approaches can work together to create a more complete picture of what is going on today and lay the foundation for a different tomorrow.

Today, Monash's projects are delivering powerful results, allowing Don and Keith and their colleagues to tackle ever-broader health care issues. Indeed, as the hospital scales the successes arising from the design process, it faces a challenge not yet experienced by many of the organizations we've studied: how to move beyond pilots to scale and integrate these new projects into the everyday work flow.

Initiative: General Medicine Redesign

Monash advanced their design journey based on the realization of leaders in the Monash Department of General Practice that continuing "business as usual" would fail to meet the growth in demand driven by an aging population with ever-expanding life expectancies and aspirations for independent living. The design team began their work, in 2007, with a simple premise: place effective patient care center stage and ensure that frontline medical teams can deliver it.

During the **What _is_** stage, the team examined the workload of junior staff, establishing what work could be done with existing staff and whether additional staff would be needed as a result of projected trends in inpatient activity. Surfacing the concerns of key staff members, including nurses, allied health professionals, and both junior and senior medical staff, was critical because the team wanted to understand the issues needing immediate attention. The work practices of junior and senior medical staff, as well as their relationships with other team members, like nursing staff, were reviewed.

On the basis of the information they gathered, they established an overriding principle that constituted a kind of design criteria for idea generation in the **What _if_** stage: _Frontline teams are responsible_ *for the delivery of the patient experience, always. Everyone else in the organization is a member of support staff, including the CEO and board members.* This principle led to two key questions:

1. How can we make it possible for the key members of the frontline team to do their jobs every minute, every hour, every day?

2. How can we empower them to support delivering a joyous patient experience?

This first redesign identified multiple structural change opportunities:

- instituting interdisciplinary bedside rounds to enable synchronous and timely information exchange, making nurses and medical leaders jointly accountable for all aspects of care;
- creating a boundary-spanning role, occupied by senior nurses, to manage overall flow and facilitate transitions in care across boundaries;
- implementing advanced training to better align the skills of junior medical staff to task complexity; and
- providing enhancements to existing performance reports to support accountability for flow performance.

The team started their experiments in an area for which they had responsibility: medical staff operations. The first operational test was the implementation of a morning report with senior medical staff present. Almost immediately, this very first step was challenged, not by frontline staff or management but by the senior staff themselves. "This was incredibly threatening to everyone and was marked by an early open revolt from several members of senior medical staff," Don explained. Informal attempts to remove the leaders of the contested change ensued. Hospital executives held firm, resisting attempts to have change leaders fired, and innovation efforts continued. "Our biggest challenge was this first one, and it was the hardest," Don recalled.

The next step focused on creating a new role for a senior nurse—general medicine liaison coordinator—to act as a boundary spanner, managing relationships with the emergency department, the bed management team, ward-based nurse unit managers, and medical teams. The coordinator was charged with producing daily summaries of activity that were disseminated in personalized e-mails at the end of each day, in a "know the rules and know the score" format. This report provided a simple set of numbers that gave a quick overview indicating whether the workload and patient flow were under control.

An automated set of performance indicators that was continuously updated every fifteen minutes was also developed.

Next, they tackled a serious workload issue that had been identified: the night medical registrar was severely overworked. A decision was made to introduce a night resident medical officer to support the night medical registrar. This change produced immediate results in terms of reduced stress for the night medical registrar, increased safety for admitted patients, and improved timeliness and performance. It also sent a signal to the medical staff that the organization truly intended to be responsive to the needs of junior staff.

Three full-time senior medical staff were added soon after, "to the shock and amazement of other medical departments," Don noted. This change put a senior doctor on the ward every morning, providing more support for junior staff and an enhanced sense of coaching and apprenticeship. Senior medical staff now attended ward-based multidisciplinary team meetings at the conclusion of rounds. Their presence signaled that improved performance mattered to the organization and that staffing would be augmented to make this happen.

The project team also looked at the broader system surrounding what happened in the wards, arguing that the major downstream service supplier, the Rehabilitation and Aged Care Service, needed to change its service model. This recommendation was based on the recognition that, in a connected system, improved length of stay in the downstream compartment would have a significant effect on performance in the first upstream compartment, the emergency department. After initial success, they had a setback when an unexpected change in senior management in the Rehabilitation and Aged Care Service removed the changes. Length of stay and responsiveness deteriorated again as a result. Later, however, changes were reinstated, and within twelve months, length of stay was reduced from twenty-four days to eighteen days, again by paying attention to the small number of patients who stayed longer than was clinically necessary.

The cumulative results of these efforts—a 40 percent reduction in length of stay, with significant efficiency gains in bed capacity, and reduced sick leave in junior medical staff—were impressive and led to additional ventures.

But "two steps forward, one step back" was a reality that the Monash team grew to accept as their work moved into other areas. The reality of politics was always present. In the team's experience, achieving change was a political process that required the development of its own strategy. That strategy had to be supported by attention to strong metrics and reporting relationships—as well as a willingness to be blunt, as necessary. Don commented on the intersection of politics and design:

> All change in a closed system is a political process. The biggest opportunity for change is present when the internal narrative inside the heads of the chief actors changes. In each individual's mind, they are the hero of their own story. Understanding this simple concept has provided the greatest benefit in terms of leverage to achieve change. This has been relatively easy to achieve for members of the frontline staff, moderately easy to achieve for senior medical staff (the option to "fit in or farewell" is always available, and in some instances was exercised), and much harder to achieve for senior executives.

Initiative: Agile Psychological Medicine Clinics

In 2013, a Monash mental health team decided to focus on their adult psychiatric walk-in service, motivated by concerns that neither patients nor caregivers were well served by the existing system. Led by Dr. Melissa Casey, the Monash team was responding to troubling signals: a significant increase in adults arriving to the emergency room in crisis; a growing relapse rate, indicated by shortening intervals between visits; and clinician frustration resulting from spending too much time filling out paperwork rather than seeing patients. The hospital's existing emphasis was on triaging at the front end of the patient's journey, with a focus on containing the damage—people were presenting in crisis, and many were suicidal. That logic seemed compelling, but the team wondered if there was a better way.

Melissa's involvement in the redesign grew out of her frustration that previous attempts at reform had only explored one side of the story—the organization's "wants." She knew of many workshops over the past five years in which clinicians had been asked what they wanted in a new design. Documents were written and debated, over and over, but no agreement had ever been reached.

In 2012, she had joined the executive steering committee, where yet another version of a draft document was debated without achieving agreement. Her belief was that the supply-side focus—in a system where everyone was delivering different parts within the supply chain—had too many competing needs and perspectives involved. There could be no alignment, Melissa believed, without the voice of the consumer.

Though she was not responsible for adult community mental health, Melissa offered to do an intensive one-month analysis of demand (on top of her normal job). She got the go-ahead from the mental health program head, Anne Doherty, and enlisted the help of Keith and Dr. David Clarke to do a deep dive into the demand side of the design story, with the aim of better understanding the patient experience. Unlike nearly all of the other studies we talk about in this book, their work did not start with ethnographic research, because of political challenges in gaining permission to interview emergency room patients. Instead, they turned to data analytics and mining, using existing data contained in Monash's information technology systems. They complemented this analysis with direct observation, shadowing clinicians. We believe that their experience provides an important counterargument to the quantitative versus qualitative research dichotomy we so often accept in the innovation field, demonstrating how either research methodology can be used to inform the design thinking process and illustrating ways that the two approaches can work together.

Melissa's analysis—quantitative and qualitative—uncovered many hot spots of opportunity for redesign in mental health. She then ran a series of workshops with the front-end clinicians, and together they formed a hypothesis to be tested in the form of a service prototype. They bonded into a team based on unity of purpose, with the senior and most expert psychologists wanting to come on board.

Their first task was to examine the demand for service by looking at patient volumes by clinical diagnosis and access point. This research meant accessing three different, unlinked information technology systems that did not communicate with each other. The first was PTS, the front-end triage phone database. PTS was the entry point for people engaging from their homes, a 24/7 service that literally provided a lifeline to those in crisis. The second database belonged to the emergency department. It captured information about patients who physically arrived at Monash's three emergency rooms and was not connected with other data systems. Finally, there was CMI, a third database, belonging to the mental health system, both inpatient and outpatient. To develop any sense of what was happening at the front end of mental health, Melissa had to link data from these three unrelated systems.

Such a data mining task would have daunted the most courageous and committed clinician, but not Melissa, who had an unusual repertoire of past experiences and skills to call on. Though extensively schooled and experienced in neuropsychiatry, she had also managed large-scale change in the Australian Taxation Office's data-intensive environment for fifteen years.

Melissa selected a sample of patients and followed their journeys across all four experiences—phone, emergency room, inpatient clinic, and outpatient clinic. Focusing on a twelve-month period, she began with the PTS phone triage database, looking at each patient engagement. Then, armed with individual patient numbers, the team linked PTS patients with the emergency department system, and for every person engaged with both the emergency department and PTS they found the overlap with the third database, the CMI mental health system.

Having pulled together the engagement data, she faced the challenge of how to make sense of it. A design consultancy Monash was working with, ThoughtWorks, suggested using a timeline to lay out each patient interaction in sequence, a technique they had recently applied in another consulting engagement for a telecommunications client. This suggestion led to the creation of a journey map that integrated all of a patient's mental health experiences with Monash.

The results were surprising and triggered an "aha" moment for the team. The story of one particular patient, Tom, really hit home. Following a suicide attempt, Tom was referred by another hospital's acute psychiatric ward to Monash's adult mental health service for outpatient treatment. Just two months later, after treatment, Tom was readmitted to the hospital with another overdose. During that period, the timeline revealed, Tom experienced significant activity as a patient, having thirteen different case managers, seventy touch points, and eighteen handoffs.

What Tom hadn't experienced, it seemed, was treatment that made a difference in the longer term. When David looked at Tom's story, he had a revelation: "There was no *care* there." Clinicians realized that their present system was providing patients with an

BENEFITS OF A BROAD REPERTOIRE

Melissa Casey offers a great example of the important role played by an innovator's set of life experiences, or repertoire, and the benefits of exposure to a diverse set of experiences.

Remember Geoffrey's broad background? We see it here with Melissa as well. Her past work encompasses both highly analytical work *and* patient care. As a result, she is able to bring a unique mindset and skill set that allow her to identify opportunities that highly capable individuals with exposure to only one of these areas cannot see. She studied economics and accounting in college and took a job in tax as an auditor after graduation. Finding it unsatisfying, she transferred to the management team doing large-scale change work in the central taxation office. In that role, she was introduced to design thinking more than twenty years ago, while working to redesign Australia's income tax system, with an eye on the human dimension.

Wanting to go deeper on the human side, Melissa pursued doctoral and postdoctoral studies in neuropsychiatry and became a therapist. While doing clinical work, she saw a colleague struggling with a major restructuring. Putting her old hat back on, she offered advice. And from that, she came full circle back into change work, this time in health care rather than taxation.

Tom's Story

We wondered about our patient's experience

A journey map of one patient's experience.

experience that was not at all like the one they wanted to deliver. Christine Miller, Monash's deputy director of psychology, observed:

> We can think all kinds of things about how we believe the system is working, but then, seeing the reality of how it was really working, it was shocking to see how far from our intentions reality had come. Patients needed someone to be present for them. Despite a flurry of activity, nothing was changing for them. We needed to feel the blockages and struggles.

Furthermore, Tom's information was recorded in five different information management systems and fifteen different patient records. Clinicians' sense of overwhelming paperwork, it seemed, was also well founded.

The team was ready to design—almost. Before turning to ideation, spurred by stories like Tom's, the team members decided they needed to revisit the basic purpose of their work. Melissa explained:

> In health care, we often think of purpose on the supply side, around what suits the organization. But that only gives you half the story; the reason why we exist is to meet the purpose of clients. Despite a wealth of data, we still haven't gotten to the heart of purpose. We're only going to get that when we understand from our

client's point of view what it's like engaging with us. And not just clinically. Especially in mental health, it's the nature of their experience as well.

Often, systems drive to their own purpose, however unintended, which may or may not match the mission of the organization. This is what Monash's mental health data demonstrated. Mapping their patient processes and examining the patient experience over time revealed the true nature of the system. What the Monash mental health service was delivering was completely different from what the clinicians—and the organization—wanted. Melissa observed:

> We were viewing each contact between staff and patients as episodes of care and not seeing the whole system. In the moment, we were treating the consumer in what we thought was the best way possible. But, from their perspective, and looking at the cumulative sum of their experiences and needs, we weren't responding well.

Given this deep understanding, the mental health team asked themselves what the purpose of any new system design should be. For an answer, they reached back to their roots in psychology and were inspired by the work of Erik Erikson, who, building on Freud, argued that a good and wholesome life is being able to live, love, and work. "People are presenting to us because there's been some fundamental fracture in some of these core elements of being able to live, love, and work," Melissa explained. She continued:

> That, then, should be our purpose, taking it back to that basic level. When people engage with us, what we're trying do is help them get back on trajectory where they can start a recovery journey. Of course, we know that somebody's not going to get over having schizophrenia, but we are trying to get to the heart of the person's life and, within the

JOURNEY MAPPING

Journey mapping is one of the simplest yet most powerful tools in design thinking's arsenal. It captures stakeholders' journeys as *they* experience them, paying particular attention to the emotional highs and lows as each stakeholder seeks to accomplish the job to be done. It is usually summarized in a flowchart or other graphic format. Journey mapping can be used throughout the design thinking process and is especially useful during **What *is*** to capture the current journey.

context of what they've got to work with, optimize the outcomes that they can actually have, help them find purpose and meaning in their lives. That's why we needed to go back to the basics of what we need as human beings to live a fulfilling life.

Armed with this sense of purpose, the team captured a set of insights from their exploratory work:

· *All roads lead to the emergency room if patients want to see a physician urgently.* If the team wanted to impact outcomes, members would need to design a system that incorporated what happened at what was usually the first face-to-face contact, in the emergency room.

· *Many adults present in crisis and receive primarily crisis treatment.* Examining the nature of the care encounter in the emergency room revealed an important gap: at the front end, emergency medical services—often drugs—were available, but longer-term therapeutic services were not. Melissa explained:

> Say a patient intended to kill himself and took an overdose. He or she would go into the emergency department and be treated for that particular incident rather than the underlying mental health condition that had predisposed him to vulnerability in the context of a life stressor. The patient would react by, say, taking paracetamol and would come into the emergency department. She would be treated and then discharged. So people were coming back frequently. They had gotten over their biological incident, but the underlying mental health disorder that was creating the vulnerability in the first place wasn't being treated. They were often just discharged to their general practitioner for follow-up.

· *The team realized that Monash needed to focus on what patients needed now and how clinicians could help, versus spending time discovering and analyzing the patient's history.* Clinicians were traditionally trained to use a structured assessment process. What the patient mapping revealed was that patients who presented frequently were being assessed repeatedly. Rather than conversing with patients about their current issues, clinicians were asking them the same set of standard questions over and over again.

- *The paperwork burden had become a serious inhibitor to delivering patient care.* "We are just inundated, as I think everywhere around the world is, with paperwork, particularly related to regulatory needs," Melissa said. "As each new change comes out, we develop a new form. Rather than looking at the system as a whole, we just respond to the immediate pressure." Here, again, the unintended result was a disruption to the clinician's ability to focus on the patient. "How can you relate to another person," Melissa asked, "if you're head down, filling in all of these forms during that patient's session?"

Redesigning the Mental Health Experience at Monash

Armed with the insights they uncovered during their attention to the **What is?** question, the mental health team was ready to ask **What if?** They prototyped a new clinical process aimed at creating a therapeutic working alliance that asked patients about their needs and monitored, on a continuous basis, whether patients believed their needs were being met. The focus of the new clinic, which they named "Agile" in a nod to its embracing of the principles of Agile development, would be on improving longer-term outcomes instead of only triaging for suicide risk reduction and symptom management.

To accomplish this aim, Monash moved specialist treatment to the front end of the processes and set a goal of offering every patient a follow-up appointment within seventy-two hours of an emergency room visit or phone call to PTS. The intention was to keep patients safe in the short term by providing crisis services, but then to quickly move into treatment to reduce patients' fears while helping them gain confidence and remain safe in the long term.

The new approach would assign a patient to one clinician, who would "hold" the patient as their primary contact. Patients would be asked to use a session-rating scale for each session, to provide feed-

AGILE DEVELOPMENT

Agile, a methodology for developing software, has a lot in common with design thinking. An alternative to a traditional software design approach that emphasizes sequential planning followed by testing, Agile works in fast iterative feedback cycles and emphasizes cross-functional collaboration. We will talk more about how Agile and design thinking methodologies can work together, in chapter 10, which relates the story of the Transportation Security Administration.

back about how the clinician did, what the experience was like, whether it met their needs, and what they wanted to address next.

The paperwork process would also be streamlined. To figure this out, the team gathered all forms required in the existing process and imagined an actual patient answering the myriad, often duplicate and triplicate questions. They determined which questions were essential to preserving the patient–doctor bond or therapeutic alliance and which had to be retained for governmental and Monash health protocol and regulatory reasons. They tried to eliminate the rest.

Learning through the Learning Launches

The team selected one clinic site to conduct their initial learning launch and then iterated week by week. After staff worked out the initial recipe for success, Monash expanded to two other Agile clinic sites. Throughout the process, Melissa was mindful of the need to stay open to new changes:

> I wanted us to remember that we're always learning. There's no such thing as putting in a change and then we're done. What we've found is that we've had to make modifications as we went, and we really used the prototype for twelve months as an intense learning experience.

One key issue was getting staff who had not been on the design team to change from crisis control to longer-term thinking. Integrating the hospital's new referral concept required both an emotional and a practical investment. "I use the analogy of paramedics knowing how to keep people in their ambulance alive, and they do that very well and they're entirely focused on that," Melissa explained. "If you were to ask paramedics what treatment any patient was going to get in the emergency room, they're not even thinking that way." The Agile clinic concept required them to think more broadly:

> We didn't understand that, right from the start, we were asking emergency department caregivers to do a different sort of assessment, not just get patients through their crisis situation. Thinking about referring to Agile meant that staff had to do their work assessments differently.

At first, few referrals to the clinic came in, and the seventy-two-hour appointment slots weren't fully utilized. Only when Agile clinic personnel were literally in the emergency room or on the phone with emergency department staff did staff refer mental health patients for therapeutic sessions. When Agile staff weren't present, the emergency room returned to its old crisis mode and any spike in referrals disappeared. Melissa and her team had, of course, consistently advertised the Agile service to emergency room personnel and explained the new process and referral pathways in staff meetings, but those interventions couldn't overcome the status quo of old practice. "We needed to do something fundamentally different," Melissa explained. The team decided to try to influence other parts of the systems to accelerate the change.

Their first experiment aimed at increasing referrals. The Agile team decided to open up the referral process to any mental health clinician and to general practitioners in the community. Ten sessions of therapy were offered for people with depression or anxiety. On a Friday afternoon, the team sent out an e-mail to general practitioners and mental health staff with the offer. By Monday morning, every potential appointment was booked, many by the original clinicians who had previously not been referring. The tipping point leading the original clinicians to act was apparently the possibility of losing an option that they'd previously been ignoring.

Moving Forward

Within a year, the Agile clinic demonstrated major improvements. Its key measure of success, increasing the time between presentations, was achieved: the interval between patients seeking men-

DON'T FORGET THE ON-RAMP!

As innovators, it is tempting to think of our job as being over once we have answered the four questions and created and tested what we know to be a valuable new product or service. But, as the Agile clinic staff discovered, the task is not complete until you have figured out a way to get other key stakeholders to adopt your new idea. This involves designing an "on-ramp" that helps them gain awareness about your innovation, try it out, and incorporate it into their practice. Attending creatively to the on-ramp is critical, lest your great new idea languish because of a lack of awareness. Designing the on-ramp often requires a whole new design project—the four questions must be answered all over again, just as carefully as you answered them when you created the solution itself.

tal health care grew longer after the Agile clinic model was introduced. A pre- and post-intervention comparison quantified that Monash patients' overall re-presentation rate decreased by 60 percent. Meanwhile, key indicators of patients' mental health all improved, as did patients' satisfaction with the quality of their experiences.

TEST: CLINICAL AND CONSUMER OUTCOMES

CLINICAL Outcome measures	Description	Pre	Post	Improvement
HONOS (Health of the Nation Outcome Scales) (clinician report)	Measures consumer outcomes in four domains: behaviour, impairment, symptoms and social.	9.9	3	70%
K10 Kessler Psychological Distress Scale (consumer report)	Measures anxiety and depressive symptoms	35	26	26%
Demoralisation (consumer report)	Measures loss of meaning, dysphoria, disheartenment, helplessness and sense of failure.	63.6	46	27%
Basis 32 Behaviour and Symptom identification Scale (consumer report)	Measures major symptoms and functioning experienced by people with mental ill health	64	38	40%
Session rating scale (consumer report)	Measures therapeutic alliance between therapist and consumer. Each session is rated by the consumer on relational bond, agreement on goals and tasks of therapy.	74% = average satisfaction score for all sessions		

Outcomes of the Agile clinic.

Melissa observed:

> Patients are still coming back, but after longer intervals. Equally important, caregivers are enthusiastic about the new system as well. Staff love it. Clinicians felt that the prior system was blocking what we really wanted to do, and we now feel that we can actually do it and are rejuvenated.

Monash, she reported, is "tapping into new staff energies."

Most difficult, the team said, was moving up the on-ramp from learning launch mode to transitioning to "business as usual." Monash has opened two additional Agile Psychological Medicine Clinics and two other, related clinics, Agile Complex Mood and Agile Recovery from Trauma. In scaling and integrating the new approach, the prototype team has been instrumental. But the proof mentality still lives on. "We think we've proven our idea and so people should just get on with it!" Christine explained. "But they haven't." Melissa elaborated:

> We've proven it in our world but not theirs, which is just an indication that we haven't proven it at all. We can say that our clinical outcomes and patient satisfaction have improved and that we're co-designing and iterating with consumers. And the psychologists and clinicians that we've had working on the Agile clinic have really embraced it, as it is so energizing and so wonderful to be part of. They're getting consumed by that experience and so they think, "Well, why can't other people see it?"

As Agile staff worked to manage the change process, Melissa reflected on how people influenced systems development and how systems, in turn, influenced the behavior of people:

> Why is there such a lag time between discovery and practice, a disconnect between the know-what and the know-how in health care? I'm really interested in looking at the human phenomena when we think of design and change because, bottom line, that's where it's at. You know, our intellectualization of the process is only one component. I think it often works to our detriment in health care: we have intellectualized and abstracted phenomena so much, we've lost the relationship to what actually happens.

Initiative: Long Patient Stays

In August 2014, Monash began to tackle the challenge of extended-stay patients. Long-stay patients represented only 2 percent of patients but used 25 percent of hospital bed days, so minimizing long stays had significant value. And since few people *want* to spend extended time in a hospital, it had obvious value for patients as well—each additional day's stay tended to have less medical efficacy and to produce more stress for the patient.

Monash's design team began by drafting a short design brief to lay out their objectives. The twelve members of the long-stay team then immersed themselves in the **What *is*** stage, both in analysis of the avalanche of existing quantitative data and in the experience of long-stay patients, conducting extensive interviews and using patients' real-life description of their needs to deepen their understanding of the problem. They created journey maps that captured patient experiences. They also spoke to frontline medical staff to understand obstacles to delivering care. Emerging from these conversations was a strong sense of what the new system needed to accomplish, which the team elected to formalize in a single statement: "The MMC Long-Stay management system ensures that patients who are at high risk of an extended stay in the hospital receive appropriate, high-quality, safe, and waste-free care in partnership with the patient and caregivers."

One key insight that emerged from Monash research was that each case was unlike any other; patterns were difficult to find. Another was that the patients enjoyed simply being asked how they were. That simple human connection helped their emotional and, therefore, physical state.

To engage staff in generating new possibilities during the **What *if*** stage, Don and Keith broke the design thinking process into short, intense ideation "sprints" to accommodate team members' rotating block schedules. Out of these came a comprehensive set of solutions. Chief among them was the opportunity presented by better tracking and monitoring of patients with elevated long-stay potential, in a way that was easy and intuitive for busy clinicians. This need led to an idea that resonated with all: an iPad app to allow frontline team members to quickly and easily enter long-stay risk factors, like infection. Besides predicting long-stay risk, this information would support doctor/patient decision making and allow staff to track issues as they arose. It would also enable staff members to request assistance with patients who were "stuck" because of hospital processes and systems.

The app prototype also included such information as "courtesy card" surveys, which asked patients what was bothering them (care related or not) and had a quick, color-coded scheme so that each caregiver could quickly compare the patient's situation against a set of risk factors for becoming "stranded" in a long stay. Finally, the aggregate information from the app promised to cut down meeting time among operations managers, who would be able to swiftly review all the needed information about patients at risk of long stays.

As part of determining **What *wows***, the team worked to create a vivid picture of what the future under the new approach might look like, prototyping a detailed journey map that traced the new and improved experience of patient "Larry Longstay."

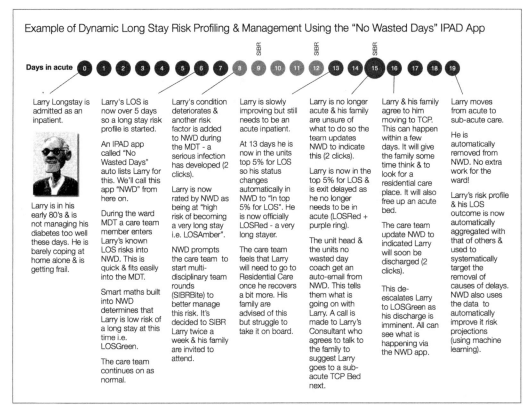

A journey map showing the experience of a patient at risk of a long stay.

In the **What *works*** stage, team members iterated through multiple learning launches with the concept. Keith and team member Damien Burns first worked with a carefully selected single group composed of early adopters. Initial results were encouraging, and Damien suggested bringing a second team into the testing process. Keith, on the other hand, was a believer in going slow: "It is too fundamentally important to go about it except in a learning manner. We want to make sure we give it the best possible chance to work."

Adding the ability to message other departments for things the nurses could not handle themselves was next on the agenda. Keith and Damien wanted to introduce site management messaging before extending the launch, because it showed the staff how they benefited. They expected iterations to go on for years.

The findings of these learning launches led to an increasing focus on the app's usefulness to front-line staff in identifying patients who were at risk of long stays, and then working to prevent additional days in the hospital. Multiple learning launches produced an unexpected benefit: they created a conversation space around the importance of the project and facilitated the development of trust between frontline teams and executives.

Don talked about why he saw this as critical:

> I am more and more convinced that the value of prototypes and learning launches is that they make concepts tangible and create a conversation space for engagement. Language is about the creation of shared meaning. This is achieved through conversations that establish trust and that lead to commitment. Systems matter more than software. Design tools work on the conversation and embody the nature of the commitments that bind us. The ethical transformation of people and their commitment to work with each other that underpins design thinking is based on people listening before they act, not a set of inflexible requirements. In essence, complexity demands loosely coupled systems rather than evidence of compliance. To enable and support this, a conversation space based on trust must be opened up.

Even before the app rolled out, the team noticed that the average number of long-stay patients had already begun to drop dramatically.

Other Monash Projects

Two other projects currently under way illustrate the breadth of Monash's use of the design thinking tool kit. One—on hand washing—targets a micro-level set of behaviors, but an important one. Hand washing is a critical defense against hospital infection and its heavy toll in both human and financial terms. Though the project is still in its early stages, the power of reframing their view of noncompliant staff not as villains but as stakeholders who need a better reason to change their behavior became clear to the team and helped members generate ideas they had not previously considered.

At the other end of the spectrum, the hospital's latest and, in some ways, most ambitious project, Monash Watch, was getting under way as this book went to press. Don noted that they could not have considered a project of this magnitude without having already tested the design thinking waters in the other projects we have talked about in this chapter. Monash Watch targets "super-utilizers"—patients who are estimated to be less than 2 percent of the total patient base but who use 20 to 25 percent of hospital resources. It combines a unique telehealth approach to building rapport and constant monitoring of outpatients' health, both mental and physical, with new payment mechanisms that will pay for keeping patients *out* of the hospital rather than for services rendered when they are in it.

The strategy involves nearly daily telephone contact with four hundred super-utilizers, to address social and psychological aspects of their health in an effort to improve the patients' physical conditions and reduce hospitalizations. Patients will report health issues to telecare guides, who will develop and maintain a personal rapport with them and gather specific information to be fed into an accumulating database. In other tests, such self-reported health data has proven surprisingly accurate. Work in Ireland by Dr. Carmel Martin indicated that telephoning patients halved their hospital visits. "Having done three smaller learning launches—and having discovered an Irish trial of something similar—we're about 85 percent sure this will work," Keith noted. To design Monash Watch, two staffers developed deep insights from thirty intensive ethnographic interviews of the generally elderly super-utilizers, learning that, even though the patients experienced multiple hospitalizations annually, physical care was often secondary among their concerns, in the overall context of their lives.

Don and Keith have worked hard to give the project the runway it needs to succeed. The design team backed away from a similar concept last year, when Monash's former CEO would only fund it for three to six months. But soon thereafter, when Victoria's Department of Health and Human Services (DHHS) began seeking proposals aimed at decreasing hospital admissions, they were ready. Of the ten hospital groups that could have applied, only Monash and one other decided to try something radically new.

When a new super-utilizer is admitted into the study, DHHS will pay Monash the equivalent of the average cost of three annual hospital visits. The hospital succeeds by keeping the patient healthy and out of the hospital. Estimates suggest that Monash will break even on cost if Monash Watch decreases hospital visits by 15 percent.

Once a person in the at-risk group has been admitted or discharged and meets DHHS requirements, a Monash staffer (a telecare guide) will be assigned to that patient. In regular phone calls, the telecare guide will engage in friendly dialogue focusing on how the patient is feeling. A computer program will analyze the incoming data while the telecare guide develops a social rapport with the patient. If the computer and/or the guide recognize a problem, a health coach (or nurse) can decide whether to send an ambulance to the home, to have the patient seen by a care provider, or to reassess the situation during another day's call.

Because metadata programs are evolving rapidly, Monash expects that, soon, each patient's narrative will be analyzed ethnographically in a process of continuous feedback and learning. Every aspect of Monash Watch is an experiment, and the team expects that the questions, the script, and the specific services provided beyond the telephone will all be investigated and iterated throughout the learning launch.

Scaling Design Thinking at Monash

Across the many stories of design thinking at work at Monash, a common theme emerges: mobilizing the clinical staff to look at design thinking's four questions in order to reframe problems, develop a deeper understanding of needs, translate the needs into new opportunities, and see what works in practice. In fact, the HealthCare InnovationbyDesign team has coined a fifth question—What *next*?—that we like so much we intend to steal it!

In the larger context of cultural change at Monash, making systemic design thinking core to problem solving has required more than just an invitation to staff to play with ideas and tools; it has necessitated creating a structured process that is accessible to all. "Some people have the view of design thinking that if you get a whole bunch of people in a room with Post-it notes, something magical happens. And afterward, you don't quite know how you did it," Don observed. Instead, he said, "You have to make it clear that there's a rigorous methodology in place that people can learn. We want to be *leading* edge, not bleeding edge. You need a very structured methodology that lets you safely work through the elements."

At Monash, that methodology has focused on the four (now five) questions. Having determined that the design thinking methodology works in their medical center setting, Monash is again at the leading edge of health care practice—this time looking at how to *diffuse* design thinking throughout the organization. They have thought long and hard about how to effectively and cost-efficiently scale their design efforts and build a core competency in design tools and process.

This quest has led them to rely heavily on the power of asynchronous online learning to reach busy staff. Don and Keith have led the way, enrolling interested staff in an online course offered by Darden and then mentoring participants as, working in teams, they apply their learning to an actual Monash project. One student was Dr. Cathy McAdam, head of general pediatrics at Monash Children's Hospital. "The key to it for me," she said, "was actually having the group do it, so that we were learning together." She and her classmates watched videos at home and then gathered to review them. Commitment to the group gave her the accountability she needed to push forward on assignments, despite her busy schedule.

Keith observed, "This approach has given us a way to inquire which we didn't have before." Cathy echoed Keith when she noted that the online course provided her with the tools to devise the type of services her patients needed most. Important to her specialty, she adds, the course helped her to devise ways to measure how pediatricians could better meet the needs of consumers, patients, and families. For example, in one design thinking project during the online class, Cathy prototyped and experimented with several iterations of a survey for pediatric visitors, observing:

> What I wanted to do was create a way of measuring impact so that if we put in new innovative models of care services, like video conferencing appointments, we can actually see whether it's had an impact that's measurable to families. Because otherwise the hospital will only look at how much it costs and how much clinician time it involves.

The online course discussions helped Cathy become comfortable with "the idea of testing something that may not be perfect and actually moving forward, rather than waiting until you've got everything 'perfect' and then launching something and wondering, 'Aw, gee, why did that flop?'"

Reflections on the Process

At Monash, we see the value of introducing a rigorous, structured design thinking process that couples deep quantitative and qualitative analysis of patient needs with a spirit of engaged experimentation, all facilitated by medical leaders who walk the talk, fight the battles for change, and provide capability-building opportunities through online instruction that focuses on real projects.

As Monash looks forward to taking design thinking to new levels, the HealthCare Innovation-byDesign team does not lack for dreams. Besides consistently drawing additional Monash staff and expertise into an ever-growing human-centered conversation, the team's ambition is to play a leading role in health care innovation by creating an international hub for design education and applied research and practice.

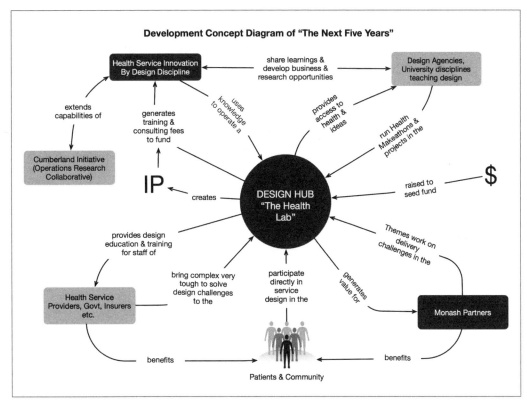

Development Concept Diagram of "The Next Five Years"

Diagram of Monash's five-year vision.

But, throughout his forty years as a clinician, Don's focus has remained the same: to help people get better. He refused to be distracted by the goal of reducing cost in and of itself:

> Cost will be stripped out by doing the right things and thinking in a designerly way. You can't focus on cost as your objective. Your objective is to provide high-quality health care and support people to remain well throughout the community. You can never lose sight of that.

Accomplishing the change, Monash leaders know, will take time. As Melissa observed, "Clinicians need to trust their leader. There is no quick way to building a trusting relationship—it takes time. There is no quick fix. It's taken five years of team building demonstrating predictability to get here."

"We're on a big learning curve," Keith noted, underlining the ways in which both the conversation and the culture at Monash have begun to shift. But significant challenges remain:

> Our view is maturing. We now need to think about on-ramps and the political systems in which we sit. We've found a way to get good ideas; now we have to figure out how to influence the system around us to actually do the work.

CHAPTER SIX

Turning Debate into Dialogue at the US Food and Drug Administration

THE CHALLENGE TO THE GREATER GOOD

Creating change in the social sector often involves more than just achieving more effective collaboration across differences within the organization; it requires engaging multiple organizations with differing missions and perspectives to work together as well. How do we ensure that conversations don't deteriorate into arguments that push these stakeholders farther apart instead of closer together? Assuming we can get the right parties into dialogue and conversation, how do we keep their different worldviews from paralyzing progress? Productive conversation across organizations can be difficult to achieve. Add in a highly politicized climate and potentially controversial topics and you have the makings of adversarial relationships.

DESIGN THINKING'S CONTRIBUTION

Avoiding divisive debates and encouraging dialogue across difference is a strength of design thinking, as this story from the US Food and Drug Administration (FDA) illustrates. Because of the nature of regulations limiting engagement with the public, federal agencies often hold public meetings to communicate with their diverse constituencies. Often, participants formulate their messages prior to the meeting, based on already-entrenched positions. In this sequential model, there is little listening and interaction. Human-centered design, as the FDA discovered, provides a process for ensuring that organizations engage in deeper, truly interactive discussions that produce greater possibilities for alignment and higher-order solutions.

A t the US Department of Health and Human Services, profiled in chapter 3, we saw a federal agency using design thinking to reach out and invite frontline employees into the innovation process. At the US Food and Drug Administration we see a different but equally compelling use of design thinking: to convene a conversation across a diverse set of constituents, both internal and external. At the FDA, which often finds itself at the epicenter of controversy, dedicated innovators are turning debates into dialogues, using design thinking to break the gridlock that can accompany working across seemingly entrenched interests.

Ken Skodacek, a policy analyst in the FDA's clinical trials program, joined the agency in 2008 with a mandate to ensure the safety and effectiveness of medical devices. A biomedical engineer by training, Ken brought more than a decade of experience in the implantable medical device industry and—equally important—a passion for partnering with others in creative conversations. Like many US federal agency employees implementing human-centered design, Ken got his initial taste of the new approach at the Office of Personnel Management's innovation lab, which we talked about in chapter 1.

Lab personnel facilitated a conversation between FDA officials and a set of thought leaders on temporary assignment to federal agencies in 2012. At the FDA's Center for Devices and Radiological Health, this group included CEOs of medical device companies, heads of investment teams, venture capitalists in the medical device space, clinicians, and electronic health record experts. Ken explained the program's purpose:

> At the FDA, we are very patient focused—for us it's all about getting the devices to the patient. And that means that we want to try to streamline our processes, like clinical trials, for making that happen. But it also means that we have to figure out what other obstacles—like reimbursement—are in the way. So we had a lot of really experienced people coming together, tackling big problems that we really didn't understand very well.

The team of about thirty FDA insiders and outsiders assembled at the lab for a "meet and greet" icebreaker, with a focus on identifying key issues. Lab personnel facilitated the conversation by using design tools. Ken described the experience:

> It was really enlightening! It helped us to better understand each other, think outside the box, and develop a picture for what we wanted to do next. Normally, you put all those

different people with different perspectives in a room and they mostly come up with ideas they don't agree on. What we found, instead, was that design thinking methods helped us step away from our roles and focus on the issues—we got to know the other person's perspective and understand how they thought. That helped the teams work together after the meeting. Usually when you're tackling a problem, it's the senior person or the more forceful person that dominates the conversation—the rest of the people aren't really engaged and so they don't really support the outcomes. This conversation totally changed that dynamic—people were on equal footing, and interested in learning different perspectives on how to address the issues at hand.

The Challenge of Government

Entrenched interests can lead either to the kind of decision-making gridlock that we saw in our earlier discussions of psychiatric care at Monash or to the adoption of "satisficed" solutions that sacrifice decision quality. Core to the challenge is the diverse array of stakeholders involved. Innovation in the FDA requires the cooperation of manufacturers, patients, health care providers, industry associations, academics, and other federal agencies. As is so often the case, attempts to improve one aspect of the system can have negative repercussions in other parts. The US Paperwork Reduction Act, passed by Congress in 1980 with the intention of reducing the burden on citizens, resulted in unintended consequences for federal agencies' ability to engage these stakeholders. This law requires evaluation of the overall impact on public resources of any government request for information. Surveying more than nine individuals on a topic necessitates completion of a formidable approval process, making it hard for agencies to engage outside stakeholders except in open public meetings, which can devolve into a handful of people speaking from already-entrenched positions on the topic and the remainder awaiting their turn to talk.

Typically, in a federal workshop, speakers prepare remarks in advance, come to the microphone at their allotted times, and present their views. When each speaker finishes, the next speaker offers a different opinion. This point/counterpoint style can be polarizing: people arrive at the meeting with their positions solidified, and any listening is filtered through their own preferences. Though useful for soliciting views, this serial engagement rarely leads to alignment and consensus. The use of human-centered design techniques can help avoid setting up such polarizing debates. Ken explained:

> In our typical federal workshop, the messages are often formed before the meeting. There's eventually an outcome, but there's not a lot of engagement getting there—or commitment to where we end up. Human-centered design allows us to bring people together to engage and learn from each other in a way that we hadn't seen as possible before.

Conflict is not introduced solely by the differing views of citizen groups, however. Government agencies have overlapping duties as well, with the result that some products are regulated by multiple agencies, each of which may view the situation from a different perspective. For instance, a helmet worn to protect a person with a medical condition like epilepsy is regulated by the FDA. A helmet worn in professional sports is regulated by the Occupational Safety and Health Administration. Put a similar helmet on a high school student and it will be regulated by the Consumer Product Safety Commission. Stakeholders can feel caught in the middle as they try to satisfy different agencies' requirements, which may not overlap. Here again, design thinking can improve and accelerate decision making by helping the agencies involved find a common focus rooted in the problem itself, rather than the more parochial perspectives that so easily form within expert silos. Let's examine some specific examples at the FDA.

WHAT IS "SATISFICING"?

Satisficing is a term that, to us, perfectly captures the flawed decision-making process we so often see in the face of different views. We think of satisficing as selecting the least-worst solution everyone will agree to. Noted economist Herb Simon coined the term as part of his work on bounded rationality. He saw satisficing as positive: it allowed decision makers to act despite their information processing limitations, by accepting *satisfactory* solutions rather than continuing to seek *optimal* ones. Satisficing is decidedly negative in the innovation space, however, where we are looking for new *higher-order* solutions that are better than what anyone brought into the room in the first place. The urge to satisfice, to negotiate solutions that accommodate difference by cobbling together pieces of different stakeholders' original solutions to create one that is minimally acceptable to all, rarely leads to breakthroughs.

Orchestrating Conversations: The Battery Story

At the time of the lab event, Ken was involved in a battery working group within the FDA. Because the FDA's organizational structure regulates products by use, a focus on batteries was not easily achieved. Within the FDA, one group handled cardiovascular products, such as pacemakers; another worked on ventilators; another oversaw infusion pumps or external defibrillators. Though all these products require batteries, the organization had no common path for battery regulations. Although seemingly simple, batteries are actually complex. Their characteristics change depending on how they are used and maintained in different environments. Device batteries need to work reliably under adverse conditions, during power outages, and in snowstorms with very cold temperatures. Battery failures can lead to serious consequences—even death.

The FDA saw value in initiating a discussion of best practices across all groups that handled battery-powered devices. The work team, wanting broader engagement, decided to sponsor a public workshop. They thought it important to bring diverse parties together, but they approached the conversation with trepidation because the FDA was not considered an expert in the battery space.

Coincidentally, at about that same time, Ken's neighborhood in DC, Georgetown, invited residents to think together about the future of their community. Ken attended the event and again found himself part of a human-centered approach:

> Some attendees were business leaders in the community. Others were residents or people who worked in the neighborhood. There were representatives from universities. And I was just amazed at the way one idea led to another, and then to another—even though you might expect businesses, for instance, to have opposing views to universities, or residents, or whatever. But it was just the opposite—the process helped us all understand each other's perspectives and build towards a common vision.

Ken left the community event inspired that a group with such diverse interests, in a place as traditional as Georgetown, could create the ambitious plan for the future that emerged from the process. He shared his experience with the battery working team, suggesting a similar approach to engage their constituents.

Recalling his experience with the Lab@OPM, he reached out to lab staff for advice and assistance. Initially, lab staffers were uncertain about facilitating a design conversation with a group as large as the battery working team envisioned—two hundred to three hundred people. They decided to solve the scale problem by breaking the larger group into eight smaller teams of about thirty people, and then subdividing into groups of ten. Lab staff then trained eight FDA employees to facilitate that discussion.

The event that Ken's team planned and implemented offers us the opportunity to take a deep dive into the mechanics of orchestrating a successful design conversation among diverse stakeholders. We choose the word *orchestration* deliberately; the need for advance planning and forethought, the assembly of the right players in the room, and the need for a conductor's deft hand helping them to work together make it an apt metaphor. We often find a puzzling paradox in attempts to facilitate these kinds of strategic conversations. On one hand, leaders are excruciatingly sensitive to all that can go wrong. On the other hand, they naively believe that inviting a group of people into the room and asking them to "talk to each other" is enough. Such an approach is a prescription for embarrassment and disaster. Successful design conversations—especially across difference—require a level of attention to detail rivaling that of a successful military campaign. The battery workshop gives us a chance to explore what a well-orchestrated conversation looks like.

Designing the Workshop

Successful designing begins with knowledge and planning. Knowledge, in this case, was provided by the lab's training, utilizing a tool kit from LUMA Institute (whom we met at the lab in chapter 1). As they planned the agenda, Ken's team incorporated design thinking into their own process, using design techniques to brainstorm ideas for organizing the two-day event. They invited each facilitator to suggest which tools to use and in which order. Using LUMA's human-centered design planning cards as a planning tool, each facilitator placed his or her preferred tools on the wall. Then, as a group, they moved the cards around as they refined the agenda. They used the resulting roadmap to lay out the details of the facilitation in terms of time, responsibilities, room layout, and goals.

To Ken's surprise, the most inexperienced facilitators sometimes had the most creative suggestions:

> On day one, we had planned to create these posters for the different ideas. Typically, we'd take a picture of each and just save it, but someone suggested putting them on a projector and having them scrolling in the morning on day two, when attendees arrived. Then somebody else suggested putting them up around the room, instead, so that people

could walk around and look—like an academic poster session. That worked well because you not only had people looking at the posters but the people who created them got engaged. That encouraged a dialogue that wouldn't have taken place if we had put them up on a screen. If it's on the screen, you don't have people talking to each other. They're not roaming the room. They're not intermingling.

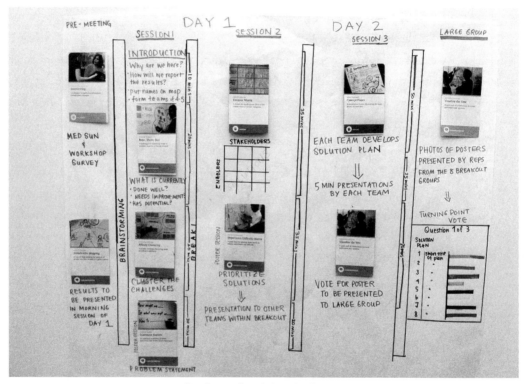

Roadmap of workshop facilitation.

The intention of the resulting plan—to identify challenges and propose and refine initial solutions—was straightforward. Making it happen with 240 people in the room was not. That required the carefully planned flow and pacing of exercises.

Team composition would also be critical. As the date for the event drew close, the battery working group collected information on attendees in advance, which allowed them to set up diverse teams representing battery manufacturers, medical device manufacturers, and health care providers. They queried attendees about their hopes for the workshop. The group was concerned that most attendees responded that they wanted to see what the FDA was going to *tell* them about how they intended to regulate batteries and battery-powered devices. Yet the team's vision for the workshop was the opposite: the FDA did not have an answer; instead, the federal government hoped to engage stakeholders to learn more about the challenges and possibilities.

The two-day event was held in July 2013. In addition to the 240 people who attended in person, approximately seven hundred more participated online. The workshop design included a session in which selected attendees sat around a conference table and participated in an on-camera discussion. Online attendees were able to post questions and thoughts, with facilitators selecting thought-provoking questions for display on a screen in front of the panel for response, the first time this approach had been incorporated at the FDA.

In his introductory talk to the assembled group, Ken began by setting expectations, acknowledging that the pre-meeting survey suggested that attendees had come to hear what the FDA had to say. Instead, Ken explained, the FDA's goal was to engage the stakeholders in the room to define how they could best work together. "That took the pressure off of us to be the experts, and we became facilitators to bring people together to have a conversation," Ken recalled. He also shared a rough stakeholder map, a diagram showing the different constituencies in the room.

Day one of the meeting then kicked off with traditional prepared talks by experts, with the presentations kept short and to the point (ten to twelve minutes each). "We wanted to keep things aggressive so we didn't lose people's attention," Ken offered. In the afternoon, they broke into smaller teams (dividing the 240 participants into eight groups of thirty as planned) and began the human-centered design sessions. This agenda focused on the identification of the challenges facing the group and the drafting of possible solutions, using a variety of design tools.

In the first activity, each participant was asked to quickly share his or her name, organization, and stakeholder group. Participants were then sorted again into smaller, diverse groups of ten, a critical design element. "Because people didn't know each other, they were all on an equal footing," Ken explained. "It encouraged them to speak up and engage in the conversation in a much more natural way than if they were able to form groups on their own."

Identifying Challenges

Next, the group used Rose, Thorn, Bud, a design method from LUMA's tool kit, to identify challenges. Attendees were asked individually to use pink sticky notes to identify what they believed to be done well (roses), blue for areas needing improvement (thorns), and green to identify potential (buds). Each participant was encouraged to write multiple items of each type. This exercise encouraged each participant to reflect on his or her own view of **What *is*** before sharing it with the larger group. Next, the individual participants shared their notes, and the group clustered the collective set, highlighting areas of similarity and difference. There was no debate about whose view was better or worse. Instead, the focus was on understanding and exploring how each member of the team saw the situation.

PROBLEM FRAMING

Rose, Thorn, Bud

A technique for identifying things as positive, negative, or having potential

UNDERSTANDING

Rose, Thorn, Bud

QUICK GUIDE

- Identify a topic for consideration.
- Assemble a diverse group of stakeholders.
- Give each participant a pen and 3 sticky note pads.
- Explain the topic and the color key.
- *Rose* = Pink (indicates things that are positive).
- *Thorn* = Blue (indicates things that are negative).
- *Bud* = Green (indicates things that have potential).
- Instruct each person to generate many data points.
- Include one issue, insight, or idea per sticky note.

HELPFUL HINTS

- Tell participants to write multiple items per color.
- Resist the temptation to describe solutions here.
- Limit the time frame and the amount of discussion.

© 2012 LUMA Institute

LUMA Institute card describing the Rose, Thorn, Bud tool.

Next, again individually, each participant was asked to create at least three "Statement Starters." The statements each identified an area of opportunity that participants saw as important and focused attention on actionable challenges. They then shared the statements with their group, which together agreed on a single one to continue to work with. The time in which to select the particular challenge the team would work on was limited—extended debate was not allowed.

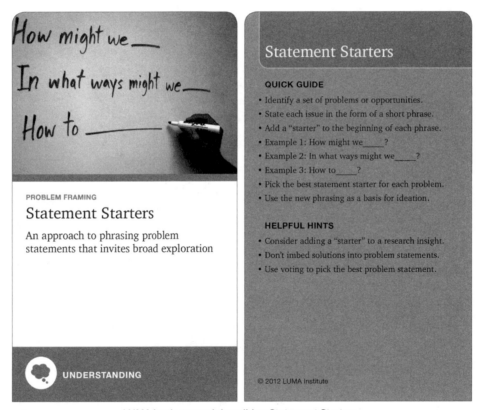

LUMA Institute card describing Statement Starters.

Brainstorming Solutions

After a short break, groups addressed the **What *if*?** question by brainstorming ideas to solve their identified challenges, using another LUMA Institute tool, the Creative Matrix. The goal was to create at least one solution for each box in the matrix; groups of stakeholders (each with a column) interacted with a particular technology (contained in the rows). At this point, the goal was to encourage divergent thinking about possible solutions.

The ideas from the Creative Matrix that the group found most compelling were then prioritized and placed on an Importance/Difficulty Grid that positioned each idea according to its relative importance to attendees and their assessment of the ease with which it could be implemented—this focused on convergence again. In their final activity that day, each group presented the Importance/Difficulty chart to the larger groups.

Problem Statement: How might we...?	Patients & Healthcare Providers	Hospitals & Healthcare Technology Managers	Medical Device Manufacturers	Battery Manufacturers & Suppliers	FDA & Other Regulatory Agencies
Technology & Digital Media					
Facilities & Environments					
Events & Programs					
Policies & Laws					
Wildcard					

LUMA Institute's Creative Matrix tool.

DIVERGENCE/CONVERGENCE IN DESIGN THINKING

Design thinking makes use of cycles of divergence and convergence around each of the four questions. When participants each wrote out their individual thoughts in the Rose, Thorn, Bud exercise, the process invited divergence in order to get differing perspectives on the **What *is*** conversation. Clustering these perspectives for similarity moved the group toward convergence, and the Statement Starters exercise completed that convergence and focused their transition into **What *if***. The Creative Matrix then encouraged divergence again.

Refining Solutions

Day two focused on refining and testing the proposed solutions, using a different set of human-centered design tools. When attendees arrived, all the charts created the previous day were on display in the breakout room. The charts acted as a kind of prototype that summarized each group's thinking in a way that members from other teams could quickly grasp. One member of each group was asked to stand by the group's chart to receive feedback; other group members toured the gallery of charts to give feedback to other groups. Groups were then given a chance to revisit their solution plan based on feedback received. They captured the revised solutions on Concept Posters. After another set of short presentations to other teams in the breakout room, the group of thirty voted for one poster to be presented to the larger group of 240. They then rejoined the large group. Pictures of the other posters were taken for future reference.

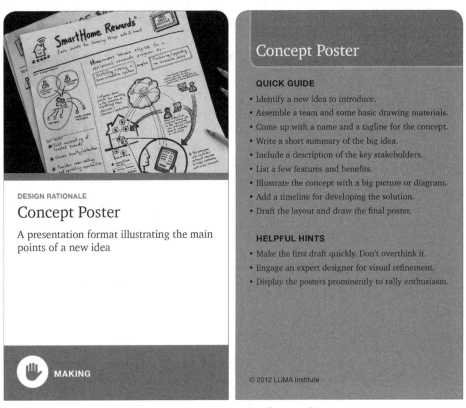

DESIGN RATIONALE

Concept Poster

A presentation format illustrating the main points of a new idea

MAKING

Concept Poster

QUICK GUIDE

- Identify a new idea to introduce.
- Assemble a team and some basic drawing materials.
- Come up with a name and a tagline for the concept.
- Write a short summary of the big idea.
- Include a description of the key stakeholders.
- List a few features and benefits.
- Illustrate the concept with a big picture or diagram.
- Add a timeline for developing the solution.
- Draft the layout and draw the final poster.

HELPFUL HINTS

- Make the first draft quickly. Don't overthink it.
- Engage an expert designer for visual refinement.
- Display the posters prominently to rally enthusiasm.

© 2012 LUMA Institute

LUMA Institute card describing Concept Posters.

In the larger group, each of the eight teams whose poster had been selected by their breakout group gave a five-minute presentation. Facilitators were not allowed to present. The ideas presented were diverse. One group, for instance, suggested compiling a comprehensive guide for clinicians and users titled "The Hitchhiker's Guide to the Battery Universe." Another focused on the creation of a self-managing battery system.

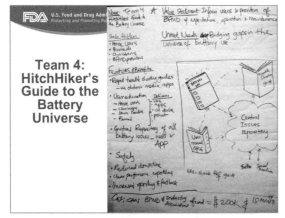

Concept Poster of a
comprehensive battery guide.

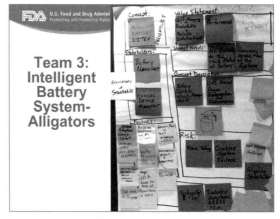

Concept Poster of a
self-managing battery system.

Testing Solutions

To get an initial sense of how well the resulting solutions appealed to the larger group, all participants were asked to vote (using electronic voting devices) on three questions:

1. Which concept will have the most significant impact?
2. Which concept can be implemented quickly and easily?
3. Which concept would you be willing to support, based on your expertise?

The session concluded with the announcement of the results of the votes: the self-managing battery system was seen as having the most significant impact and the most support, while the "Hitchhiker's Guide" to batteries was voted as the quickest and easiest to implement.

The feedback on the workshop was overwhelmingly positive: 87 percent of attendees registered satisfaction, with the breakout sessions seen as particularly helpful. In contrast to a typical government public workshop consisting of a panel of speakers with little opportunity for the audience to share their thoughts, this approach created a new dynamic. Attendees were shocked that a government agency would be so desirous of having an open dialogue without solutions already in mind. Ken talked about what his team learned:

> When we put a medical device manufacturer and a nursing health care provider and a hospital technology manager who maintained the device batteries together, they fed off each other's ideas and perspectives and engaged in a dialogue that moved the conversation forward.

Outcomes from the workshop took different forms. The most obvious was a typical FDA output: a guidance document. The intention of the guidance document was to capture the different views and learnings. "In the absence of our meeting, we certainly wouldn't have had those views," Ken explained, and offered an example:

> For instance, we learned about a big issue with sterilizing battery-powered medical devices. When you sterilize something, you typically heat it to a very high temperature or you use very special chemicals on it. There's a perception from the end user that if you do that with a battery-powered device, it's not going to work. This was something that we had never considered before. It was identifying potential issues like this that were in our blind spot that was the most valuable for us.

Attendees from outside of the FDA also moved forward with actions as a result of the conversation. AdvaMed, an industry trade association, took on the task of creating a best practices document. Bruce Adams, an executive at Cadex Electronics, a producer of battery testers and chargers, came away from the FDA conference excited about the open dialogue and the chance to connect with other producers, regulators, and users, especially from the health care field. "I think the FDA did a great job," he said. He continued:

> It was well organized, with all the right people, a broad cross section of participants, many joining remotely via web access, the breakouts and hosted interviews, and then

the wrap-up with human-centered learning to gather enthusiasm to drive improvements in the market. I hadn't participated in an FDA-hosted think tank like that before and I was impressed.

Even more impressive is that Cadex used the conference to explore new ways of thinking internally. Conversations with regulators, manufacturers, and users at the conference encouraged them to develop a web-based service to judge whether medical batteries were functioning at peak efficiency. Building on the connections made at the conference, Cadex is working with cell and battery producers to build a bench tester capable of saving three to four hours per battery in the testing process, and is also seeking a method of remote monitoring. Hospitals with 150 beds, Cadex learned, are so dependent on battery technology that they need a full-time staffer dedicated to year-round, full-time testing. Cadex is using the co-creation methods they learned at the conference to work with hospitals to save that time, a goal that grew directly from the FDA's battery conference. Bruce explained:

> One of our big takeaways from the conference was just how much human error impacts confidence in battery-powered devices. If a battery device is unplugged for any period of time, people just don't know or trust its capability. If we can solve how to get real-time state of battery health communicated between the device, the hospital, and manufacturers, staff can make more intelligent decisions on when any battery needs to be replaced.

News of the success of the battery workshop spread within the FDA. Members of another program, Emergency Preparedness/Operations and Medical Countermeasures (EMCM), faced an equally vexing challenge. They approached Ken's team about using a design approach for their upcoming workshop on respiratory protective devices (RPDs).

Harmonizing Processes: The Respiratory Protective Devices Story

RPDs were an area of long-standing difficulty within the emergency preparedness field. Stockpiled by the federal government, by some states, and by the Centers for Disease Control and Prevention, a reliable supply of RPDs was important for protecting the public at large in the event of major public health crisis. The swine flu pandemic of 2009 had demonstrated confusion in the field related to RPDs and had left regulators keenly aware of deficiencies in the current system. Though the issues were very different from those faced by the battery group, the core challenge of working across diverse constituencies (in this case, agencies, manufacturers, and users) was similar.

RPDs fell under multiple regulatory authorities, depending on their use: under the FDA as medical devices; under the Occupational Safety and Health Administration as personal protective equipment; and under the National Institute for Occupational Safety and Health (NIOSH), an arm of the CDC, as disease prevention equipment. Unlike with batteries, the FDA had extensive expertise related to RPDs. Even within the FDA itself, multiple groups were involved—the premarket device review branch as well as the Office of Counterterrorism and Emerging Threats, the parent organization of EMCM. All of this complicated the process for manufacturers, who had to deal with multiple federal agencies with different approval requirements.

Suzanne Schwartz, the director of EMCM, had a mandate to harmonize processes both within and across federal agencies, to provide a more reliable stock of RPDs for use in the event of a pandemic by removing some of the burdens on the manufacturers. EMCM also hoped to reduce confusion among other stakeholder groups in the large RPD ecosystem, such as among health care delivery organizations, which were unsure about products to purchase and stock in hospitals. Much of the confusion had to do with which type of approvals the products required: Did they need both NIOSH and FDA clearance, or was NIOSH certification sufficient?

Aftin Ross, an EMCM fellow, was assigned to lead the planning and facilitation of the human-centered design portion of the workshop. As with the battery meeting, the RPD planning group selected the attendees with care, creating a stakeholder map at the outset to ensure that all relevant stakeholders—manufacturers such as 3M and Honeywell, regulators, academic researchers, health care managers and clinicians, and trade organizations—were invited to take part in the conversation.

THE STAKEHOLDER MAPPING TOOL

For the kinds of complex, multistakeholder problems often found in the social sector, stakeholder mapping can be a critical tool. It is easy to get caught in designing for end users while postponing consideration of the perspectives of other key stakeholders who will be crucial to the implementation of any new idea. Laying out the web of organizations involved in advance helps to ensure that the whole system is in the room when the conversation starts, and that teams are composed to maximize diversity.

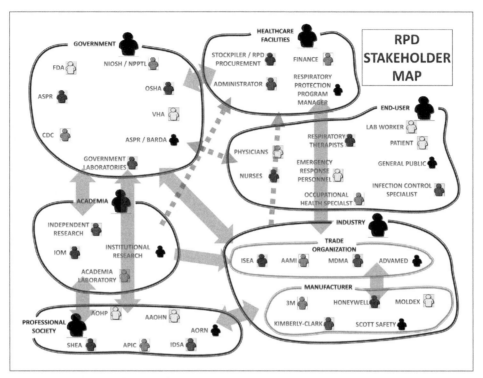

Stakeholder map for respiratory protective devices.

The planning team did extensive work beforehand, meeting privately with the other federal agencies involved, to get them to the table. Even getting their internal partners at the FDA into the room required significant work on the team's part, as Suzanne explained:

> It's worth pointing out how much it took to even get other groups within the FDA to actually come into the same room for these meetings. They often participated via teleconference even though we're all in the same building! So we decided not to offer a telecom line. Everybody comes into the room together.

Meeting face-to-face, Suzanne felt, shifted the discussion in positive ways.

On May 21 and 22, 2014, the stakeholders convened to talk about challenges in the RPD space. In a series of breakout activities, they used design tools similar to those used in the battery workshop to identify challenge areas, and then they selected several to drill down into and proposed solutions to address them. Groups then presented their challenges and proposed solutions to the larger group. Once again, they used human-centered design techniques to give feedback on and refine the solutions proposed.

As the conversation proceeded, the team at EMCM discovered new insights that caused them to reframe their own definition of the problem. Aftin explained:

> We found that some of the challenges we were focused on, from the agency perspective, were not the major issues for our stakeholders. This was very good for us to understand as we started to develop potential policy solutions. We also saw that, even though some of these problems were not necessarily within the FDA's purview, they belonged to other stakeholders who were present, and they wanted FDA involvement in what came out of the human-centered design work. And they wanted copies of the products that groups presented during the summit meetings.

Ken, too, talked about what the FDA people learned:

> It is easy at the FDA to see standards as being what matters, but in the meetings it became clear that the standards didn't incorporate real-life experiences. We began to see a new reality: this particular standard is useful, but it's not comprehensive enough to really guide us, or it doesn't provide the solution that we need to overcome this challenge.

Aftin agreed:

> When we came in, we thought that the standard, the testing, was really the main issue. What we learned from the summit was that, for our end users, it was really about the practice, the training, the education, knowing which device to use when, and making sure people had the appropriate fit for the device—all these training-related characteristics that were beyond the science question that we were concerned with. They were really about how do we best implement this in practice.

Aside from the concrete outputs of the meetings, this broadening and reframing of the agency's own view was a key, albeit intangible, benefit of the conversation. As we saw already at Monash Medical Centre, solving a problem defined only from the supplier's perspective risks wasted resources, as solutions may do little to create better value for the users or achieve the outcomes desired.

As with the dialogue on batteries, diverse ideas emerged during the RPD discussion, ranging from streamlining regulatory process, to training, to tracking devices within the hospital. Early on, the planning team had debated whether to constrain the conversation to specific topics. In deciding, instead, to allow the session's participants to set their own boundaries in problem definition, the FDA team allowed for maximum learning. As Aftin noted:

> We had gone back and forth in advance as to whether attendees would address the questions that we wanted them to address if we didn't insist on it. Well, to a large part, they didn't. But that turned out to be OK. What that told us was that what we maybe thought was an issue or problem was only an issue or problem for us.

Again, the assembled stakeholders were very positive about the experience; they liked the opportunity to take part in a working session instead of listening to presentations. The summit gave the stakeholders, including EMCM's internal working team, new information to consider while working to harmonize processes. Aftin commented:

> I think that the human-centered design activities really allowed us to put lots of things on the table—and even if people didn't necessarily favor those ideas, they at least actually were put on the table. This was very important because the outcome that ends up resulting may not be what people expect when we start. If we hadn't used some of those human-centered design activities, these would have been a tougher pill to swallow.

As they moved into policy development, the feedback and refinement resulting from the conversation paid off. The conversation allowed EMCM to produce better policies—ones that other stakeholders, having been part of the conversation, were now poised to better understand.

Reflections on the Process

The two FDA stories illustrate the potential of gathering together a set of diverse players from across the ecosystem and guiding them carefully through a new kind of conversation that avoids early negotiation and compromise and that aims for the creation of a productive dialogue rather than an adversarial debate. Such a structured process encourages the kind of creative collaboration that produces higher-order solutions to real-world challenges. Without this, people with expertise in different silos can easily talk past each other.

Though these conversations on batteries and RPDs, as well as the FDA's role in each, were significantly different, design-led conversations and tools proved equally valuable in optimizing everyone's problem-solving potential. Suzanne reflected:

> Design thinking has been such an extraordinary tool for us internally because this is an area that is heavily emotionally charged for the groups that are involved, many of whom are very wedded to certain ways of doing things. Without the tools, these would be much more difficult conversations to have. The tools made it more about the problem as opposed to making it about the people involved. Just having the markers and the Post-its on the table and putting people to work removed that emotional charge that I think would otherwise have existed.

For Ken, design thinking allowed the FDA to reach higher levels of engagement, which led, in turn, to greater openness to new possibilities:

> It's an amazing way to have people feel empowered and engaged. If you have a meeting of even ten or twelve people, what happens is a few people end up dominating the conversation and everyone else is just nodding or thinking, "I could speak up if that other person would shut up for two seconds."

Besides promoting design thinking's "totally different way of getting people to be open to different perspectives," Ken argued that the creative collaboration represented by the battery and RPD conversations is becoming more and more critical for addressing complexity, especially as change in the medical regulatory device ecosystem accelerates:

> When the FDA controls all aspects of the process, then maybe you don't have to bring in the other stakeholders. But, in many cases, a government agency is at the crossroads of an issue—we don't have complete control over it. And that's when bringing people together and having a dialogue is really critical to making progress and addressing all of the important issues.

Suzanne agreed, noting that bureaucracies face inertia that is hard to surmount without collaborative thinking and action that broadens participants' perspectives on critical issues:

> The real challenge that we face in government is that we are a huge bureaucracy. It takes a lot to move things. We have found design thinking to be an excellent tool to help us move incrementally as well as stepwise. Making it about the methodology makes it about focusing on the problem rather than the person or the culture or the entrenched beliefs. It allows us to neutralize these charged discussions. By getting people comfortable with these exercises, folks are finally able to move away from attachments at the cultural and personal belief level and look at the problem in a more neutral kind of a manner.

CHAPTER SEVEN

Fostering Community Conversations in Iveragh, Ireland

THE CHALLENGE TO THE GREATER GOOD

We have looked at challenges that cross the boundaries of individual organizations. But what if the challenges lay within a community? Without the structure of specific roles and responsibilities, how can the conversation be orchestrated? The construction of community conversations has a long history of experimentation with different approaches. Despite significant effort, results have been mixed for some of the reasons we have already discussed—entrenched interests, conversations that go nowhere, and lack of local ownership of solutions—with the result that outcomes fail to materialize as momentum is lost.

DESIGN THINKING'S CONTRIBUTION

Design thinking can offer more than just a structured process for facilitating better team and organizational conversations; it can be scaled to foster and sustain a community-wide conversation that challenges participants to move beyond analyzing problems to generating solutions that can be shared and tested. Coupling design thinking with a process called a charrette, the Institute without Boundaries (IwB) in Toronto, Canada, teamed with the citizens of Iveragh—a beautiful Irish region on the Ring of Kerry that is beset with problems of unemployment and depopulation—to create a community-wide conversation that helped to imagine new possibilities in ways that pushed beyond good intentions to make them tangible and testable.

The Ring of Kerry on the Iveragh Peninsula is one of Ireland's most visited tourist destinations, and for good reason: dramatic ocean scenery, ancient Celtic ruins, and the beauty of the Skellig Islands and the MacGillycuddy's Reeks mountains. Yet this beautiful spot wrestles with the irony that few tourism dollars trickle down to the rural population. Tourists fly into and out of the airport near Killarney, spending almost all their money in that city's restaurants, pubs, and hotels. From Killarney, they tour the Ring of Kerry in a single day, driving the coastline road around the Iveragh Peninsula in buses too large to access the small parking lots and the roads leading to most of the region's archeological sites, family farms, and adventure opportunities.

But the region's challenges go beyond capturing tourist dollars. Farming, a key source of income in the area, has suffered, as the unintended consequences of national and international political decisions, plus a dearth of market-bound transportation options, have gradually nudged the younger generation off the farm. Today, the average age of a south Kerry farmer is sixty-seven, and those remaining compete with cash-rich factory farmers and ranchers around the world. In general, unemployment on the peninsula is high, and well-paying private jobs are few. Throughout the area are neighborhoods of empty new houses, called "ghost estates," built to be second homes for weekend vacationers from Dublin, Cork, and Limerick, who never came. Factories have closed, having succumbed to ever-greater international "subsidy shopping," and Iveragh's citizens have learned through the painful collapse of the so-called Celtic Tiger that if it sounds too good to be true, it probably is.

But behind the distanced economic language of unemployment, loss of tourist dollars, manufacturing flight, and unsold houses is a much more human—and painful—problem: Iveragh has lost its children.

"We have lost a generation," Noreen O'Sullivan, the Cahersiveen community librarian lamented to us, "and we feel great sadness at having lost our young people." Noreen grew up in the area but left to begin her education and then her career as a librarian. She was one of the fortunate ones, able to come home when the local library had an opening, but her three children have left, first to get an education and then to find jobs.

A local gardener, John Joe O'Sullivan, also described the loss in personal terms:

> I live on a road which back in '69 had twenty-nine children. Now, no school bus comes because there are no children left on that road. There are no pregnant women. In the

past, I'd have to step off the footpath because of the pregnant women and their prams. Now, there are none.

With several closed elementary schools, south Kerry's high school educates only two-thirds of the students it held a decade ago. Retired high school principal Michael Donnelly explained:

The area needs to do something. When I was principal in 1999, there were 780 students. Today, there's a huge decline. In any community meeting today, there is a dearth of people in their twenties and thirties. And the young, vibrant, enthusiastic are vital to any community.

The desire to bring their children back led the Kerry County Council to an unlikely partnership with a Canadian design school—the Institute without Boundaries at Toronto's George Brown College—and introduced them to the power of combining design thinking with a decades-old process from the architecture and urban planning world: the charrette.

Seeking to achieve social, ecological, and economic innovation, the IwB is an educational program focused on collaborative design. The IwB merges students from diverse academic and professional backgrounds with partner organizations around the globe to understand and tackle real-world challenges, with the aim of expanding decision-making creativity and cultivating the resources to support any innovative ideas developed.

Jean Byrne, a Dublin transplant to Iveragh, was a catalyst in bringing the IwB across the Atlantic. With deep family roots in Kerry, Jean and her husband had vacationed on the Iveragh Peninsula for decades, building a second home they called Anam Cara ("soul friend" in Irish), with sweeping views

WHAT IS A CHARRETTE?

Adapted from century-old architectural practice, a charrette is an intensive collaborative process that aims to bring the entire system of stakeholders physically into a room together to create a range of new solutions for a given challenge. The emphasis is on moving between small work groups and the entire collective in fast, iteration-focused, and feedback-driven cycles of idea development.

over the rugged Atlantic. A neighbor, local farmer Michael O'Connor, invited Jean to attend a community meeting in Caherdaniel, a small village on the peninsula, to share with them her work using design thinking as a tool for civic engagement in Dublin. As a result, she was invited to join the local community group. The village was in the process of finalizing a five-year development plan. From Jean's perspective, they were missing a more significant opportunity: leveraging the area's natural beauty as a focus for developing economic activity and a sustainable community. Another problem she observed was that the small communities along the peninsula were all struggling with the same issues, but, as she described it, "They saw their problems in isolation rather than seeing the bigger picture that solutions might lay in connectivity and cooperation rather than competition."

As an outsider, but with a deep love of the place and respect for the community, Jean persevered, looking for opportunities to broaden the conversation, for reasons she explained:

> There is no place more beautiful or soulful to me in the world. I feel so fortunate to be
> able to spend time here and so grateful. I believe that we care for what we love, and that
> is my motivation for the work that I do.

She learned that the IwB, with which she had worked in Dublin, was investigating rural areas and seeking a research location.

> I thought the Iveragh Peninsula would be an ideal place for them to study, and I saw
> the opportunity for Iveragh to benefit from it. I also believed that this might be a way to
> enable the local communities to embrace a bigger picture and give them the opportunity
> to experience design thinking as an approach to problem solving.

She approached a fellow committee member, the former school principal Michael, and introduced the idea to him. Together, they approached the chief executive of the Kerry County Council, Moira Murrell, to explore the possibility of working on a project with the IwB. The council secured a small grant from the Design and Crafts Council of Ireland to invite the IwB to Kerry to make a presentation to Moira and her senior team. The IwB facilitated a workshop called Imagining Iveragh, which used a design thinking approach to explore the challenges of the region and to work collaboratively to define themes for the IwB's research. It was organized with the help of Noreen O'Mahoney from the Kerry

County Council and Barry MacDevitt, CEO of Design TwentyFirst Century. They invited more than fifty people to attend, from the various communities as well as from state and university sectors, and Moira gave the go-ahead for the IwB to utilize Kerry in its 2015–2016 research.

Having seen the combination of design thinking and the charrette process before, in a project for the Dublin City Council, Jean was enthusiastic about the power of coupling these two methods:

> I have evidence to see that design thinking works; I have seen it firsthand. Taken together, design thinking and charrettes give people the opportunity to work through complex problems together in a short period of time. My experience is that some extraordinary things can come out of even a week's work using the methods of design thinking combined with the charrette.

The IwB director and dean of the Centre for Arts, Design and Information Technology, Luigi Ferrara, analyzed the Iveragh situation:

> In Kerry, you have the classic condition of an agrarian area, developed in a magnificent way in that agrarian era. It's a spectacular setting full of history, suffering the effects of global centralization, with the resources of agrarian life depleted. The industrial era has passed it by; the postindustrial is passing it by. We're trying to work with Kerry to reimagine projects that would reenergize and revitalize the region and actually bring new flows of global interaction into the region. We're trying to redesign the relationship of the local and the global to make it a favorable relationship, instead of unfavorable.

Helping Communities Move Forward

The question of how to help communities come together to address challenges has been of interest to researchers and community organizers for decades. The complex and interrelated problems they face make the challenge of fostering productive, in-the-moment conversations that nurture sustainable improvements problematic. As early as the 1950s, social activists were experimenting with bringing community members into complicated conversations around issues such as public health, transportation, and economic revitalization. Methodologies like community search conferences and, more recently, World Café surfaced. All share with the charrette method an emphasis on broad participation within a structured and intense conversation format. But many of these efforts have been stymied by predictable challenges: achieving cooperation across entrenched interest groups, bringing coherence and closure to conversations that can go in circles, and creating local ownership of solutions to maintain momentum.

To improve these results, design thinking contributes a set of tools for structuring the conversation that encourages a strengthened sense of community, along with alignment, local ownership, and action around a particular new future. Together with a charrette format, it has the potential to build momentum and optimism around new designs, rendering subsequent implementation of the proposed solutions more likely.

We have emphasized that one strength of design thinking is its insistence that we immerse ourselves in the problem space and ask **What *is*?** in ways that allow people with diverse perspectives to come together to develop a less parochial, more nuanced view of current reality. But communities can become so mired in discussions of problems that it can be a deterrent to moving forward; it is possible to stay *too* long in the conversation about today's problems. Design thinking also insists on movement from **What *is*** into **What *if*** and a discussion of testable solutions. In this way, design thinking advances the conversation along a specific timeline, forcing a search for alternatives and an action orientation to pursue them. This focus on generating new possibilities, rather than just endless analysis of problems, pushes people out of theoretical debates and toward action. This focus on action is, in Luigi's view, critical:

> One of the reasons I think charrettes are so successful is because you have to produce something. That forces your thinking. It is easy to stay safely in the debate space and never have your hypothesis interact with reality to get feedback about whether or not it is true. This is what makes everything slow down. It's what paralyzes bureaucracies. You can debate forever. This is where design gets interesting. You have to translate your sentiment into an embodiment that others can see. A fundamental part of design is making things sharable in the world. That forces collaboration, because you have to agree on an output. And that changes the thinking. You can say we want to be the world's best city, but that is really empty until you confront the design challenge: operationalizing the value. So what is the best city? All of a sudden, a bunch of qualities come out, and those qualities need to be shared.

As he pondered what made his experience with the IwB different, Michael noted exactly this dynamic during the Imagining Iveragh project:

> This was a very interesting exercise that made us think in a different way. We'd been analyzing and defining the problem for years. This conversation was about solving the problem. It meant that there could be a solution. Maybe our problems weren't just an inevitable part of society evolving that we just had to accept. In those previous discussions, we had been concentrating on our difficulties rather than our strengths. This focus made us think about possibilities instead. There were reasons for the children to come back! It showed us there were things we could do.

Luigi added:

> When you are in a charrette process, you have to commit. You have to go beyond "I want to make nice things for people" and show them how. This moves you beyond good intentions into the world of effects, where you can gauge, measure, and get feedback. That's the super power of design. Otherwise, there's no evidence; there's no test of whether anything works. You just remain in an endless loop.

Chris Pandolfi, IwB academic lead and faculty member, described a charrette as the opposite of design by committee, where people react and comment on the design of others. In a charrette, designers co-create and become invested in the project. It is "design with stakeholders," he explained, as opposed to "design by experts." Design experts have solid input, but so do government officials, students, businesspeople, seniors, journalists, and marine biologists, as in Kerry's case.

The Charrette Process

In July 2015, a yearlong collaboration began between the IwB's faculty and students and the Kerry community. After a series of charrettes and continued iteration of ideas, Kerry locals and the IwB faculty and students created a strategy for addressing the region's troubles.

Preparing for the Charrette

The IwB works behind the scenes to make their charrettes productive and to keep momentum going throughout the process. Heather Daam, IwB academic project coordinator, explained:

> The co-design and feedback from the locals come in a lot of different forms. You get so many different perspectives, and then, as soon as you go out and speak, new stories come out. In approaching people who haven't been primed or networked before, their reaction offers a lot of input.

The IwB argues that formal training in design skills is not needed to produce a successful conversation. Luigi explained:

> Design is done by everybody. There are acts of design in everything you do. There's an act of intention when you structure the world around you to achieve certain things: the choice of clothes, where you live, how you live. Design is embedded in everything. It's like the fundamental shared language. That's why it is so invisible. But when you force people to engage and to work together to design, their hidden design skills emerge.

IMAGINING IVERAGH PROJECT TIMELINE

July 2015: IwB faculty travel to County Kerry to meet interested parties, including the Imagining Iveragh steering group, and to learn how locals envision their own future. From a one-day workshop, the IwB begins developing a design brief, identifying four areas of opportunity.

September 2015: IwB students in Toronto are introduced, via Skype, to Kerry policy makers and begin studying existing data. Over the next two months, students design proposals as part of their curriculum modules and simultaneously develop the Kerry charrette's design brief, based on the project opportunity themes identified in July.

November 2015: A dozen IwB graduate students, supervised by IwB faculty members, spend eight days doing field research work via meetings with local Iveragh stakeholders at area tourism and economic sites, including archeological sites, schools, and tourism businesses, and a bus tour of the famed Ring of Kerry. Next, undergraduate students from two Irish universities join the IwB students, and a five-day charrette process kicks off with a short trip to four specific sites, one in each of the four opportunity areas. Students meet with interested local residents, policy makers, and businesspeople. Assisted by locals at key moments during the charrette, the students brainstorm ideas and conclude the charrette with presentations to all.

February 2016: At the Toronto International Charrette, an annual IwB event that brings together more than two hundred students, faculty, and industry experts from organizations around the world, the Kerry charrette concepts and curriculum module are further developed, alongside new ideas, into detailed project proposals for sustainable economic development in Iveragh.

June 2016: The IwB produces final concepts and presents a detailed proposal to representatives of the project partners.

The outcome of deep preparatory research is what the IwB refers to as the "brief," a detailed document that includes an itinerary aligning charrette teams around specific opportunities and guiding them through the process of generating innovative ideas. An IwB brief includes guiding principles for making decisions and working through potential solutions. As participants build on prior data and ideas, thinking is expected to evolve, requiring new briefs.

Imagining Iveragh Kicks Off

Beginning in July 2015, the IwB held a one-day workshop in Iveragh to kick off its design process with key stakeholders, active residents, and other state and academic individuals who might be interested in or have expertise to offer the project. During this time, they also invited any and all into a weeklong design session with international college students, later that fall. Jean was impressed by both the variety of participants and their enthusiasm:

> We had parents of young children; we had academics, farmers, and people from county council who, when we identified problems, came in with funding. We were absolutely delighted. The county CEO and her team and others, like tourism-focused Failte Ireland, came. They saw the bigger picture and heard ideas that they hadn't thought of themselves.

Luigi offered:

> It's enthusiasm that generates the most innovation. It's the commitment. If it was just expertise or intelligence or knowledge, then the most successful people in the world would be people with the highest marks in high school. What makes people truly successful is lack of fear and the willingness to commit. If you're not committed, you don't succeed. The willingness to go beyond your comfort level and create together is crucial. No one becomes successful on their own. That's very rare.

Attendees shared some of their perspectives on both the pain and the joy of their reality in Kerry, each unique to the individual. "In the rush to industrialize farming, we've lost the understanding, implicit since the beginning of agriculture, that food is a process, a web of relationships, not an individual ingredient or commodity," one farmer told the IwB.

"Even after decades of seeing the same scenic views, when you take a moment to stop whatever it is that you're doing and just look upon the water, sometimes it feels like you're seeing it for the first time, and I love that," a housewife offered.

"It's ironic that hotels and restaurants don't support and buy from local farmers and want to increase tourism at the same time, when what the scenery tourist comes for is highly dependent on farmers grazing the land," a bartender pointed out.

On the basis of these initial conversations and the results of the workshop, the IwB faculty identified four areas of opportunity to be explored:

1. *County Kerry as a destination.* Imagine County Kerry as a destination rich in history, cultural events, and ecology that entices different types of visitors and tourists. The notion of County Kerry as a destination will be explored, with a strong focus on lengthening the tourism season, creating an environment that entices young people to settle in the region and establish roots.

2. *Science and ecology in Kerry.* There is a timely opportunity to create a systematic plan to make County Kerry a leader in research and knowledge in the field of science and ecology, and to capitalize on this role with ecotourism. Harnessing the region's ecological importance can result in economic development at both the public and private levels.

3. *Culture and heritage in the Kingdom of Kerry.* County Kerry is an important archeological and historical area. The region's cultural and heritage assets can be used as a catalyst to make County Kerry an important site for the development and appreciation of Irish history and culture. Harnessing the value of the history, folklore, language, and traditions of County Kerry will empower the community and set the stage for cultural and economic development.

4. *Innovation and new industry in Kerry.* There is an opportunity to explore the assets of the county and how they can be used to develop new types of industries, such as in the areas of energy, farming, communication, and technology. Sustainable economic development in County Kerry requires better interregional communication and more partnerships with the rest of Ireland, Europe, and the world.

Running the Charrette

Part of the IwB's facilitation goal is to set a high bar. The faculty want to create a vision for transformational change while also managing expectations of what is possible, what it will take, and the time frame for implementation. Key to facilitating good conversations during charrettes are a simple set of engagement rules: respect for each other, a commitment to working together as equals, and a focus on a purpose larger than oneself. Facilitating a dialogue and setting the stage are key. For example, on the first day of a charrette, no one can say no. Team members are reminded that they can arrive at "no" later but also that minds are often changed and a higher-order solution based on the original idea may emerge.

In November 2015, the IwB returned to conduct field research and the first of the charrettes. In this, each twelve- to fifteen-member team of IwB and Irish college students was dedicated to one of the four designated areas of opportunity. They then divided into smaller groups to analyze the area and share thoughts. All team members participated in the original definition of the problem, discussion of the design brief, and presentations to the larger student group and any interested locals. The IwB faculty felt that it was important to identify any interpersonal communication problems surfacing in the teams. Teams were reminded that everyone was working together, that ideas were welcome from everybody, and, finally, that *difference* makes life more interesting and produces a richer solution. As in other community-based methodologies, titles and hierarchical roles were minimized during the charrette process. Deep listening was the goal.

Brainstorming

A charrette's intensive brainstorming sessions encourage participants to think outside the proverbial box. The IwB provides tools to keep participants on track without stifling creative thought, with each team selecting what works best for them. They offer no formula, just a variety of ways to nudge reasoning toward innovative but realistic possibilities.

The IwB suggests numerous tools and techniques to help participants think practically yet creatively. Many of these tools, like storyboarding and creating personas, are familiar design thinking tools. To kick-start brainstorming, the IwB emphasizes four tools in particular:

1. *The flip.* Flipping involves understanding the barriers that need to be overcome, making a list of them, and then identifying a *bad* way to deal with each one. Brainstormers are then

asked to flip and identify the opposite approach. Besides providing fun for participants, flipping forces people to see things from different perspectives and gets creative juices flowing.

2. *The far-out.* Participants are asked to push every idea and every thought to the extreme. By listing even the most far-out suggestions, participants realize that it's much easier to moderate an extreme concept than to belatedly nudge a safe idea in the other direction.

3. *100 ideas.* As fast as possible, brainstorming participants write out and visualize one hundred ideas without any judgments, in a maximum of fifty words per idea. Each idea should be accompanied by a quick sketch, photograph, or other means to help visualize the idea.

4. *Archetyping.* Participants are asked to dig deeper than the problem at hand, into what it represents. They might consider, for example, that shoes aren't fashion accessories or a product but covers for feet. Breaking the issue down to its most basic archetype is the point. From there, participants build a new method of thinking about it.

In its design-focused brainstorming, the IwB reminds participants to stay positive in all discussions, to keep a record of all ideas, and to look for opportunities to combine concepts, but not to elaborate too deeply on any given train of ideas, because good brainstorming seeks quantity over quality.

In February 2016, the IwB continued the discussion in a second charrette, bringing hundreds of students together in Toronto to discuss the issues affecting rural and semirural zones in general. The Kerry-specific design process concluded with a "Dean's Charrette" in the spring. As teams developed and reshaped their ideas, there were frequent communications between them and the Iveragh officials, residents, and, in particular, Jean and Michael.

A BETTER WAY TO BRAINSTORM

Announce a brainstorming session and you can expect groans from a substantial portion of your audience. We have all suffered through the "How many uses can you come up with for a paper clip?" approach to brainstorming, which leaves the Georges among us tongue-tied as we stare at the blank piece of paper or flip chart in front of us. Design thinking approaches brainstorming differently, as the IwB's method demonstrates. First, it is data driven. It takes the information we learned about our users during **What *is*** and uses it to inspire our creativity. Second, it provides trigger techniques—like flipping—to help encourage new ways of thinking. Third, it facilitates quick, iterative rounds that allow us to build on the ideas of others.

The final report, delivered in June 2016, described five concepts. At the center of the final proposal was what the IwB called Weave, a location in a now-closed elementary school that would "foster collaboration, community building, and an entrepreneurial spirit in the Skellig Kerry region." Besides encouraging "entrepreneurs, students, community advocates, scientists, artists, and researchers to come together and create new initiatives and businesses," Weave would house offices and provide support for the four other potential projects.

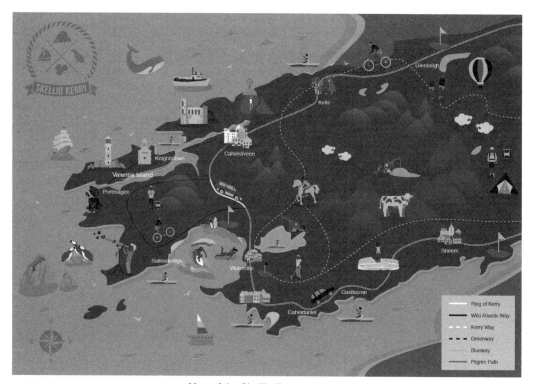

Map of the Skellig Kerry pathways.

The first project, Skellig Kerry—a response to the "County Kerry as a destination" area of opportunity, identified at the July 2015 workshop—tied County Kerry to the world-famous Skellig Michael monastery just off the Iveragh Peninsula. It sought to encourage longer tourism stays by utilizing key natural, cultural, and historical assets along a series of pathways for cycling, walking, and kayaking. Although the Skellig islands are only a tiny part of the Iveragh Peninsula in south County Kerry, the

IwB hoped to connect their international reputation as a World Heritage Site and *Star Wars* filming location with the area's famed Wild Atlantic Way to promote site *using* rather than just sight*seeing*. The Skellig Kerry concept developed out of an original "outdoor museum" idea that took advantage of extensive but dispersed archeological sites from prehistoric periods, such as the famous ringforts, and the water resources of the Atlantic Ocean.

The Cosan project took adventure tourism along a technological path by providing tourists with wristbands and a phone app that could act as emergency signals, if needed, while highlighting and promoting local restaurants, hotels, attractions, and maps of the pathway system. Helping to build the Iveragh's adventure tourism brand, Cosan drew on the electronic health tracking trend (e.g., Fitbit devices) to monitor human health indicators while adventurers cycled, climbed, or paddled.

The next project, Innovation Iveragh, housed in Weave, coordinated five outdoor pavilions originally referred to as "Pearls." The concept built on prior discussions highlighting the value of modern farming—including the new industry of harvesting seaweed—and south Kerry's "dark night sky" preserve (the only one in the Northern Hemisphere), which regulated light sources to enhance stargazing. Designed to encourage visitors to bring their own transformative projects and innovative ideas and to collaborate with local experts, Innovation Iveragh sought to create a regional gateway for investors looking to incubate and launch new industries.

Finally, the Muinin ("pride" in Irish) Project developed a "Transition Year" process in Iveragh's school systems to keep local high school graduates in the area. The components of the Muinin Project were linked with the other proposed projects. For example, the transition students would work at Weave, help build the Skellig Kerry pathways, and aid international mentors in Innovation Iveragh. Promoting a sense of belonging and Iveragh identity in these students would, the IwB students projected, address the long-term desire to repopulate the area with young families and achieve the greater goal of keeping the new generation in Iveragh.

The concepts were all interrelated, both conceptually and geographically. This arrangement allowed for flexibility and adaptation to ever-changing local reality, because Iveragh officials could select among concepts, combine them, and develop sensible timelines—important, given the reality of budgetary constraints. Fixed solutions, the IwB believed, could quickly become obsolete in a changing environment.

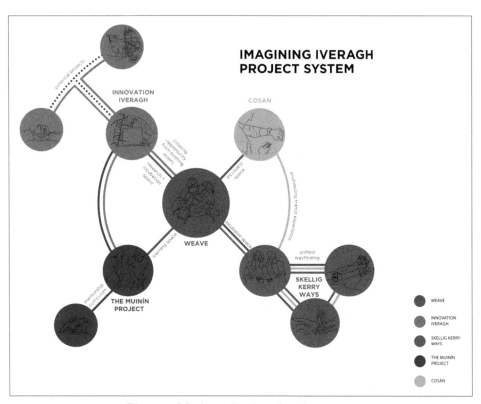

Diagram of the Imagining Iveragh project system.

The Evolution of Ideas

The final proposals received input from a number of sources throughout the year and evolved through a combination of curriculum modules, the November and February charrettes, and further iteration and collaboration with partners and key stakeholders. The outdoor museum, for example, began with a cable car that would soar over a hard-to-reach archeological site. It transformed into using gondolas for transportation over the MacGillycuddy's Reeks mountains and a dozen archeological sites. Later, recognizing that the cost and environmental and time factors rendered this idea impractical, students settled on a single gondola to the top of one mountain with phenomenal views of the Skellig Islands. In subsequent iterations, the gondola concept disappeared, but the idea survived in the Skellig Kerry pathways—an on-the-ground system that allowed active tourists to find and enjoy dozens of hidden archeological sites.

Another idea that initially generated buzz during the November charrette was the Pearl project. The team's original idea of a single research and visitor center had morphed into five satellite Pearl domes, each highlighting a different aspect of the area's uniqueness but able to be combined with other groups' concepts. Though the word *Pearl* had disappeared by the final report, the concept lived on in another form, the Innovation Iveragh concept, with its five pavilions.

Keys to Success in Collaborative Design

The IwB team identified several factors as key to the success of the Imagining Iveragh project, in particular, and to the success of charrettes in general.

Working Face-to-Face

The first success factor was putting everyone physically together in the same room. The charrette, like design thinking, is essentially a social tool. As Luigi expressed it:

> Face-to-face works so much better! The charrette is about breaking down sequential specialization methodologies and bringing in collaborative creation methodologies. The most sophisticated tool to do that is not necessarily mechanical or digital; some of the most sophisticated technologies are social. So face-to-face is a super powerful technology. Face-to-face, with all the knowledge in the room, is one of the principles of systems thinking. Get all the knowledge in the room.

Visualization

As is true in so many of our stories, visualization was a constant. It was used throughout the charrette, providing multiple ways for people to talk with each other. In Imagining Iveragh, teams used drawings, computer designs, mapping (of both geographic and economic realities), and literal models to communicate with each other and with local stakeholders and policy makers. Visualization helped people of different backgrounds and nationalities, or different sensibilities, ages, and experiences, to understand each other's meaning. During the Kerry charrette, for example, it was common to see silver-haired, buttoned-down Michael peering over a rather less formal but equally dedicated young student to view an animation on the student's laptop. As Michael suggested improvement ideas, the student responded with nods and fingers flashing on the keyboard.

Prototyping

Prototyping is one variant of visualization. It enabled participants to interact in more concrete ways with the ideas proposed. Luigi explained:

> When you prototype, it is a simulation. Everyone thinks simulations are these powerful computer things, but simulation is when you grab a Kleenex and fold it. You are making a rough version that is an imitation of the final version. It is important to visualize, simulate, and then interact. But interaction is most important, because then you can really see whether a concept behaves with people in the actual environment the way you hope it will.

He elaborated:

> The tendency is to try to preplan everything and have the answer ahead of time, but if you can see an answer already, you haven't created anything new. You are still in the world of the known, not the world of the unknown. By prototyping, you enter the world of the unknown. You learn about it, and then you can actually reiterate and perfect your solutions. Most things fail for details. Not because their thing was wrong but because the details were not worked out. And the only way to work out the details is to prototype, get it in use, revise, reiterate until it actually works.

PROTOTYPING

Prototyping early and often, one of the core tenets of a design thinking approach, involves creating rough visual representations of an idea. A prototype tells a story, allowing team members not only to ensure their own alignment on a new idea but also to seek more accurate feedback from stakeholders. Prototyping forces design teams to pay attention to details they might otherwise overlook.

Setting Timelines

Timelines were an important part of the IwB's process. By visualizing the timelines for each project, with the details of implementation beachheads clearly specified, residents gained a plan that could be worked on incrementally. Luigi explained why timelines are critical:

> Considering things in time is very powerful. We don't leave people just a design; we leave them a set of actions over time. That's what they start to follow. That's why time-lining is such a powerful process. When you visualize the timeline with the action steps and the small designs that you have to get done, that together would change everything, people have something to work towards.

All of the final Iveragh concepts came with both a timeline by project and an overall timeline that illustrated how the ideas interacted. The Skellig Kerry project timeline, for instance, began with a traditional guidebook in 2017, added an electronic guide in 2018, and specified that the actual "wayfinding" (electronic signposts) would be added in 2019, when the pathways were projected to be finished.

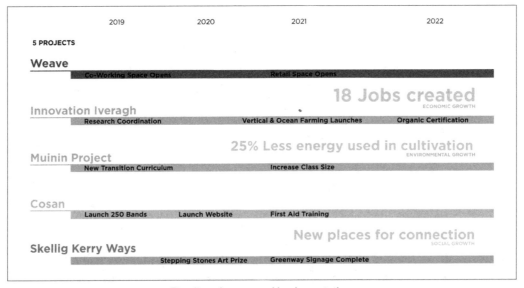

Timelines for proposal implementation.

Timelines also helped communities figure out how to make small bets fast in their efforts to reinvent the economy, which often is challenging for most people to envision. Certainly, Iveragh would need to renovate the closed elementary school to transform it into the Weave centerpiece. But smaller experiments also were possible, as the timelines demonstrated. Skellig Kerry, the adventure tourism concept, began with branding. The assets for this adventure tourism concept—mountains for downhill cycling, the Atlantic for kayaking, the winds for surfing and parasailing, and the famous walks—already existed on the Iveragh Peninsula, and three trails similar to New Zealand's famous treks were already on the drawing board. The initial actions involved combining existing adventure tourism guides and seeking cooperation from small hotels, restaurants, and facilities to offer multiday stays, and then communicating the packages to the targeted tourists—generally young, professional, and risk-inclined young couples from Europe and America, rather than the older, sedentary tourists who circled the Ring of Kerry and the Wild Atlantic Way in buses.

Creating Champions

A final element, perhaps most critical to implementation of the IwB's ideas, was finding champions among community members. These champions emerged early on in the design process and became the connectors who forged the other relationships required to actually build the new future. These connectors helped galvanize the community to action and maintained the momentum after the charrette.

In fact, it was the impact of the charrette on the lives of the people involved, above and beyond any specific actions taken, that was Luigi's dominant measure in evaluating the success of a charrette:

> I actually think the proof is in how people's lives are changing. That's really hard to capture with metrics. And it takes time. A lot of the things we've accomplished in charrettes have taken time to gestate before they come true. The most powerful part is what they do to the people who have been in them. Sometimes I am not even worried if change happens. In fact, when I started I thought we had to finish all the projects. But what really needs to come from a charrette is that people are given agency and that things start to change—that people are empowered to change.

Reflections on the Process

Noreen O'Mahoney, economic and tourism officer for Kerry, reflected on what made the design thinking experience powerful:

> For economic development in rural areas like Iveragh, the rural area has many opportunities, many attributes, but needs some fresh thinking and maybe outside perspectives. Design thinking and action research bring collaborative thinking with the researchers, the communities, the local governments, the locals to act together to come up with actions and solutions. In a more traditional process, you'd have hired a consultant and gotten recommendations. The consultants would interview the community, but only about that project. This was more environment based. The researchers are involved with the community. The community is the one who, at the end of the day, has to be invested.

Luigi concurred:

> To create and implement solutions over time is to imagine the unfolding of a solution, not a silver bullet. There is no silver bullet. It's not one thing; it's an interaction of things, of people working together. The reason collaborative design is so critical at this moment is that we've spent five centuries developing specialization as our methodology. We solved problems by acquiring knowledge. This process towards specialized, abstract knowledge has been critical. But having reached higher and higher levels of specialization, and achieved that intense domain of knowledge, our next step becomes how to integrate across specialized knowledge to solve the increasing complexity of the world, to take the world forward. Wicked problems have always existed, but it has become clear that we can't solve problems within a single specialization. Everything is interconnected. Today we need people working together.

Whether it's called user-centered design, service design, or design thinking, this process of thinking together, of interaction and insight seeking, using tools such as a charrette, makes possible a new kind of conversation and a new future.

After ideas blossom and stakeholders align around a particular set of opportunities, then fiscal and political constraints are added to the mix and assumptions are scrutinized. Some possibilities may confront realities that impede their implementation; any given idea may or may not be financed. But, by ensuring creative thought, by working in intensive collaboration, we believe that exciting possibilities capable of surviving the **What *wows*** and **What *works*** tests will emerge.

In Iveragh, it all started with a few forceful folks: a catalyst, Jean, with a strategy for problem solving, and a leader, Moira, with the courage to try a new approach. "Jean found the opening, and she pushed it very hard," Michael commented, "and we are all better off because of that. If Jean was easy to say no to, this would not have happened."

Jean acknowledged:

> Sometimes you have to be a good bit "bulldozerish" to change mindsets. Hopefully, like the US decided to put a man on the moon and then did it, perhaps Kerry can use and harness the IwB's results and perhaps go to the moon.

Back in Cahersiveen, town librarian Noreen O'Sullivan would settle for more-modest change:

> For a group to include us, to consult with and involve local people, it helps the community buy in and support the project. Everyone got so enthusiastic. We had a full house listening to the proposals. We'll embrace whatever projects are finalized. Whichever ideas get selected, it can only be a huge positive, if the project helps people to stay here and not have to leave. We have such a wonderful quality of life here for those who can stay.

CHAPTER EIGHT

Connecting—and Disconnecting—the Pieces at United Cerebral Palsy

THE CHALLENGE TO THE GREATER GOOD

How do you facilitate bringing together those who have needs with those who can potentially meet those needs, and help these groups to work together to accomplish some greater good? Can you galvanize different stakeholders, who have differing needs and inputs but need each other's resources, to work together to generate new solutions? And can you win the support of your organization's key stakeholders to accommodate such a strategy?

DESIGN THINKING'S CONTRIBUTION

Innovation in the social sector often requires building connections across what, in business, we would call the supply chain. Design thinking can offer a methodology for initiating these connections and architecting the networks capable of both generating new ideas and translating them into reality. In this story, United Cerebral Palsy (UCP) explores expanding its mission beyond seeking donations and offering services, aiming to foster the connections needed to invent and incubate new products. Taking a design approach, they created Innovation Labs—traveling design thinking events that invited people with all kinds of disabilities, caregivers, engineers, entrepreneurs, and design students to improve the quality of life of those with disabilities. Then, unfortunately, the real world intervened.

When we first heard the leaders of Life Labs at United Cerebral Palsy tell their story, we felt as though we were looking into a crystal ball and seeing what the charitable organization of the future would look like. UCP had always been a forward-thinking organization, pioneering innovations like the telethon that have become fund-raising staples. Throughout their almost seventy-year history, UCP's mission has remained constant: advancing the independence of people with disabilities, enriching their lives, providing support to their families, and advocating for their inclusion in every facet of community life. But it was their bold new experiment to better accomplish this mission that caught our attention. It reversed the traditional paradigm and rethought the basic business model of the charitable organization itself; instead of *asking* for help to assist those they served, they wanted to *offer* help.

Central to this strategy was their Life Labs operation. Originally conceived as a kind of development lab for assistive technology, Life Labs was intended to evolve into an entrepreneurial hub for the development of products and services to improve the lives of those with disabilities, using design thinking to get there. Marc Irlandez, Life Labs's former director and technology leader, talked about the journey to that shift:

> Originally, Life Labs was meant to be a kind of R & D practice—but we quickly learned that we didn't have the resources, we didn't have the expertise or the manpower to do that type of work. But we had a lot of ideas. And so we went exploring—not only about what we could do but what people with disabilities were really hopeful for, what they were looking to do.

A pivotal moment in this exploration came during a meeting with a new start-up called AbleGamers, a small nonprofit with a goal of making video gaming accessible to those with disabilities. That meeting sparked a revelation for Marc:

> We loved what they were doing but recognized that UCP was never going to fight that fight. Not only did we not have the expertise—that just wasn't going to be on our agenda. But our missions intersected, and we wanted to be part of that kind of work. And, at that moment, I recognized that it was going to be laser-focused organizations like AbleGamers that were going to be instrumental in accomplishing our mission, not us.

We weren't going to own and execute the agenda. Helping those fledging nonprofits, helping the guy in his garage create a piece of technology for his loved one—that's where Life Labs could make the greater impact. This was not something that we were going to do alone.

Life Labs's contribution could be to spawn and nurture a network of entrepreneurs. Though technology would play a role, it would not be *their* role. As Marc described it, "The innovative thing that we wanted to do had nothing to do with the technology—it was the *relationships* that we would build that would allow us to make an impact out there."

When Josef Scarantino joined Marc's team, his experience in the maker movement added another building block. Creating an accessible maker space for people with disabilities could have a big impact, they believed. Marc could trace his own interest in the maker movement back to his first week on the job at UCP. A documentary he watched that week featured a young man with a disability who was writing a book by using a tongue interface his father had created in their garage, with help from a local engineer. It was apparent to Marc that the device would not be of interest to big companies looking for large markets, yet not everyone had a loved one capable of creating such a product. "But it totally changed that boy's life," Marc noted. "Now he's writing books."

Equipping people with tools—both literally and figuratively—and helping them to learn to create became a goal of Life Labs. Marc explained:

> It didn't have to be a father. People with disabilities should themselves be able to have a 3-D printer or a soldering pen or whatever it takes to fabricate tools, because our commu-

THE MAKER MOVEMENT

The *maker movement* manifests design thinking's iteration process, in which tinkerers devise, design, try, test, and retry to build something. What makes makers a movement is that social spaces designed to aid people in these efforts have popped up in cities around the world. In these spaces, makers can pay a nominal fee to use tools such as welding machines, 3-D printers, lathes, drill presses, table saws, and filmmaking equipment. These "hacker spaces" promote learning by doing, through networked, peer-led approaches.

nity is the most reliant on technology. The able-bodied use all these gadgets as luxuries, but for people with disabilities they are a necessity, so they're already hacking things. They change everything—because they have to. That's a true maker movement, because you're doing it out of passion and your own need.

Meanwhile, a UCP colleague attending the South by Southwest Conference in Austin, Texas, heard a talk given by people from a London-based nonprofit group called Enabled by Design that was doing novel things. Back at home, the Life Labs team reached out to them to learn more about an event they had organized, Enabled by Design-athon. It struck a chord, and the Life Labs team took the kernel of that approach and adapted it to their own mission. Their three-day event brought diverse teams of engineers, designers, people with disabilities, and caregivers together to invent and prototype new products and services. After the first year, UCP elected to change the name of their version to Innovation Lab, reflecting their hope that it would become a real-world laboratory for experimentation and collaboration. Josef told us:

> We've always liked the hackathon idea of putting things into a pressure cooker and seeing what happens, but what attracted us to the Design-athon versus a hackathon was that people with disabilities were actually involved. Rather than bringing preformed teams together to see what they can do for people, the users are involved.

The Innovation Lab captured the essence of the maker movement and used a design thinking methodology that relied heavily on the Stanford design school model, which they called Innovative Thinking, to structure the process. But then UCP went a step further—it made the creation process *social*. This social dimension itself met an important need of people with disabilities: "The social aspect is the number one thing that the disability community wants," Marc explained. "Forget about policy or support programs or whatever. The social side is what people with disabilities want the most. We take all these things for granted."

Like the event that inspired it, UCP's Innovation Lab would ask people to come together to solve problems with strangers. The first Innovation Lab took place in Washington, DC, in the fall of 2013. It involved a lot of bootstrapping.

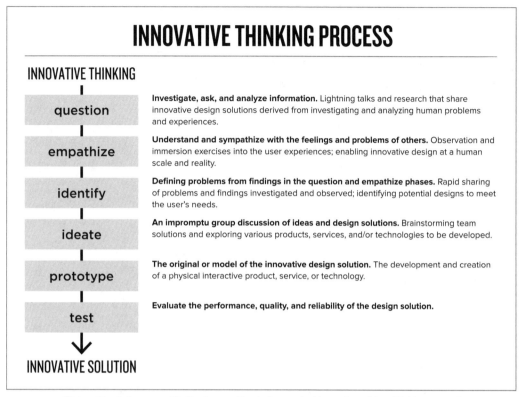

INNOVATIVE THINKING PROCESS

INNOVATIVE THINKING

question — **Investigate, ask, and analyze information.** Lightning talks and research that share innovative design solutions derived from investigating and analyzing human problems and experiences.

empathize — **Understand and sympathize with the feelings and problems of others.** Observation and immersion exercises into the user experiences; enabling innovative design at a human scale and reality.

identify — **Defining problems from findings in the question and empathize phases.** Rapid sharing of problems and findings investigated and observed; identifying potential designs to meet the user's needs.

ideate — **An impromptu group discussion of ideas and design solutions.** Brainstorming team solutions and exploring various products, services, and/or technologies to be developed.

prototype — **The original or model of the innovative design solution.** The development and creation of a physical interactive product, service, or technology.

test — **Evaluate the performance, quality, and reliability of the design solution.**

INNOVATIVE SOLUTION

The methodology used in the Innovation Lab, created in partnership with Marymount University and based on the Stanford University Institute of Design (d.school) model.

Finding Partners

One element critical to the success of the Innovation Labs was attracting the right kind of partners. Life Labs already had a set of corporate relationships, and they started there. The timing was fortuitous, as Marc explained:

> We had already lined up partners for Life Labs, and had been working with them, trying to find common ground, figure out where their interests lay, and how we could get them involved or get involved in what they were doing.

Sponsors responded enthusiastically to the Innovation Lab premise. "Now you're giving me something that I can really throw our weight behind!" is how Josef recalls their response.

Marc was clear that the effort was new territory for them all and was going to require courage: "All the parties had to be very brave with what we were doing." Google, in particular, stepped forward immediately, as Josef described:

> Google started to get involved by doing a lot of in-kind support. It can take a long time to get actual funding from Google, because they want to ensure there is sufficient impact on the community. And so they wanted to show their support, but they were looking for ways to show that in-kind support through event coordination of venue, catering, things that really do eat up a lot of resources. And that's where they came through. The key is really finding partners who have an intersection with your mission. I think that the mistake a lot of nonprofits make is to immediately go ask for funding when there are so many other opportunities for partnerships.

Marc elaborated:

> If you write a check, tons of people don't know about it. This was more successful for Google because their engineers were totally jazzed about what we were doing. They're an engineer-driven organization—getting their engineers in that mindset is an important thing for them. How do we design for communities that aren't really represented in engineering communities or in design communities?

Google's sponsorship brought credibility to the event—both with participants and with internal leadership.

Curating the teams was another critical piece of setting up the success of the Innovation Lab, with the same emphasis on diversity that we have seen in so many of our other stories. Josef described why:

> At the Innovation Lab, it's about the process. It's not really about creating this widget—it's about the process of getting people together and working across different areas. When we curate the teams, based on those who have registered, we try to bring together

a mixture of designers and engineers but also caregivers and people with disabilities. We try to be as diverse as we can.

They found the ideal team size to be six to eight people, with at least one member representing the disability community—a caregiver or a person with a disability. This created a challenge around how to market the event to people who were new to design. UCP reached out to its network of caregivers, both to promote the event and to let them know that they, too, had great value, even if they weren't an engineer or designer. Marc observed:

> Everyone comes with one or more missing components: I'm not a designer, or I'm not an engineer. I don't have a disability background. I don't have a disability. No one is all of them, but that's the whole point—so you're missing a part; that's perfect!

The UCP team also found another enthusiastic partner in universities. Always on the lookout for ways to incorporate experiential learning, to move out of the classroom and give students the experience of creation in real life, they found the Innovation Lab opportunity compelling. Eight universities were represented in the first Innovation Lab, from as far away as Michigan, Syracuse, and Boston.

The Innovation Lab Event

The Innovation Lab was designed to be a three-day event, commencing with an evening kickoff on day one, followed by two full days of workshops.

The first Innovation Lab, held in Washington, DC, began with a series of "lightning" talks. Only five minutes long and aimed at giving a short introduction to a topic of interest, like universal design, they gave attendees a chance to get to know each other. One former board member reviewed the business case for designing for people with disabilities, emphasizing that it needn't be about charity and could be about building a business. "People loved that message," Marc noted.

"People with disabilities don't want to be treated as a charity," Josef explained. "They want to be treated just like everyone else."

An important role of the Innovation Lab was to increase awareness and engage others in advocating for people with disabilities. Marc noted:

> Their voices are just not heard. They don't need the type of help where you start pushing someone in a wheelchair—but people don't know that. What we need is for you to fight for more ramps, for the policy around it.

ENABLED BY DESIGN-ATHON

DAY 2
NOV 6, 2014
SCHEDULE

8:00 AM	Tea/Coffee + Registration
9:00 AM	Welcome by Sprint Relay
9:15 AM	**3D Printing for People with Disabilities Talk** — Robert Gootzit, PCS Engineering
9:30 AM	Team Activity
10:30 AM	**Part I – Explore** — Exploring challenges related to accessibility.
12:00 PM	Rapid Report Back
12:30 PM	Catered Lunch & Networking
1:00 PM	**Part II – Ideas** — Brainstorming ideas, building on the insights and experiences gathered in the Explore stage. Enjoy lunch with your team, courtesy of Google.
2:30 PM	Rapid Report Back
3:00 PM	**Part III – Make** — Teams begin turning their idea into reality by working on their prototype.
5:30 PM	Close of Day 2
6:00 PM	Happy Hour

#DESIGNDC14

DAY 3
NOV 7, 2014
SCHEDULE

8:00 AM	Tea/Coffee
9:30 AM	**Part III – Make – cont.** — Teams continue working on their prototype.
12:00 PM	Catered Lunch & Networking — Enjoy lunch with your team, courtesy of Google.
1:00 PM	**Part IV – Share** — Show and Tell session of team projects.
3:00 PM	Judging
3:30 PM	Winners Announced & Wrap-Up

A typical Innovation Lab schedule.

On day two, dedicated team facilitators, as well as a set of mentors who would float from team to team, arrived thirty minutes early for a pep talk and instructions. The facilitator's job was to keep the team on track, and each got a detailed printout of the schedule for the two days.

The session kicked off with a speaker from the Small Business Administration talking about federal funding opportunities for start-ups. Then an executive from a sponsor, Sprint Relay, who was herself deaf, gave an inspiring talk about her personal story. Another talk was given by representatives from a local prototyping company that focused on 3-D printing, working with start-ups to create their products. They talked about 3-D printing for people with disabilities and 3-D printing of prosthetics, and they brought along a few machines and engineers to be available to the design teams during the workshop.

The Innovation Lab session then unfolded in three stages typical of design thinking processes: Explore, Ideas, and Make. The exploration portion was handled differently than in traditional design thinking approaches, in which ethnographic research would be done in advance. The Explore stage began, instead, with empathy exercises in which team members imagined the experience of those with disabilities. Team members who themselves had disabilities or who cared for people with disabilities were present to help everyone understand the challenges they faced. Teams then jumped into selecting the focus for their next two days of work together, knowing that, during the final day's competition with the other teams, they would be judged on the usability, accessibility, and desirability of the designs they produced.

Soon, the teams gave the first in a series of rapid reports to the group at large—this one on the names the teams had selected. Then, teams shared where they were headed. They had the opportunity to pivot after hearing other teams' quick pitches, which sometimes gave them different ideas. They then transitioned into the Ideas stage, using paper and cardboard to do rough prototyping. With about an hour left until the end of the day, they gave another rapid report. Teams then worked at their own pace as they pulled together their pitches.

By the start of day three, teams were expected to be in the third stage. The Make stage focused on taking rough prototypes to the next level of development and constructing stories around them. People showed up early on day three, ready to jump in, as they foresaw the end of the day closing in on them. By noon, they needed to have their pitch polished and their presentations ready. Marc observed:

> On day two, people are scared that they are going to be in front of people sharing something on day three—they just can't imagine being ready. But when they come in that morning, they're sure that they're going to have something. They're just working to get it done, which is a totally different dynamic.

EMPATHY ACTIVITY

Dexterity

Gloves

Put on the gardening gloves or rubber gloves and:

- find a pen at the bottom of your bag
- tear open a Band-Aid and stick it on your face
- zip and unzip a plastic click-lock bag
- Plus, think of two of your own challenges using the gloves.

Non-Preferred Hand

Without the gloves, fill in one of the Australia Post forms using a pen held in your non-preferred hand. Keep to the squares!

Think about potential scenarios and people who might have altered dexterity.

What challenges would they face in everyday life?

How might it make them feel?

Please note:

These empathy activities can help to understand how different impairments might affect real world tasks and empathise with those affected.

Enabled by Design-athon: Sydney 2014

An empathy exercise used in the Innovation Lab.

STORYBOARDING

Storyboarding is a staple of the film industry, as well as a useful tool in design thinking. A storyboard lays out a sequence of events visually, capturing a stakeholder's journey in pictures, almost like a cartoon strip. They are particularly handy to illustrate concepts that aren't tangible, like processes, and can serve as a great springboard for co-creation.

The teams worked feverishly, preparing the prototypes of their concepts. These prototypes took different forms, including storyboards, videos, and photo mock-ups of products in use. The objective was not just to show the product but also to tell the story of how it would meet the needs of people with disabilities in unique ways.

One team created a messenger-style bag, modified for ease of use, using a storyboard to walk their audience through how it could make life easier for those with disabilities. Though the idea hardly seemed revolutionary, it represented exactly the kind of innovation that Life Labs hoped to achieve, taking a standard bag and modifying it to add features like magnetic closures and an accompanying wristband to be worn by the user to make opening, closing, and retrieving objects from the bag easier. These seemingly modest alterations, easily doable by home hackers, had the potential to make life far easier for a person with disabilities.

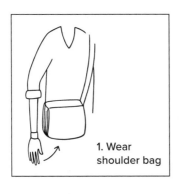
1. Wear shoulder bag

2. Tap with magnetic band to open

3. Remove item from bag

4. Press bag shut with wrist

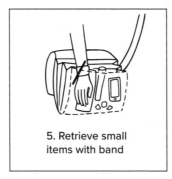
5. Retrieve small items with band

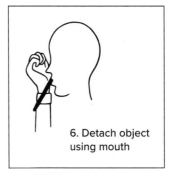
6. Detach object using mouth

Storyboard showing the features of a bag modified for ease of use,
re-created from a more detailed Innovation Lab storyboard.

Judging started at 3:00 p.m. with judges given a chance to ask one or two questions. An announcement that prizes would be awarded created an element of surprise, providing an energy boost. In addition to the modified bag, the prototypes presented were diverse. Another team created a "companion app" that could help people with disabilities navigate the public transportation system. A third created a wheelchair that could climb stairs. The idea "Stars at War," a software program that translated colloquialisms for people with autism, won the competition. The session ended by 4:00 p.m., with the teams deciding what they wanted to do with their prototypes. UCP did not want to own the ideas. One team at the DC event elected to open source their design.

The success of that first Innovation Lab was a big win, despite a limited bankroll behind it. As Josef described, "That was a really big boost for UCP in general because that whole event was bootstrapped. It was done with very little funding. It's funny, because having very little funding pushes you to get very creative."

Outcomes

The level of engagement of the Innovation Lab attendees was a key metric of interest to the UCP team. "It's more about creating stories that feed into the mission of UCP in a broader sense," Josef explained. Marc added:

> The people that attend are future donors or future sponsors, as are their companies. The most important outcome to me is people coming out of it and saying, "I like the process. I'm going to have that in mind when I go back to my job"—whatever their job is. It will have changed their approach to their work. You don't have to be an expert on disabilities, but you do have to have that interest. That's the first step.

Josef noted that the event helped to spark new interest in how design can help people with disabilities, a topic that many attendees had not previously considered.

Over the next several years, Life Labs ran a series of Innovation Lab events around the country, all using a similar format.

The Next Life Labs Step: The Incubator

The creation of an incubator for start-ups was the next part of the Life Labs strategic plan. Complementing and extending the work of the Innovation Labs, it would add mentoring, investing, access to UCP's affiliate network, and a direct connection to users to facilitate testing of the new products and services developed. The aim was to create a mechanism to support follow-through on the ideas generated in the Innovation Labs entrepreneurial ecosystem. The hope was that, with the incubator in place, the ideas generated in the Innovation Lab events would be more likely to be developed into real products and services. Marc observed:

> For people doing work in disabilities, testing can be a big hurdle. How do you get someone with dementia into the design process? We can make that connection. If we can get these companies to survive a little bit longer, help them get a product to market, some of them will keep going. We're creating a safety net for those willing to market and sell to this marginalized population. We'll help them get to that population and make the idea sustainable—and they'll get a paycheck while they create great products for our population. That's our intention. We need more people trying.

Josef added:

> You hear stories of innovators that have created a $50 version of a $10,000 product. We want to see that replicated! It's not unusual to have a prosthetic that's $50,000, and yet you can 3-D print prosthetics for $100 or less.

The Life Labs team visited the Cerebral Palsy Alliance, a UCP affiliate in Sydney, Australia. There, they met with a team that created chairs specifically contoured to the body of individuals with disabilities, intended to fit each person exactly. Unfortunately, as the team explained, by the time they measured and then fabricated the chair, their client's body sometimes had degenerated further and the chair no longer met that client's needs. The team realized that they needed a faster way, as well as a cheaper one. They hoped that the combination of the quick Innovation Lab events, coupled with the availability of incubator support, would expedite the development process.

In fall 2015, Josef was appointed director of Life Labs. He reflected on next steps at that time, as they set a goal of hosting Innovation Lab events in more than six different cities in 2016:

> I think people will come to think of the Innovation Lab as a bridge between highly skilled individuals across different professions and those in the community expressing need and the desire to be a part of the solution. We've tried hard to keep the focus on the process rather than the outcomes, but that will change as Life Labs moves toward creating a business incubator and the Innovation Lab becomes a pathway to the incubator. But I really intend to keep the focus on the design process as much as possible. I think people crave collaboration and social interaction more than they crave entrepreneurship in its traditional sense.

Reflections on the Process

The urge to create, Marc believed, was powerful, but the connections to produce the new product or experience, to find the market, were often missing among the kinds of amateur makers that UCP sought to assist. He noted that Life Labs's incubator hoped to make those connections and to find buyers for niche, but crucial, services and products for people with disabilities:

> People want to create something—that's a lot of what designers and engineers want. Just tell me—I want to create a company, but tell me what the world needs. What are the problems out there? And they want to solve them. One thing that I've learned in the last two years is the importance of learning how to work across industries—never pigeonhole yourself into one area. That's the brilliance of the Innovation Lab: getting designers with caregivers, making use of people from such a variety of industries.

Marc encouraged others to try a similar approach to connecting creators with those in need:

> You don't have to be an expert to hold this type of event—or come from a disability background. You don't have to be an expert to do something innovative in an organization. You don't have to be an expert in assistive technology to create things at an Innovation Lab. You just have to have the curiosity.

Curiosity, Josef noted, can be so easily lost, but without curiosity new ideas will lie undiscovered:

> When you become an adult, you lose some of that curiosity. That's the great thing about maker spaces—they give adults the opportunity to get a little curious again. There's fun in that. Having fun is important. It doesn't all have to be about creating business and making money. Have fun, because there are some really brilliant things that come out of that.

Postmortem

Sometimes reality intrudes and having a great idea isn't enough. Life Labs no longer exists; it was shuttered in early 2016. Having pursued a different kind of vision for a Web 3.0 version of a charitable organization, Life Labs fell apart for real-world reasons not necessarily connected to design thinking. Leadership support for Life Labs and its proposed innovation incubator evaporated as funding challenges and management changes swamped the organization. UCP's six Innovation Lab events planned for 2016 were never undertaken, and the incubator concept was not advanced, after Life Labs failed to convince key stakeholders that it had created a sustainable way to overcome funding problems. Josef joined Marc in taking his design skills elsewhere, while UCP is today going through a change of administration and dealing with a sagging donations market.

Many of UCP's larger organizational problems involved questions of identity and brand, including how each of the eighty or so self-governing affiliates saw the international operation and its relation to the reality of the many disabilities, including autism spectrum disorder and Down syndrome, that UCP now seeks to address in addition to cerebral palsy. Though Life Labs and its incubator could potentially have connected product designers with people affected by any of the other disabilities, and in the process achieved greater economies of scale, many local affiliates failed to see Life Labs's relevance to their own work.

Because less than half of the people UCP served actually have cerebral palsy, and 85 percent have multiple disabilities, even the name United Cerebral Palsy is under fire today. About 20 percent of UCP's independent affiliate organizations have already changed their names and mission statements, and pressure is accelerating for a name change for the national organization. Powerful forces are pushing for retrenchment to the core mission, and the dues from the independent affiliates that sustained operations at headquarters are beginning to decline.

In our view, Life Labs was an inspired idea—one we believe will be re-created in other contexts in the future. The approach had many positive attributes:

- Like the conversations we looked at in the FDA, it brought people with different backgrounds and perspectives together to learn, share, and create.

- As in the Kingwood story, it invited those with disabilities, and their caregivers, into the conversation in a meaningful way. In doing so, it changed the people who participated—they saw the world of disability in a different way and perhaps saw a new role for themselves.

- As with the community conversations in Kerry, it insisted that participants translate their ideas into concrete concepts and then make these concepts tangible and testable through prototyping.

- Finally, it gave a team the experience of laying out their design logic for others and allowed them to give and receive feedback.

We believe that, given the time and support to help the nascent Innovation Lab ideas seek commercialization through the planned incubator, Life Labs could have accelerated UCP's mission to advance the independence of people with disabilities, enrich their lives, provide better support to their families, and advocate for their inclusion in every facet of community life.

We know that innovations sometimes fail, not because they don't create value but because of timing, external changes in the environment, or internal changes in the organization. That is one of the reasons why we recommend keeping an inventory of ideas that

TOP DOWN VERSUS BOTTOM UP

The question of whether design thinking (or any change for that matter) should be driven from the top down or from the bottom up is an intriguing one in the innovation space. We touched on this in chapter 1 and will return to the subject in chapter 15. We are great believers in the power of grassroots efforts and have seen the impact that they can make. Many design champions are not waiting for senior leadership to give them permission to innovate. In fact, one great aspect of design thinking is its inherently subversive nature, and that nature is much in evidence in our research.

Bootstrapping strategies do succeed. These "stealth" strategies often are led by an intrepid band of design enthusiasts, take advantage of leadership indifference, and seek support from credible outside sponsors instead. They are framed in a way that is nonthreatening in an Innovation I world and are often portrayed as problem-solving strategies, without headlining "design thinking." These early endeavors achieve small successes, provide data to argue for bigger moves, and build from there.

At the same time, internal management support is often crucial. Imagine Marliza Rivera's Whiteriver project without the support of HHS's Ignite Accelerator—success would have been unlikely. If anything were possible, we would like to see design thinking coming from both the top down and the bottom up.

don't pass the **What *wows*?** and **What *works*?** tests on their first try. In our research, we consistently see ideas succeeding on their second—or even third—attempt. Hence, we expect to see the Life Labs concept resurrected in another time and place.

But some lessons here do relate specifically to design thinking. Life Labs was not just the victim of circumstances beyond its control. UCP's former chief operating officer, Chris Thomson, recalled the Life Labs experiment in positive terms but talked about the limits of merely raising awareness versus actually bringing products to market:

> Life Labs was an incredibly inspired idea that ran into real-world problems. It was a very successful participant experience and very useful for spreading awareness and for helping us with the hacker-maker-builder community, but it never answered the questions around how to generate the revenues to sustain it. For getting people thinking about ideas, it was incredible, but for actually bringing products to market for people to help themselves, not so much.

What are the limits of creating great experiences? Even in a world where profitability is not an objective, designing an experience that gives careful thought to the underpinnings of a self-sustaining financial model in a predictable way is critical. That's why we ask the **What *wows*?** question and insist that design thinkers take their prototypes to key stakeholders (and not just users) for feedback. All invention comes with risk, and no innovator can control all outside forces, but thinking through the financial viability of an idea, and not just its desirability, before significant resources are expended is needed.

As Josef reflected on his experience at Life Labs, he also shared concerns that spoke to the role of leadership and the need for a supportive context for such initiatives to succeed:

> I don't think these developments reflect on the mission of Life Labs, but I do believe that any design thinking initiative must be more than just a program that allows an organization to check off the "innovation" box. Design thinking needs to be embedded deeply into the ethos of the overall organizational mission, and this type of focus absolutely requires leadership from the top down or it risks ending up stale, unsupported, and, worse, misunderstood.

As design thinking gains popularity in both the business world and the social sector, it will face new challenges engendered by its burgeoning popularity. Josef mentioned these in our last conversation:

> My concern with design thinking is that it has reached buzzword status and is largely misapplied and misapplied as a panacea for every organization's challenges. When it doesn't work, the organization incorrectly places the blame on innovation and quickly moves on. My view is that design thinking is a highly valuable tool in a toolbox, but by no means a universal multitool. It needs to be used correctly and given support and time to work properly.

Like Josef, we worry. It is easy to allow our enthusiasm for design thinking to turn us into the infamous young boy with a hammer who sees nails everywhere he looks. As Jim Scully of ThinkPlace in New Zealand observed, "I worry when design thinking turns into a religion." We see the explosion of interest in hackathons and workshops and sometimes wonder what will follow. One- and two-day events can provide an essential energy charge to inspire interest and get design thinking off the ground, but these need to be followed by more in-depth training in the tools and by the opportunity to apply the method in real time to real issues. Otherwise, as with so many organizational fads that we have seen come and go, people leave the workshop excited but then resort to business as usual when they find their desks swamped with work due yesterday.

Without disciplined attention to rigorous application of these methods and tools, and careful forethought about the back end of testing and experimentation in the real world, as well as the front end of empathy, design thinking will not live up to the promise we see in so many of our stories. Similarly, it is vital to enlist the support of key funders and to offer them a sustainable financing model; otherwise, even wonderful ideas created in carefully crafted processes will not see the light of day.

CHAPTER NINE

The Power of Local at the Community Transportation Association of America

THE CHALLENGE TO THE GREATER GOOD

"Think globally, act locally" is a phrase that we have come to accept as an almost universal truth. But what if it's not always true? Mandated top-down solutions to deep-seated community problems often fail to take into account critical dimensions of the problem that only local knowledge reveals. What if thinking, as well as acting, locally is better? In this story, we see the power of local thinking about a tough issue: the transportation needs of low-income workers.

DESIGN THINKING'S CONTRIBUTION

Rather than defining a problem centrally and recommending implementation of broad initiatives, design thinking offers diverse community-based players the opportunity to jointly frame problems and form solutions rooted in the unique circumstances of their communities. The Community Transportation Association of America (CTAA) used design thinking as a guiding structure to empower local partners. Over a year, the association's educators led seven local teams through the process together—sharing insights and observations as they went and creating the best of both worlds: local problem definition and solutions and shared learning.

Headquartered in Washington, DC, and working with local communities throughout the United States, the Community Transportation Association of America invites both organizations and individuals to join in achieving their mission of "creating mobility for all Americans regardless of where they live or work." CTAA's central focus is education and advocacy around transportation challenges facing citizens, especially seniors, veterans, people with disabilities, and low-income workers. Carolyn Jeskey, director of community engagement, calls herself "an educator and incentivizer" and has devoted twenty-plus years to transportation-related challenges. She explained why:

> Our transportation system is good and serves millions of people every day, but there are many people with unique needs that current transportation services don't yet serve well. The work that CTAA and I have been doing for all these years is working to create mobility that responds more empathetically to those with unmet needs. For instance, in a system that runs 8:00 a.m. to 6:00 p.m., how do you build a transportation system that works for people working a 10:00 p.m. to 6:00 a.m. shift? We've been advocating for better services for those whose needs have not yet been met, like trying to get services for aging in place and more self-sufficiency in lower-wage communities.

Convinced of the value that design thinking could bring to their work, CTAA partnered with Peer Insight, a DC-based innovation consultancy that fuses design thinking with entrepreneurship principles. Together, they developed the Design Thinking for Mobility tool kit, and Peer Insight trained twelve CTAA staffers to facilitate use of the same four-question design thinking methodology that we have talked about in earlier chapters, with the goal of empowering local communities to seek their own solutions.

Amy Conrick, Carolyn's colleague at CTAA, commented on how deeply the value of community self-governance was embedded in their approach:

> From its beginnings, CTAA believed strongly in the power of self-help, giving communities the tools, support, and education needed to create local solutions. Through its decades of work, it also recognized that no outside organization could ever know a community's characteristics, needs, and resources better than those living within the bounds of that community. An old saying in the transportation business that reflects the

uniqueness of each town, city, and village is "If you've seen one community . . . you've seen one community."

In 2012, CTAA made a commitment to the design thinking process, with the aim of taking local teams beyond action planning into actual implementation of solutions. Carolyn worked with Amy to launch the Job Access Mobility Institute (JAMI), which used a design thinking process to lead discussion and programming to address the transportation issues faced by unemployed and underemployed people. The proposal listed the objectives for the institute:

- bring together broad-based regional partners from the transportation, employment and training, economic development, and business sectors, and others, to solve a specific job access mobility challenge in their community;

- catalyze innovative employment transportation service delivery solutions that respond to the transportation challenges of job seekers and low-income workers;

- teach a user-centered design approach for creating or improving job access services; and

- model a process that partners find both rewarding and compelling, in both the near and long term, to create solutions to other mobility challenges.

Carolyn explained their rationale:

Our whole goal was to get the teams to feel confident that they could think anew about ways to meet their communities' needs. A lot of times, everyone is being told, "Here is the solution, and now you fit the people in it." We wanted the process to develop through the variety of minds on each team seeking to understand the low-income experience. Our whole emphasis at CTAA is about being customer centered, and design thinking is a great process for that. We want to help people think based on what the customer needs and not so much what a funder requires. That's easier said than done, because your funding is very important. But if you give the design process a chance and you price things right, somebody will buy it, whether it's an agency, a foundation, or the end user. The inspiration is just to try to do things that are new and different and that better serve customers who have complex mobility needs.

This emphasis on bringing together diverse community players was a long-standing value at CTAA, implemented long before design thinking arrived on the scene. Design thinking seemed well suited to the task. Concepts like journey mapping and jobs-to-be-done analysis, which are new to many fields, have long been in use (under different names) in the transportation field because of the nature of transportation itself. "Mobility is so connected to origin and destination and trip purpose," Carolyn explained. "Nobody wants to just take the bus—why are they taking the trip?" The need for this kind of broader systems perspective was especially evident when the focus was on lower-income employment opportunities, with the biggest issues for low-income workers consistently being transportation and child care. "People's lives cross systems, and you can't create change alone," Carolyn observed.

In spring 2012, having obtained Federal Transit Administration funding, CTAA sent out a request for proposals, encouraging applicants to form diverse teams within their communities, with the aim of helping low-income workers and others with less mobility get to jobs. CTAA's intention was to use the JAMI process to spur conversations among people representing different parts of the systems, who did not generally work together. Galvanizing these kinds of networks, they believed, created a long-term capability for local problem solving that had positive impacts on the community and that reached far beyond the specific area of opportunity in any current request for proposals.

CTAA analyzed the submitted JAMI proposals and selected seven teams from different settings around the country—from urban New Jersey to sparsely populated Texas counties, and from trendy Marin County, California, to low-wage suburbs of Portland, Oregon. Teams were chosen on the basis of CTAA's assessment of their commitment and readiness to bring a design approach to solving a job access mobility issue identified within their community.

THE JOBS-TO-BE-DONE TOOL

The jobs-to-be-done tool looks at *why* people do the things they do. What is the job that they want the solution to help them accomplish? Jobs can be functional—like getting to work on time, in the CTAA case. But often the most important jobs are *emotional*—reducing the anxiety that comes from being late for work, for instance. Paying attention to both the functional and the emotional aspects of the stakeholders' needs is often critical to value creation.

Team Leader: Each team needs a team leader who will convene the team and maintain the momentum during the duration of the September to March Institute experience. To the extent possible, we are looking for the team leader to come from the economic development or workforce development sector.

Team members must include participation from

1) One or more mobility experts, such as a public or private transportation provider (of bus, van, vanpool, carpool, taxi, bike-sharing services, etc.), transportation management association, ridesharing coordinator, mobility manager, transportation planner

2) One or more economic development experts, such as from an economic development agency, chamber of commerce, business park association

3) One or more workforce development experts, such as a Workforce Investment Board staff or board member, One-Stop Career Center director, community college leader, sector-based coalition member, community-based employment and training provider, TANF agency manager, business services representative, career specialist, employee assistance professional

4) One or more consumers, representatives or advocates for job-seekers or other populations, such as veterans, older workers, persons with disabilities, low-wage earners, homeless persons

5) Other team members chosen at the team's discretion, such as a local official, technology expert, foundation, community or neighborhood organization, or other sector

Team composition requirements for the Job Access Mobility Institute.

TEAMS SELECTED

- City of Tualatin, Oregon
- Essex County, New Jersey
- Kerr-Tar Workforce Development Board region, North Carolina (Caswell, Franklin, Granville, Person, Vance, and Warren counties)

- Marin County, California
- Mercer County, New Jersey
- Northeast Iowa (Allamakee, Clayton, Fayette, Howard, and Winneshiek counties)
- Texas Coastal Bend (Brooks and Jim Wells counties)

The program they designed used a series of explanatory webinars, Skype meetings, and in-person visits to gather data and inform the **What *is*** stage of the research, followed by a summit that would bring all seven teams together to the DC area to envision **What *if*.** After the summit, teams would again meet online for additional webinars and, supported by CTAA facilitators, complete the **What *wows*** and **What *works*** stages.

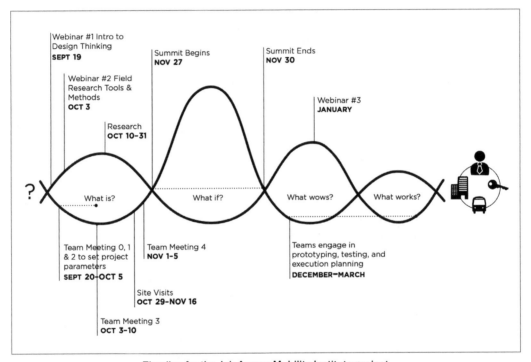

Timeline for the Job Access Mobility Institute project.

To begin, teams developed their design briefs and began their exploratory research. The webinars helped the teams to scope their challenges in order to identify the specific opportunity they would explore and plan their research strategy. As they selected particular design tools to focus on, Carolyn urged groups to consider journey mapping:

> I find journey mapping one of the most powerful tools. When I do my training, I always
> show the journey map example of a low-wage mother with two children, trying to get to

work. I make a point of conveying that it's really great to improve an experience within a single touch point, but the impact will be greater [if you are able] to improve the whole journey! If you can just have someone take a free shuttle trip instead of a cab, that's fantastic. But what if you worked across the whole journey and solved for the child care and other challenges at the same time? How could you really improve the experiences of residents in low-wage jobs?

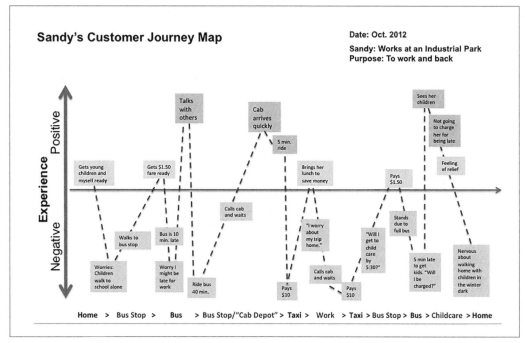

A mother's journey map.

As they went to work, the teams' perspectives on problems became more complex. Amy, who also facilitated one of the teams, offered an example:

My team was looking at improving options for non–car owners to travel to work. Their original challenge focused on getting more funding to expand employment transportation options. The economic development representative on the team noted that when employees lacked a way to get to work, it led to employees being late or absent, or sometimes even quitting, which impacted a business's bottom line, yet few business leaders considered this as an issue of concern. Another member observed that many in the community thought that how "those people" (that is, people without access to cars) got to work was not their problem.

This discussion caused the team to reconsider their direction: before they pursued funding to expand employment transportation options, they needed to build awareness of and empathy for workers who didn't own cars. They reframed their question to "How can we build community support for expanded employment transportation options?" As Amy described it, "They realized this was the question they had to address first if they ever wanted to be successful in answering their original question. And that refocusing led the team's research in a totally different direction than originally planned."

The teams' creativity often extended to *how* they accomplished their data gathering, not just the insights themselves. Marin County, California, for example, hired and trained homeless people to conduct interviews to learn more about the issues keeping the truly poor out of the workforce. They believed that these peer-to-peer conversations would yield more honest and accurate information than if their own staffers conducted them. (Marin County would bring their homeless part-timers back a year later to spread the word about their transportation project's learning launch.)

Learnings coming out of the **What *is*** stage varied across the seven teams. The team from the Texas Coastal Bend, for instance, discovered that the area's existing transportation services, though admittedly meager, were almost unknown to the heavily rural Spanish-speaking population, many of whom were without vehicles and were experiencing some of the highest poverty levels in the state. Another important learning was that area schools and colleges were desperate to get their entry-level employees consistent access to work. They were unable to depend on weak transit operations that offered no evening or weekend service because of budget cuts. Hence, large numbers of the working poor struggled with almost two-hour commutes, often shared, in run-down vehicles. When that car needed repair—a fairly normal occurrence—business and school operations were impaired by employees' inability to get to their jobs on a reliable schedule.

In late November, teams convened in Washington, DC, for the 2.5-day Job Access Mobility Summit, for detailed work in the second phase, **What *if*.** All teams engaged in brainstorming ideas at the summit, sharing their ideas with other teams and CTAA advisors, in addition to prototyping two or three solution concepts. Being together cemented a strong esprit de corps across the seven teams. In several subsequent webinars over the next year, they would thank CTAA for forcing them into the "non-smoke-filled room," as one team member joked.

Returning to their own localities, teams were supported via webinars and virtual meetings with CTAA advisors. The teams further developed their ideas, sometimes reiterating several times, including revising their design briefs as well as their concepts. "Ideas are not eureka moments," Carolyn explained. "They come from recombining old ideas and technology from the past. It's about combining several ideas together, coming up with a solution platform." Teams were then asked to surface assumptions, which she considered especially critical:

> When we teach, we'll ask, "Why did you choose that idea? What's behind it? What makes
> it a good idea?" That's why we need to specify the design criteria—because then you can
> allow multiple ideas in and then see where they take you. Rather than landing on an
> early solution, we supported the teams in considering more than one solution.

Prototyping, in order to test these assumptions, came next. Each team was offered $3,000 to develop materials to put before potential customers and stakeholders for feedback and input. Carolyn considered this step essential in reducing risk:

> The idea is to just go out and try something in a low-fidelity way before you launch it.
> This gives you the time to de-risk the solution and to improve on it so that people will
> want to use and support it. That is what we were trying to incentivize.

Developing actionable ideas was a focus throughout the process. The way to succeed with funders, Carolyn and Amy believed, was *not* to design for them, prioritizing their perspectives and desires over the needs of users of the service. Instead, they wanted the teams to demonstrate to funders that ideas derived from a deep understanding of the transportation needs of low-income workers could succeed in practice and could accomplish the funders' larger objectives. "Showing the funders the research they've done, what they have done to de-risk the program, is critical," Carolyn believed. "From the very start, we talk in terms of desirability (people want and need your service), feasibility (they have the partners to stand it up), and viability (it is financially sustainable)."

To help teams think in compelling ways about these three aspects of success, CTAA had developed a reporting system that used color coding for each. On a monthly basis, each team was asked to capture their thinking, using a "building blocks canvas," a version of the Business Model Canvas (similar to the one used in the HHS Ignite program in chapter 3) that CTAA had adapted to their purpose.

Ultimately, all seven teams came up with valuable ideas and described a new sense of teamwork and cooperation among their teammates, few of whom had known each other prior to the design thinking exercise. Two teams—New Jersey's Mercer County and the Texas Coastal Bend—immediately found funding to support the scaling of their learning launches.

Following the Dollar in Mercer County

Mercer County knew its issue going in: most low-paying jobs were in two new industrial parks off I-95, without transit service available during shift-change times, but most low-income families lived in older urban neighborhoods nowhere near I-95. Most industrial park workers survived on irregular and often unreliable carpools, and workers who could get to transit faced $25 one-way "last mile" cab rides to and from work. The team's early emphasis, however, was on how to educate employers about these transportation issues and how to communicate the availability of possible new services to potential employees accustomed to believing that jobs at the industrial parks were off-limits because of transportation issues. A survey of businesses in the industrial parks revealed higher turnover rates than desired, at least partially driven by transportation problems. Though most businesses had no idea how much individual turnover was costing, estimated expenses to train each new employee ranged from $11,000 to $15,000, according to two employers. Up to half of employees arrived in informal carpools, and the two largest employers had a 2:00 a.m. shift change, long before NJ Transit began running buses anywhere.

Learning what both businesses and low-paid employees needed, through surveys and ethnographic interviews, allowed the team to devise four different concepts, one of which was a shuttle service from the nearest transit stop, Hamilton Square, to the industrial parks. When one employer, Amazon, offered to fund the shuttle, the team elected to focus on that concept during the **What *works*** phase. They pushed NJ Transit to commit to timely bus service in order to assemble employees at the shuttle's origin point. That key assumption—that NJ Transit would alter its schedules and times to fit Amazon's shift changes—wasn't fully tested until NJ Transit joined the Mercer team and the first ZLine (as the new service was called) prototype shuttle rolled.

THE MERCER COUNTY PROJECT

Problem: Low-paying jobs in business parks along interstate highway are far from population centers and transit service.

Concept: Begin a shuttle service, funded by Amazon and called ZLine, from a nearby transit hub to the business park, and alter the NJ Transit service to that hub.

Learning launch: The ZLine shuttle opens in July 2014. Within six months, it carries 250 people each day, 40 percent of whom say the shuttle is crucial for their employment.

Iteration: ZLine service is expanded to include a second vehicle. Transit timing is improved. More round-trips are offered.

Next iteration: Getting other industrial park companies to be aware of and willing to help finance ZLine service.

Only months into the learning launch of the new ZLine shuttle service, demand forced the operation of a second van. Today, the shuttle operates seven days a week in the morning and evening hours, and NJ Transit ridership is up significantly. With the shuttle subsidized by Amazon, employees save a $20 to $25 daily cab ride from Hamilton Square and face fewer issues with unreliable informal carpools.

CTAA's insistence on team diversity proved crucial to Mercer's success. Even though the Mercer team didn't originally include a member from NJ Transit, the team, especially the chamber of commerce representative and the community college job training rep, bonded quickly. Midway through the process, the team was expanded to include NJ Transit and the state's Business Action Center. The governor's office eventually named the Mercer team the state lead for dealing with workforce transportation issues, and other communities now come to Mercer County for advice on transportation for low-income workers.

Cheryl Kastrenakes, executive director of the Greater Mercer Transportation Management Association, was enthusiastic about design thinking, noting that her JAMI team could not have solved the issues without the "fun and collaboration" it brought. She offered:

> My main takeaway was starting with understanding the end user, even their mental state. You're designing something for them, and that's where you have to start. You've got to let go of the constraints, like money, and just throw "it" out there. It's really hard to tell people in the public sector not to think about money, to just come up with the ideas and then "we'll see." Money is always the issue.

The Mercer team kept the funding issue in sight but never allowed it to halt their brainstorming and assumption testing. "Design thinking helped us think bigger and participate better and to begin working collaboratively across different areas," Cheryl continued. "That was very important."

Traveling Full Circle in the Texas Coastal Bend

Another JAMI project, covering eleven thousand square miles in the Coastal Bend region of South Texas, faced an even more challenging problem than Mercer County's job–housing disconnect. With virtually all of the jobs near Corpus Christi an hour or more away by car, the rural Coastal Bend region had the lowest per capita income and the second-highest number of individuals living below the poverty level in the Lone Star State. Taxis were out of the question for the majority of workers, and the area was too sparsely settled for effective transit service. The commuters who managed to get to Corpus Christi primarily did so in crammed and unreliable carpools.

During the **What *is*** phase, the Coastal Bend team applied the learning from the webinars and coaching, and interviewed stakeholders, including those at colleges who needed to hire janitorial and other service staff. They built personas of low-wage workers. Two of the team's insights generated particular interest: (1) people were uninformed about even the weak transit options available; and (2) the affected colleges and schools, especially, wanted additional transportation possibilities.

Brainstorming at the November summit first expanded and then narrowed their focus. The Coastal Bend team ultimately arrived at multiple concepts, one of which arose after the summit, during a subsequent CTAA webinar. As Martin Ornelas, director of the Transportation Coordination Network of the Coastal Bend, described it, the team felt frustrated, "like a circle trying to receive a square peg." Someone said employment was low not because people couldn't get to jobs but because no one could get to *training centers*. A team member responded that her college's training classes were sparsely attended, which caused a third to wonder, "Is it the rule that our project has to transport *workers*?" That constraint, it turned out, was not in the request for proposals. CTAA's stated goal for the JAMI was "to support communities in designing *new* or *improved* employment transportation service delivery solutions."

This was Coastal Bend's "aha" moment, which shifted the team's thinking. Martin said:

> We went in with an idea we thought would work, and we ended up with something quite different. That was a very clear example of the evolution of our concepts throughout the process. Intellectually, all the design thinking stuff sounded like a college-level exercise that was fun, but then it turned out to be very practical.

THE TEXAS COASTAL BEND PROJECT

Problem: Insufficient transit service from rural, low-income counties to job and higher education centers in Corpus Christi, over an hour away.

Reframing of design criteria: Low-income, rural youth have little conception of job possibilities and few ways of getting to those jobs.

Changing perspectives in brainstorming: Leaping to the next generation, the team considers an idea to help high school students learn about public safety career possibilities through community college classes.

Concept: A daily hour-plus bus run from rural towns to a summer public service academy for high school students, funded by police and fire chiefs concerned about finding the next generation of employees.

Learning launch: Extending the public service academy transportation program to more counties and more students, including heavy promotion.

Iteration: Parlaying local success into a federal grant to run daily bus service from rural high schools to two city colleges more than an hour away, providing transportation for both students and low-income employees, thereby addressing the original problem.

Next iteration: Finding nongrant funding to continue the bus service while adding additional pickup locations.

Looking for an answer to **What wows?**, the Coastal Bend team took three napkin pitches to the relevant stakeholders. Idea 1, a vanpool for a local hospital, didn't excite the head nurse, who had never before thought about how her employees got to work. Idea 2, pitched at the chamber of commerce, also failed to resonate; workforce transportation was interesting to the chamber but was not a primary concern. But idea 3, providing transportation to a public service academy aimed at high school students, gained instant traction. High school kids jumped on the concept of transporting them to the Del Mar College Public Safety Academy for a summer program for students interested in public safety careers. Perhaps the students, not yet jaded by the daily grind, visualized the concept with more imagination, allowing them to grasp the team's storytelling easier than nurses and executives who didn't want another concern put on their plates. Martin remembered:

> The idea was very tangible and very quickly validated by those who would benefit from the service. We were kind of reframing it in real time when one of the kids said, "We're going to be gone all day," and we realized he meant, "I'm going to be starving." Then it was a matter of solving the practical kinds of things, like food.

The biggest reframe came when one team member met with a county fire chief concerned about his staffing problems. This encounter led to a transportation forum with area fire, police, and rescue personnel. The chiefs soon figured that forty potential recruits a few years out were worth some investment today. They funded bus drivers from two locations, and a small bet was launched. Students were delivered from two high schools to the Public Safety Academy. Fueled by donated lunches coordinated by an area health service, students learned how to use firefighting and police equipment, rappel from buildings, take fingerprints, give elementary first aid, and even complete some bureaucratic functions of public service.

Aware of the photographic opportunity, the Coastal Bend team publicly promoted the project as an investment in children and community-wide improvement. A media day and a well-attended graduation ceremony helped spread the word, and the project expanded in 2014, taking more students from more high schools to the summer academy. Buy-in came from both ends as students talked about the fun they had learning radio codes, fingerprinting, and forced-air breathing, and officials got favorable publicity for being farsighted. The feedback allowed the team to form additional partnerships with other city governments, the courts, the district attorney's office, private developers, and another economic development commission. Martin told other teams during a webinar:

> That was certainly one of the lessons that was not anticipated—the increased level of engagement by community leadership in making this a success, not only morally, by participating; financially, by contributing; and also by rewarding these students as they returned to their communities.

Another unanticipated benefit, Martin noted, was that, by registering at Del Mar College to attend the Public Service Academy, rural kids received free access to Corpus Christi–area transit, which introduced them to available public transit options. Even more significant, students were given a sense that they could succeed in a university setting.

Building on the second year of the academy's success, Del Mar College has now revised its class times based on transit, high school counselors have begun promoting the Public Service Academy, and the Rural Economic Assistance League, a local nonprofit, has been prompted to expand bus service to three more counties. The summer academy bus link has been expanded to reach seven of the twelve counties in the Coastal Bend region. The academy's success led the JAMI team to seek and obtain a Federal Transit Administration operating grant for daily bus service linking Del Mar College and Texas A&M University–Corpus Christi with Coastal Bend high schools.

Meanwhile, the summer academy trips are continuing, with more area police and fire departments donating funds and support, further underlining the proven success that laid the groundwork for the now-daily commute runs for college students and workers. So the learning launch of buses that took high school students to a summer camp has come full circle, leading to additional opportunities for low-income job holders, the original mission of CTAA's JAMI, all the while injecting creative thinking into all aspects of Coastal Bend transportation. "After the design thinking training, now we start with one idea and get three or four," Martin observed.

The benefits of creating a local network of relationships able to move on and solve new problems is also evident in subsequent initiatives happening in the Coastal Bend region. When Martin's organization, the Transportation Coordination Network, needed space to train dispatchers and drivers for the oil and gas industry, he called another JAMI team member, Anne Cunningham, from Del Mar College. Anne quickly found space for the dispatcher training and piggybacked on it to provide course credit and state certification for enrollees. What had started as the need for a room morphed into a recruitment tool for the college, while professionalizing area trucking and transit.

Another outgrowth of the JAMI design thinking conversation in South Texas was a new development, the Natatorium in Alice, Texas, built as a multimodal transportation site to encourage all transportation options, even muscle-powered options. JAMI team member Gloria Ramos and Martin took city and county officials on a trip to a multimodal transit center in Brownsville, Texas, to see and understand how mass transit, bike and pedestrian transportation, vanpools, and private carpools can actually enhance economic prospects. These officials had been introduced to the JAMI work through the Public Safety Academy's media day and graduation ceremony. Next, they became involved, stepping up to become champions for future "out-of-the-car" thinking by insisting that the state's Department of Transportation provide alternative transportation to the Alice facility. Martin explained:

> Our "prototype" was a field trip [to Brownsville], and we had people see what we were talking about when we talking about multimodal. You need to see it, feel it, touch it, and at least imagine the inner workings, and we were showing our officials that "now you can imagine what we can do here in Alice."

The cultural change in the Coastal Bend region isn't complete, of course, but mindsets have altered across the community. Even a particularly skeptical partner came to recognize the power of design thinking. Martin reported:

> She had the planner mentality, and they think with different parts of the brain. We had to say, "Wait, you stop our dreaming when you get to that specificity. Right now, it's imagine

time." Now that we've gone through the process and she's seen the product, she's got the details and the metrics she needs. Once you learn its components and you apply them, design thinking becomes a way of doing business, a way of thinking, especially in the area of community empowerment. It's a great way of getting from point A to point Z.

He continued:

> I really think we were blessed by being accepted to participate in CTAA—maybe not in the formalized, structured way, but in a way that the outcomes are plentiful and that, through the results of that process, it has facilitated other work.

Martin, like many who have used design thinking, noted the "iceberg" effect, in which unforeseen gains lie beneath the surface:

> No one ever thought that simply taking the academy kids through the Del Mar College registration process would have benefits. But just getting the Del Mar identification was very impactful on them because many of them had not ever stepped on a college campus and never expected to. Their level of pride was immeasurable but very tangible.

These kinds of unanticipated benefits, Carolyn said, are reasonably common when design thinking is applied, but they can rarely be predicted. Understanding the unarticulated needs and desires of people is the only way to discover solutions that can work, she argues, and for that reason, CTAA has become, as she described, "the empathizers in chief."

Reflections on the Process

By insisting on an assortment of activities and perspectives on each team, and then providing the structure of a problem-solving methodology that was both human centered and flexible, while allowing for reframing of the situation when a unique understanding or opportunity arose, CTAA reached out from Washington, DC, into communities around the country and changed the conversations, demonstrating the best of what it means to be both local and global. Rather than dictate, CTAA guided and trained, promoted and supported, but left the thinking and doing to truly diverse local teams.

"The growth of the relationships is bountiful," Martin observed, noting that the new networks formed in his region have led to increased ability to fund projects as well. "We were able to secure two additional grants. Without any hesitation, the partners continue collaborating in every possible opportunity. We have a third grant submitted." Coastal Bend is now focusing on health improvement through transportation mobility management.

In her role as an educator, Carolyn spends time thinking about how local mobility leaders across the country can apply the values and phases of design thinking. "I'm trying to figure out what are the basics, so people can benefit from the process but don't get overwhelmed by it. A few key activities can go a long way toward solving complex mobility challenges." Those activities include having in-depth conversations with customers and stakeholders to gain insights into their lives, considering a number of options, identifying key assumptions about potential solutions, and testing those assumptions before launching a solution. She explained, "Just a few small steps. Otherwise, folks are like, 'Whoa, this is too complicated for me!' So I just keep simplifying to the most essential activities to conduct that will make a difference."

In transportation, officials often lack opportunities to work at the systems level. As a result, piecemeal solutions that target just one part of the problem can seem almost inevitable. Design thinking's up-front exploratory stage, as we have seen in earlier stories, helps truly diverse teams arrive at shared views of current reality—especially with regard to the lives of the people that the team members intend to serve—and create innovative solutions to even unidentified problems. In a climate of tough political realities and limited budgets, it can help teams reduce risk and arrive at practical ideas, balanced within an understanding of resource limitations yet encouraged by a shared vision of a better future. Design thinking's bias toward action and experimentation can help build enthusiasm for change within the larger community and produce more desire for involvement in co-creating a new future. Carolyn explained:

> When local mobility leaders join with other community leaders to inquire deeply into people's lives through journey mapping, ethnography, and stakeholder feedback, projects can advance in our political culture and minimize the transportation challenges often faced by on-demand, low-paid hourly workers. We want to support change makers who apply for our team-based institutes by giving them additional strategies to improve mobility in their com-

munities. We want them to be confident that they can lead a group through often complex challenges. But we also—most importantly—want them to touch base with the real users, to have an expansive view, and then to figure out "what wows" for the population at hand.

For participants across the seven teams, it was a powerful experience. Linda Moholt, from Tualatin, Oregon, a low-wage suburb of Portland, reflected:

> It's been a wonderful experience. This project, this ability to work with design thinking, allowed us to create a pilot project, which we submitted and got a doubled grant. And more important than getting the doubled funding was that it brought local partners to the table to help initiate and execute the new program. We've absolutely used every piece of the [design thinking] training to write the grant in a different way, to bring the partners to the table, and now we're going into full operational mode . . . It's been an incredible experience.

"Every grant we do has design thinking in it now," Carolyn said. "Give people the tools to be community conveners—that's the premise of our training. What we are really trying to do is change the conversation."

"Our whole goal was to get the teams to feel confident that they could think anew about ways to meet their communities' needs," Amy added.

To us, it certainly looks as though CTAA is succeeding and, in the process, calling into question the old truism that only action needs to be local; their work shows us that thinking can reside there, too. CTAA's experience demonstrates that identifying and solving problems locally, rather than globally, has big advantages.

CHAPTER TEN

Bridging Technology and the Human Experience at the Transportation Security Administration

THE CHALLENGE TO THE GREATER GOOD

"Build it and they will come" is an innovation philosophy that is probably as old as humankind. While producing some outstanding products, it often subjugates the human experience to technological possibilities and regularly produces products, services, and strategies that no one wants. Nowhere is this more evident than in the world of technology-driven innovation. How do we blend human needs and technological possibilities?

DESIGN THINKING'S CONTRIBUTION

Technology-driven and user-driven innovation might appear to anchor opposite ends of the innovation spectrum. But what does innovation look like if these two forces work together? Few organizations today face thornier challenges than the US Transportation Security Administration (TSA). Established to safeguard America's transportation system after the 9/11 terrorist attacks, TSA's airport policies and procedures have raised the ire of travelers.

Despite the seemingly inevitable trade-offs between heightened security and passenger checkpoint flow, TSA's commitment to create a more user-centered, behavioral form of security is impressive. Their leadership in fusing technology, design thinking, and Agile-styled methodologies goes beyond the goal of creating a smoother and safer travel experience. It aims to build an alliance between security officers and the traveling public, and to put a human face on the often maligned agency.

Next to the Internal Revenue Service, TSA is the most disliked government agency in the United States. Annually, approximately 700 million people move through US airport security, and the safe and secure movement of these travelers is the responsibility of TSA employees. Their dilemma: the more upset travelers become with them, the harder it is to do their job. Not surprisingly, TSA is regularly in the media headlines, often not favorably. A review of global events underlines the challenge, and securing air travel today requires a complicated balancing act. From lightsabers to boxed muffins to live fish in bags of water, there is no end to the daily surprises that travelers bring to the airport. In the glare of publicity that TSA faces, difficult conversations cannot be ignored, but, as we will see, they can be welcomed and deftly facilitated.

To understand the challenge TSA faces, take a look at the photographs of the daily haul of confiscated items on the agency's surprisingly entertaining Instagram account. It is mind-boggling: pistols, automatic weapons, ammunition, knives, and more. But most of us don't carry weapons and are just trying to move quickly through security screening to get to our flight. Balancing speed and security is no easy feat. In a recent federal hearing on the agency, one congressman sympathized with TSA's plight: "When we criticize you today about having long lines and taking too long to screen people, next week, if there is a [security] breach, we will haul you up here and lambaste you for not being more thorough."

In the social sector, innovators are often tasked with trying to nudge people into making better choices. When the task is *security*, the ante is upped. Nudging is replaced by command and control—and then the going gets tough. Public dislike of the Internal Revenue Service doesn't prevent it from collecting taxes, but the more the public resents the security process, the harder it is for TSA's security officers to do their job, which is to uncover "hostile intent." Creating a sense of calmness and collaboration, it turns out, is essential to improving safety; when *everybody* at the checkpoint is hostile, it is harder to detect *dangerously* hostile people amid the harmless frustrated masses.

So TSA has waged a fifteen-year, sometimes discouraging campaign to build a sense of shared purpose and to win travelers' trust. Research suggests that compliance—especially around issues of privacy (such as body scanners) and security—is significantly enhanced when the party that needs to comply understands the reason behind the request, the benefits of compliance, and the cost and potential risks of noncompliance, and trusts the organization making the request.

In this chapter, we will look at how TSA has used technology and a combination of innovation approaches, like design thinking and Agile software development, to work toward this goal. TSA's experience speaks to how an organization can be both technology-driven and user-centric at the same time and can engage in a dialogue that both illuminates and humanizes its purpose under trying circumstances.

Our story begins with the arrival of Kip Hawley, a former Silicon Valley entrepreneur, who joined TSA one month after the 2001 terrorist attacks and was TSA's senior administrator from 2005 to 2009. From the beginning, Kip aspired to find new ways to both serve and educate travelers, initiating a strategy of utilizing communication technologies to build better relationships that continues today.

TSA's first foray into technology as a tool for communication was a blog to create a two-way forum between the agency and the public, with the first post coming from Kip himself. It emphasized the need for dialogue, stressed that learning was required on both sides, and promised that the discussion would be candid and impactful:

> Two million travelers come in contact with the Transportation Security Administration every day. It is an intense experience all around—extremely personal in some senses but also impersonal at the same time.
>
> There is no time to talk, to listen, to engage with each other. There isn't much opportunity for our Security Officers to explain the "why" of what we ask you to do at the checkpoint, just the "what" needs to be done to clear security. The result is that the feedback and venting ends up circulating among passengers with no real opportunity for us to learn from you or vice versa . . .
>
> Our ambition is to provide here a forum for a lively, open discussion of TSA issues . . .
>
> Please be patient and good-humored as we get underway. The opportunity is that we will incorporate what we learn in this forum in our checkpoint process evolution. We will not only give you straight answers to your questions but we will challenge you with new ideas and involve you in upcoming changes.
>
> One of my major goals of 2008 is to get TSA and passengers back on the same side, working together.

TSA then partnered with a variety of outside consultants to bring this commitment to life. One of their relationships was with IDEO, the pioneering innovation consultancy that we have met in earlier stories. In 2009, IDEO utilized a variety of traditional design tools in their work for TSA: observing and interviewing travelers, identifying key emotional characteristics of their journeys, creating traveler archetypes, and noting reactive behaviors in airports around the country.

Their research findings highlighted the importance of creating an ongoing alliance between passengers and security officers in order to reduce checkpoint stressors and render hostile intent more visible. Assuring a better passenger experience was an important contributor to this effort, they argued, and required not only a physical redesign of airport areas but also a shift in culture at every level in the agency, which required leadership and training. As the IDEO website noted:

> The transformational culture change undertaken with IDEO moved the agency to embrace the notion that its employees, from frontline security officers to management and leadership, are crucial to improving both checkpoint security and the overall experience ... After establishing the blueprint for the physical space, tone, and strategy of the checkpoint experience, IDEO created a training curriculum to empower TSOs [transportation security officers] and passengers to improve airport security. The curriculum works to create a sustainable solution for improving human interactions during a passenger's journey through airport security ... The new training includes an emphasis on understanding behaviors, people, and security measures, while instilling confidence among colleagues and passengers.

Implementation began in 2009, with a goal of training TSA's entire workforce of fifty thousand employees at 450 domestic airports. Lynn Dean, a senior advisor to the TSA administrator and no stranger to daunting tasks in federal agency strategy and communications, laid out the challenge: "Our end goal is a checkpoint where everything is seamless and calm so that if there really is a bad person or someone with intent to do harm, they will stand out more." Tired, harried, uninformed travelers inadvertently cause delays in security lines and sometimes cause scenes over innocuous errors, which diverts the attention of security screeners from those meaning to do harm or carrying contraband items. It all goes back to the problem of how to speed the process and reduce long wait lines while maintaining a high level of security.

Connecting with the Traveling Public

Given the necessity to serve and educate millions of travelers, TSA also began working on tools for communication via technology, including their website, in 2008. TSA partnered with Sapient, an organization with a human-centered approach, which aims to use technology in creative ways to solve complex problems. To further the idea of creating a calm checkpoint, Sapient's mandate was to use innovative Web 2.0 technologies to better connect with the traveling public, to improve the public's overall experience both at the airport and before arrival at the airport, and to increase the public's understanding of TSA's people, mission, and policies.

To tackle this critical project, Sapient built a diverse team of creative strategists and technologists. On the TSA side, Lynn Dean, former senior advisor in the Office of the Administrator, and Neil Bonner, from information technology, joined as co-leaders. The team used Sapient's own human-centered Agile-styled approach, which utilized what they called a Fusion[SM] workshop. Exploring this process helps us to explore how design thinking works with other currently popular innovation methods, like Agile software development. The Agile model shares design thinking's focus on the user's needs, along with iterative building of prototypes through co-creation with customers.

Sapient's Fusion[SM] workshop model has been designed to change the experience of developing requirements and to help clients visualize a solution before it is built. In traditional software development approaches like the waterfall model, requirements are specified first, and then developers construct a solution, which is then tested for quality assurance. This sequential process leaves little room for iterative co-creation with users. Untested assumptions and hypotheses often cause misunderstanding about both the meaning and the usefulness of requirements. The Fusion[SM] workshops are designed to bring together a cross-functional group to incorporate differing viewpoints and concepts into a shared vision. A key desired outcome of the Fusion[SM] workshop is a clear roadmap, including business requirements and an action plan. Sapient's process involves several phases, including (1) initiation; (2) preparation, research, and analysis; (3) the actual Fusion[SM] workshop; and (4) a synthesis and deliverables summary.

The Initiate phase first identifies an opportunity. In the Preparation, Research, and Analysis phase, high-level objectives are crafted, desired participants are identified, and an agenda is set out. This phase equates to the initial groundwork in a design thinking project, where design thinkers grapple with and scope the problem, develop a design brief, and identify key stakeholders to involve. As is often the case, the crafting of the objectives may involve several iterations. The research stage is critical preparation for the upcoming workshop. The goal is to create a common language and framework to share with and align stakeholders. Tools such as journey maps and personas are used to form a baseline that facilitates workshop conversations. The emphasis throughout the process is on using clear language that everyone will understand. Visualizations, such as traveler personas and journey maps, help clarify written language and enable a discussion. Early on, visualizations can help to shift perspective to the target stakeholder's point of view, and later they aid in getting all team members and stakeholders to envision a concept in the same way.

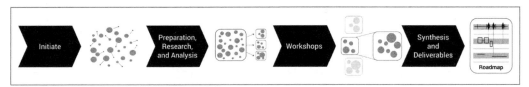

The Sapient Fusion^SM process.

The Fusion^SM workshop itself involves successive gatherings where groups meet together, break apart for focused sessions, and reconvene. Each time, ideas are captured, discussed, and iterated. The key is to be purposeful about who is in the room and to concentrate on directly relevant information that quickly moves the conversation forward. In the early stages, stakeholders come together to mine research data for insights from which design criteria are established. In later stages, the discussion revolves around designing solutions.

Workshop participants include subject matter experts, a workshop manager, a lead facilitator and breakout facilitators, and a note taker to keep everyone informed on updates and changes. The number of participants in a Fusion^SM workshop can vary, with the target between fifteen and twenty-four, though up to forty is possible.

Both the physical space and quality facilitation are important to allow participants to air different views, consider various aspects, and come to a shared understanding. Having a consultant as a trusted advisor, Sapient believes, facilitates the process: the job of the lead facilitator is to promote conversational flow while keeping the agenda on track. One key to Sapient's approach is an overarching philosophy that everyone in the room is equal, has a voice, and will be heard. The idea is to nudge even senior management to leave their organizational hats at the door.

Visualization is indispensable. Meeting rooms have whiteboards all around. The intention is to ensure visibility so that the workshop's framework is clear and understood by all. Participants cannot simply object to an idea. Instead, they are asked to build on it by addressing a challenge inherent in their objection. This requirement is similar to the improv comedy technique of "Yes, and . . ." in which one can never say no and instead has to build on the previous statement. This ensures an understanding of perspective and promotes expansion rather than critiquing of ideas.

The end result is a presentation of deliverables built with foundational pillars that include user needs and value as well as the differing perspectives of cross-functional teams and partners in the value chain. After a successful Fusion^{SM} workshop, teams are armed with a new project charter, business requirements document, roadmap, process flows, and action plans.

Exploring Travelers' Experiences

The TSA team's challenge was to explore travelers' experiences and seek ways and means to communicate with, educate, and better serve travelers, and then to fundamentally revamp the TSA website on the basis of what they learned. In a process similar to the design thinking approaches we have been discussing, their journey started with an extensive review of the traveler's journey from the points of view of different types of travelers as well as industry partners. This ethnography unlocked the door to passenger needs that previously were unknown or viewed as less significant.

The TSA team understood that keeping checkpoints calm meant paying close attention to what happens along the entire traveler journey, including what happens well before travelers reach a checkpoint. As Lynn explained:

> A lot of problems with a checkpoint shutting down start with a person who meant absolutely no harm but just had a series of things that caused them to behave really badly. A lot of problems stem from "I didn't know that before I got to the airport." By providing travelers with information at the time it is first needed, we can save passengers money, we can save them stress, we can improve security.

The TSA team knew that even getting to the airport is often frustrating, because of traffic, parking challenges, and long lines at cafés and newsstands. The security checkpoint might be the last stop on a passenger's already exasperating journey. So the team's challenge was to equip people with information they needed, when they needed it, usually before arriving at the airport. A vacationer buying wine at a vineyard, for instance, or a traveler packing a carry-on with a jar of expensive face cream needed to know about restrictions on those items. At these vineyard or packing moments, passengers might search their smartphones for what can and cannot be brought on board.

TSA pulled together a cross-functional team consisting of security personnel, employees from the TSA customer contact center, and legal counsel. Lynn singled out the lawyers as key players:

> Our legal department worked hand in hand with us. They were phenomenal. Whereas people are used to a lawyer saying no, our lawyers were saying, "We want to get to yes; we just want to make sure we do it within the confines of the law."

The use of such cross-functional teams is a key element in the Fusion[SM] process, according to Tom Sweatman, a Sapient management consultant with leadership, digital, and business strategy experience:

> It starts to create a line of buy-in across the group on whatever the initiative or the project is. Each division or specific expertise area will have its blind spots and its priorities. So you get all those key stakeholders into the room for people to bring up those priorities and those needs as a larger group—that will increase the probability of success moving forward.

The idea was to ensure that issues were raised and dealt with rather than bypassed to crop up later, when they would be harder to deal with. The team was investing up front to create a solution that looked at more variables and thus was less likely to fall apart later. It allowed team members to move from siloed, narrow perspectives to a big-picture view that promoted innovative change.

TSA also reached out to other agencies for input. The National Oceanic and Atmospheric Administration was contacted for weather information feeds, and the Federal Aviation Administration was asked for information on airport conditions. At each team meeting, Lynn made it a point to ask if there was anyone missing or anyone else who should be in the room. No one alone had all the answers, she emphasized.

As we saw at Monash in chapter 5, the team combined the use of traditional quantitative data with ethnographic research. They examined secondary research and existing survey data, including surveys on air travel as well as TSA's focus group research. They studied daily reports from checkpoints across the country. TSA web analytics and customer contact center reports were reviewed. Suggestions from the TSA Idea Factory, an online suggestion box for employees, were mined. Finally, because smartphones were becoming universal, research was conducted around how people would use mobile devices.

Primary research included interviewing a cross section of both internal and external stakeholders. Internally, TSA staff as well as frontline security officers, who do airport inspections, were interviewed. Externally, the team conducted fifteen interviews with a cross section of travelers. In addition, Sapient conducted a survey with two hundred business travelers, believing that focusing on this particular segment could yield dividends for other travelers.

Following the research, a journey map detailing traveler experiences was created. Moments on the journey map visually revealed that a lack of preparation and information created much traveler anxiety. The journey map continued to be validated and adjusted throughout the Fusion[SM] workshop process.

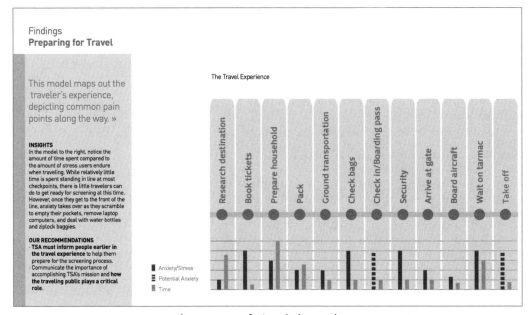

Journey map of a traveler's experience.

Focusing on Key User Needs by Traveler Segment

Detailed customer personas, representing various passenger segments, were developed to enable deeper understanding of travelers' goals, pain points, and needs. The team zeroed in on principal traveler personas—the frequent flyer or business traveler, the family traveler, and the leisure traveler—and explored how best to support those passengers' desires. By understanding each traveler journey, the team could look for ways to communicate with and educate each type of passenger.

The journey maps also illustrated the critical needs of each traveler persona. Armed with that data, the team could design the equivalent of a "minimal viable product" that would satisfy fundamental user needs. By zeroing in on key traveler segments, the team could focus on what was essential to that segment of users. This "curation" aspect is key to both design thinking and Agile-styled methodologies. In design thinking, curation happens with the identification of key insights and the creation of design criteria. These critical activities allow us to take all of the **What *is*** research and translate it into a simple set of criteria to drive idea generation in the **What *if*** phase. Instead of trying to stuff all possible features and information into any solution, the goal is to focus on paramount user desires, thereby simplifying planning and developing features that add tangible value to the solution.

The team created vignettes demonstrating how the traveler experiences the journey to the airport and how advanced information might engender a smoother journey and a calmer checkpoint. For example, business passengers who travel weekly through airports are most interested in getting through security quickly. Hence, a focus on wait times and airport status was important to them because both facilitate the business traveler's decision on when to head to the airport. The less frequent leisure traveler will be more concerned about what can or cannot be brought on board. The vacationer in the vineyard needs that information *before* making a purchase, not at airport security. From this understand-

THE PERSONA TOOL

Personas are one of the most popular design tools. They are archetypes—fictional characters that we create to represent different types of stakeholders. Though they are based on actual data gathered during **What *is*** research, they are a synthesis of characteristics of different people that we have interviewed, rather than one actual person. We use them to bring our stakeholders to life—not as demographic descriptions but as flesh-and-blood people with names, challenges, and jobs to be done.

ing of when answers are needed and how travelers could search for information came TSA's "When I fly, can I bring my . . ." tool.

Although features were developed for different ends of the usage spectrum, from infrequent to frequent passengers, tools developed for travelers on one end of the spectrum still held value for others. While wait-time information was particularly important to business travelers, this feature still could be helpful to all travelers. Every passenger scrambling to the airport worries about how busy security checkpoint lines are, because everyone occasionally misses a wake-up call or hits bad traffic.

Artifacts created during research and discovery, such as the journey map and traveler personas, became a baseline for the workshop phase, during which participants could adjust or build on them as additional information was shared. These items formed the common framework and language to move the work forward. During the workshop, TSA web strategy summary goals were clearly laid out, including primary and supporting objectives. The primary objective was to prepare the traveling public for security checkpoints and to increase the public's understanding of TSA's people, mission, and policies. Secondary and supporting objectives included providing authentic, timely, and relevant information; setting expectations about the dynamic nature of TSA's role; and portraying TSA employees as skilled and intelligent employees. Decisions made with respect to tools and features would be measured against these goals.

A strategy experience framework was developed to set out the actions to be undertaken. The framework included Engage, Attract, and Extend stages to engage travelers through the design, implementation, and maintenance of the TSA.gov website. Each stage was detailed in terms of the specific tasks to be undertaken. In the Engage phase, the website would be designed and built to reflect the user's needs and the TSA brand. The Attract stage would provide the on-ramp and would involve efforts to make travelers aware of the redesigned website. The Extend part of the process would allow for continued dialogue and feedback. A timeline or roadmap (similar to the one we saw in the Ring of Kerry story) clarified and detailed how the work would evolve.

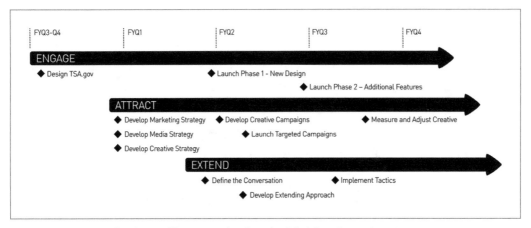

Roadmap of Transportation Security Administration web strategy.

The Best Laid Plans . . .

But the TSA team was to face their own cucumber water moment, like the one we recounted at the start of this book. The day before the intended launch of the revamped TSA.gov website, the Department of Homeland Security announced unexpected policy changes that required all agency websites to follow the same format. This change resulted in a delay of the website launch while the team reviewed the changes necessary to meet the Homeland Security guidelines.

Not to be deterred, the team pivoted to the development of a mobile phone app. Building an app was both within the project mandate to find channels of communication to engage and attract travelers and within the budget. The extensive early research for the website also provided the foundation for other channels of communication, not solely the website. And so a mobile phone app was quickly moved into prototyping. Although the first iPhone had just been released in 2007, it was already clear that people were turning to smartphones for more than text and e-mail. In Lynn's words: "We didn't want to build an app if nobody needed it, but it just seemed that every time you flew you saw people pulling out phones for every reason under the sun."

In the development or prototyping stage, TSA's iterative cycle continued. In the first instance, wireframes (frameworks illustrating the proposed features and functions) were quickly created to validate the design and features. Using fast, iterative cycles, the team moved on to create working prototypes with a robust back end. Users were asked to conduct specific tasks, and observers verified the number of clicks and amount of time it took to accomplish each task. As Tom explained:

> A lot of times when you design something, you are a little bit too close to it. What you think is an intuitive experience may not be intuitive at all. So we make sure that it is. We do specific testing to validate that the design we are trying to deliver is cleaner, more efficient, and creates a better result.

Design and testing were done in smaller sprints. The TSA team took prototype phones with the app, supplied by Sapient, and asked colleagues in neighboring departments to utilize the app—a simple but effective solution to time and access restrictions. This idea of observing the user's actual interaction with a prototype is key to successfully learning and iterating. As Lynn described:

> We knew that the app would have to evolve over time. We needed to be able to make changes if a new procedure was added or any security rules changed. We just knew we would learn throughout the process, even after the app launched. I think you have to go in knowing you are going to learn.

And learn TSA did.

Updates to MyTSA

Launched in June 2010, the MyTSA app was updated over time on the basis of feedback. One early update added the ability to type in three letters to anticipate full search terms in the "When I fly, can I bring my . . ." tool. In addition, multiple spelling formats were included—for example, *light saber* and *lightsaber*. As part of the effort to humanize TSA staffers, humor was eventually added: "Sadly, the technology doesn't currently exist to create a real lightsaber. However, you can pack a toy lightsaber in your carry-on or checked bag." If passengers look up "elephant," the response begins, "Yes, we have 'elephant' in our app!"

The tool started with one thousand items, including both permitted and prohibited articles. That list is now at 4,600 and includes multiple descriptors. As Lynn described, "We kind of counted on users helping us with what works, what doesn't work. We looked at the feedback on iTunes. People left feedback on what they liked and didn't like. And so we were able to make upgrades." Today, the tool allows users to suggest items to add to the database.

Since that time, TSA Pre✓® has been integrated into the MyTSA app. Launched in 2011, TSA Pre✓® allows travelers to apply for prechecked status, which speeds traveler movement through security checkpoints. TSA even put a call out for ideas on the InnoCentive website, asking people to submit ways to create a more efficient screening process that accommodates all levels of travelers, offering a prize of $5,000 for the best idea.

The app also now integrates a link to TSA videos on YouTube, another communications channel that was added to the mix. Users click through to simple, quick videos that help them with their journeys. Guides such as "Dress Smart," Pack Smart," "Liquids, Aerosols, and Gels," "Traveling with Children," and "Military Personnel" were added to provide information at travelers' fingertips. Another addition was a list of tips or useful information that travelers might not know, which would automatically appear at the bottom of the screen, beginning with "Did you know?" A tip might be "Children ages twelve and under can leave their shoes on at security checkpoints." The tip would be followed by details on where to go for more information.

There is no way to launch the perfect app, but it is possible to launch a well-thought-out, user-centered tool design that evolves over time in response to feedback. The key is to seek constant, direct feedback. When the redesigned TSA website was eventually launched, in 2012, learning from the MyTSA app was incorporated into the website.

Minimizing Risk with Small Steps

It clearly is a challenge to communicate with 700 million travelers in a timely and convenient manner. It is impossible to foresee all situations that might occur. Because eliminating risk is impossible, especially in a constant state of global flux, it is of vital importance for TSA to manage risk effectively by creating a portfolio of concepts and by proactively and progressively prototyping solutions that support their primary mission of service and security. If, through various tools of communication, TSA can anticipate and address unexpected situations *before* they cause problematic delays and discontent, then their work goes a long way toward maintaining calm and improving both speed and security at checkpoints, their ultimate goal.

Let's return to Kip's initial desire to open the channels of communication to better serve the public. The first new channel of communication, launched with Kip's support, was the TSA blog. When viewed from the lens of today, a blog may seem decidedly ho-hum, but in 2008 it was revolutionary. Although TSA was not the first federal agency to launch a blog, it was the first to allow people to interact and comment—certainly a potentially risky endeavor, in light of the potential backlash. TSA had cleared the blog through its own legal team, but the Department of Homeland Security demanded an explanation.

Luckily, TSA blogger Bob Burns had already become so popular that it was hard to pull the plug. In fact, each early blog post received hundreds of comments, many from travelers expressing, often vehemently, their frustrations with TSA screening procedures. The blog received national media attention, which drove even more traffic to it, with some readers *defending* TSA against egregious comments. In fact, the blog sought to stimulate this kind of conversation. It was the first effort to establish an authentic and open dialogue between TSA and the traveling public. With the blog posts and the question-and-answer conversation in the comment area, TSA started the process of communicating what the agency does and why, in order to build a better relationship between travelers and TSA staff and, in doing so, to encourage compliance.

Other communication initiatives undertaken by TSA, building on the success of its blog, include an Instagram account, started in 2013, and a customer service account on Twitter, @askTSA, started in 2015. In 2016, TSA became the first federal agency to offer its services via Facebook Messenger. "We continue to work on improving the traveler experience and security effectiveness with innovative tools such as Twitter and now Facebook Messenger," TSA administrator Peter Neffenger explained. "By using social media to enhance the service that we provide, TSA is better positioned to assist travelers in real time while keeping transportation security our top priority." These efforts continue to expand the means through which travelers can engage in a timely dialogue with TSA. These channels now even allow travelers to share photographs of carry-on items they have questions about—a visualization aimed at expediting assistance.

Both the TSA blog and the Instagram account remain popular today (hip website Jezebel recently called the Instagram account "surprisingly hilarious"), and both humanize the agency. They illustrate the issues TSA faces and the value TSA provides in securing air travel. When passengers become aware that seven or eight guns are found daily in carry-on luggage—not to mention other prohibited items—travelers develop a better understanding of TSA's challenge in maximizing security while minimizing wait times.

There is inevitable risk in taking action, in reaching out to the public to encourage authentic communication. But such actions are necessary experiments, undertaken to learn, refine, and iterate. If we learn from them, they are not failures. While there is always the risk that a concept will fail—and, in today's environment, possibly result in a social media backlash—there is greater risk, we believe, in inaction. Human-centered design helps us to manage the unavoidable risks that reaching out invites.

Reflections on the Process

MyTSA has now been downloaded more than 1 million times, which is impressive, given federal limitations on paid advertising. In 2011, the application was named Best Mobile App in Government by the American Council for Technology and Industry Advisory Council. In May 2016, MyTSA app usage was up 400 percent with a busy travel season predicted by airlines and airports. On Twitter, @askTSA, launched in September 2015, had received forty thousand inquiries by July 2016. But it isn't just other government agencies that TSA is besting. *Rolling Stone* magazine recently analyzed popular social media sites, and TSA's Instagram account ranked number four overall, beating out Grammy Award winner Beyoncé, in fifth position. "The nod from *Rolling Stone* is a bit of a coup for the oft-criticized agency," the *Washington Post* noted, continuing:

> It also is an acknowledgment at how adept the agency has become at using social media to engage the public. Whether it's inviting travelers to tweet @askTSA for answers about what they can and cannot bring on their flight or using its blog to bust myths, these platforms have given TSA new ways to build goodwill, educate the public and shore up its image.

TSA has gathered more than half a million followers on Instagram, according to the *Washington Post*.

So the desire to foster open channels of communication with travelers, which Kip initiated, continues to advance, along with the intent to educate passengers about checkpoint security and to promote TSA's people, mission, and policies. TSA continues to experiment with tools that will best serve the traveling public, whether on Twitter, Facebook Messenger, or other platforms.

But, as we saw in the United Cerebral Palsy story in chapter 8, the use of design thinking does not guarantee a happy ending. TSA continues to struggle, in the eyes of the public, and is still the butt of jokes (e.g., "TSA stands for 'thousands standing around'") and a source of complaints. As with UCP, much of this has little to do with its user-centricity and more to do with basic economics of staffing and budget cuts, as a recent article in *Politico* commented:

> The crunch comes down to simple math: since 2011, the number of travelers moving annually through TSA's checkpoints has increased by nearly 100 million, to a predicted 740 million passengers this year, while the agency's staff has shrunk to a five-year low.

Yet the tools TSA created are being used by thousands daily, and the traveling public is now more aware of TSA policies and the reasons behind them. It is a complicated balancing act, but important strides forward have been made.

Tomorrow's technology has yet to be discovered, and tomorrow's policies have yet to be unveiled. We know that change is the only constant and, especially in the technological world, undoubtedly brings new challenges. But humans are *Homo sapiens*, not the "Homo economicus" that much planning and strategy is based on; our behavior is often irrational and is rarely dictated totally by analysis. Dealing with the human animal in successfully implementing technological possibilities involves searching for insights that will help us understand our uniqueness and idiosyncrasies. Rather than merely demanding that humans adapt to technology, governments and nonprofits can better serve us, and can accomplish their missions more effectively, by using technology—as TSA has done—to communicate with us and to better understand our often unarticulated needs.

At TSA, understanding and addressing these "peripheral" human desires advances the goal of security. Acknowledging that technology plays a key role, TSA's strategy has been to systematically expand channels of communication in a manner that meaningfully meets travelers' needs. The design thinking process, coupled with Agile-styled methods, has helped the agency to highlight bias, blind spots, and unexamined assumptions and to drive better results.

When challenges are complex, solutions often need to evolve in layers that support each other. TSA did not simply build channels of communication. The agency also trained employees to support the changes in approach and considered how to improve the security checkpoint spaces, identifying many passenger touch points to potentially improve. In both design thinking and Agile approaches, the holistic systems perspective is unlocked by bringing all stakeholders into the conversation.

The TSA story is much more than a lesson in social media use. It is a story about bringing technological capabilities and human-centered insights together to attempt the almost impossible: build a relationship of trust and cooperation amid threats of violence and terror and do so in the spotlight of constant scrutiny and critique. It is a story of having the courage to initiate a conversation that may not be pleasant and the resolve to learn from both the good news and the bad.

CHAPTER ELEVEN

Making Innovation Safe at MasAgro

THE CHALLENGE TO THE GREATER GOOD

What if stakeholders targeted by a design effort are afraid or reluctant to change? Often, especially in the social sector, working toward a greater good involves inducing people to alter their behaviors—to adopt healthier lifestyles, prepare more carefully for air travel, or stay in high school instead of dropping out. But innovators, who are advocates for change, regularly underestimate human resistance to it and are surprised when their obviously "superior" solutions fail to be embraced by stakeholders. Deferring consideration of the challenges of inducing humans to change their behaviors is tempting—especially among the Geoffreys of the world—but yields predictably negative consequences.

DESIGN THINKING'S CONTRIBUTION

Design thinking insists that we construct a clear and compelling case for an altered future as part of the process, not as an afterthought, and provides powerful tools, like prototyping, co-creation, and experimentation, to accomplish this, as the story of MasAgro illustrates. MasAgro is a partnership between the Mexican government and agricultural groups that works with local farming communities to bridge the gap between farmers and research scientists and to encourage the adoption of sustainable modern agricultural methods. But subsistence farmers' entire livelihoods can rely on each year's crop, and they are understandably loath to risk abandoning tried-and-true traditional methods for new ones, even ones aimed at raising their income. MasAgro uses respected community leaders and local hubs to create compelling prototypes and experiments that demonstrate results. They offer testimony to design thinking's ability to reassure stakeholders reluctant to embrace new ideas.

W hat if we build it and they don't come? Attempts to introduce innovation—particularly practices that challenge long-standing approaches rooted in tradition—have an uneven track record in the developing world. MasAgro, an effort arising out of a partnership between Mexico's agriculture ministry and the International Maize and Wheat Improvement Center (abbreviated CIMMYT from the Spanish), is a dramatic exception. In this instance, a national government has directed the funding for a major initiative through an international nongovernmental organization because it perceives it as a way to gain more bang for the buck. More than 40 percent of participating farmers have adopted at least one MasAgro innovation—an extraordinary rate of success. Starting with a blank slate, MasAgro has designed a powerfully aligned set of elements and works in full consultation with its stakeholders, all with a goal of helping farmers increase crop yields in ways that improve their livelihood but do not contribute to climate change.

MasAgro brings together national and international organizations that partner with members of the entire agricultural value chain to practice conservation agriculture, an approach to farming that aims to improve soil management in order to achieve higher crop yields as well as long-term environmental sustainability—which results in greater long-term profitability. Often, farmers in Mexico lack access to modern agricultural technologies. MasAgro aims to help them increase their income by combining improved farming practices with high-yield varietal crops that do not negatively impact the environment or contribute to climate change. MasAgro also helps with postharvest farm-related activities.

MasAgro's director, Huntington (Hunt) Hobbs, found his calling serendipitously when he was a student at the Darden School of Business. Hunt's comments in an agribusiness class reflected an understanding of context in developing countries that impressed a group of class visitors. Shortly thereafter, he received a handwritten invitation, mailed from the Philippines, to join the CIMMYT team in Mexico. Hunt accepted the offer

ABOUT THE INTERNATIONAL MAIZE AND WHEAT IMPROVEMENT CENTER

The International Maize and Wheat Improvement Center grew out of a pilot program sponsored by the Mexican government and the Rockefeller Foundation in the 1940s and 1950s, to raise Mexico's farm productivity. Headquartered in Mexico but with offices throughout the developing world, CIMMYT's mission is to reduce poverty and hunger by sustainably increasing the productivity of maize and wheat cropping systems. Best known for work in the Green Revolution, it has developed initiatives that have led to the widespread adoption of improved crop varieties and farming practices. These initiatives, led by CIMMYT biologist Norman Borlaug, who was awarded the 1970 Nobel Peace Prize, have been credited with saving millions of lives across Asia (some say more than a billion). Today, building on Borlaug's work and legacy, CIMMYT is focused on providing affordable maize and wheat to the poor in the context of today's challenges, which include rising demand for food, climate change, and the desire for a healthier environment.

and found his passion: the desire to have an impact on feeding the world and helping the poor, small-scale farmer.

Also leading the innovation charge is Carolina Camacho Villa. Carolina is a principal researcher in the socioeconomics program of CIMMYT and works for MasAgro. She completed her PhD thesis after living in an indigenous community for a year in Chiapas, in the south of Mexico. Carolina understands firsthand the value of deep immersion and the importance of adapting to local contexts.

The MasAgro story is a lesson in experimentation through collaboration, community building, and change management. One of the strengths of MasAgro is its constant science-based experimentation to learn and improve (rapid prototyping in design thinking language). MasAgro works with all farmers, and many of the areas they serve are remote. The nature of the farming zones can vary from temperate mountainous to flat coastal areas and from humid tropics to semiarid zones. This variation also makes it challenging to scale practices and requires experiments to ensure adaptation to local needs. The farmers themselves can be very different from each other. Some have limited literacy skills or speak only a local dialect. Hunt described sitting in a room full of farmers, where several had laptop computers while others were illiterate.

Elements of the design thinking process can be seen throughout MasAgro's approach. Although MasAgro has a long history of working with farmers, their user-centered methodology starts with research and discovery, paying significant attention to **What *is***. Having developed this knowledge, they design **What *if*** experiments based on the interests and needs expressed by locals. Research workers collaborate with innovative local farmer leaders to assess **What *wows***. Then, through experimentation and iterative prototyping, they refine technologies as they apply to local conditions in **What *works***. The learning is shared with the community and the research center. Over time, the farm leaders decide what works best and share it with other locals, offering them the opportunity to follow suit.

A Three-Part System for Learning and Experimentation

MasAgro's goal is the adoption of good farming practices through adaptation to local farming needs. With that goal in mind, they set up a network, which they call a hub, where new maize and wheat technologies are developed, tested, and transferred. Hunt described how the hub works:

> MasAgro employs cutting-edge scientific teams to develop better seeds, machines, and innovative approaches. At the same time, we scan for potential needs which may benefit

from technological solutions. We then select a set of promising innovations, in this case for Mexico. Next, we take these "best bets" and test them in fields in the region we are seeking to serve; these "platforms" could be land lent to test that is owned by a university, a private sector company, or an NGO [nongovernmental organization]. A committee of informed local farmers selects the bets to move forward and reviews the results, identifying the bets of most potential interest, which are often fine-tuned based on what we learn, and go through another season of testing, sometimes again and again.

The selected innovation is not always a technology; it can be a new practice such as spacing between rows, or the planting date, or when to weed. It is then tested in "modules." A module is where the farmer uses the innovation on half of their field and follows current practice on the other half. Farmers choose which modules they want to test. Finally, local farmers are brought to the modules. The participating farmers and technicians describe what is being tested and the emerging results.

Together, the platforms, modules, technical support staff, and advisory form the network hub within which all MasAgro initiatives happen. Participating farmers then adjust as they decide what to adopt in their own fields.

The hub is designed to test, validate, and scale practices using six MasAgro technologies. The hub not only showcases proven MasAgro technologies but also serves as an experimental space for adaptation to local needs. Local farmers are offered an array of options, ranging from seed varieties, types

MASAGRO'S SIX TECHNOLOGIES

1. Appropriate varieties or types of maize (for example, yellow or multicolored), wheat, and other crops (ideal varieties for local conditions)

2. Diagnostic tools to measure soil fertility, emphasizing nitrogen, phosphorous, and potassium

3. Fertilization techniques

4. Conservation agriculture (including crop rotation and the protection of soil) for best adaptation to climate change

5. Diversification and access to new markets

6. Postharvest technologies, such as steel silos designed to protect the harvest

of fertilization, conservation, and postharvest techniques to diversification and access to new markets, and can select those that are of greatest interest for testing. The selected MasAgro technologies are then placed into experimental platforms to adjust and refine the technologies for local conditions. The technologies are designed to sustain agriculture by maintaining and/or improving the quality of the land, conserving water, and ensuring the quality of the crops.

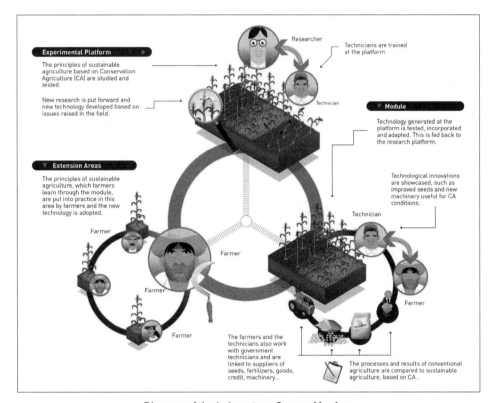

Diagram of the hub system. Source: MasAgro.

Parts of the Hub

In the hub system, the *experimental plots* of land allow for investigation and experimentation in conjunction with local farmers. The aim is to generate knowledge, data, and information, driven by the interest of local farmers in specific technologies. The advisory committee of farmers works with a team of collaborators from universities, government organizations, church groups, and nongovernmental organizations, including MasAgro's certified technicians and scientific workers, to establish needs and experiment with options in a space where farmers can easily compare the yields of traditional and more scientific farming. This collaboration allows MasAgro to learn and adapt to local conditions and needs, including agricultural and ecological needs and technical, economic, and environmental factors. Members of the local farmer advisory committee, along with innovative local farmers, decide which technologies or practices they want to try, and they help to evaluate the results of the experiment. These local farmers are often community leaders, who then share their knowledge with others in the hub.

The *modules* in the hub system are farmers' plots of land, which allow for side-by-side comparison of innovation and control plots. Control plots use conventional farming techniques, while innovation plots use one or more of the six MasAgro technologies. Local farmers volunteer to plant a module, and they choose which of the six technologies they want to try. This arrangement allows for experimentation with new technologies but also adaptation to local needs and conditions. A MasAgro technician will listen, to understand local needs, and follow with diagnostic tests. Often, the farmer and technician negotiate how to proceed with the crops.

The experiment allows for learning on both sides and tweaking of proven methods. Logbooks are used to track the process and results. In other words, the experimental modules allow farmers and technicians to hypothesize about and test potential solutions and then feed the results back into a common knowledge base. As Carolina shared:

> In place of offering a package [a predetermined solution], which beforehand was very common, now it's a portfolio of options in which, depending on the type of farmer, he will select the kind of technology that will fit for adoption and adaptation.

Carolina explained that the hubs engender cooperation among farmers, trainees, and researchers. This type of user involvement and interaction, in design thinking language, is called co-creation.

The final part of the hub, the *area of extension*, is land on which the farmer is no longer experimenting but has actively embraced one or more of the MasAgro technologies. These plots also serve as visual models for the entire local community. When the crop is harvested, neighboring farmers are invited to see the difference that the new technology made. The local farmer and supporting technician will compare the old and the new practice and describe the use of the technology.

The farming community comes together in annual hub meetings to discuss and assess issues, potential solutions, and performance. At these meetings, the stakeholders, including farmers from different regions, discuss the main regional difficulties and how they might be addressed. The pioneering farmers who try potential solutions on their own land (the modules) are ultimately solving regional challenges, and their modules showcase the results. Hub meetings serve as an important forum for sharing and feedback.

How the Hub Works

The hub system serves as a space for research and discovery at the front end of the process and for the development of possible concept solutions and experiments at the back end. Through collaboration and over time, the hub allows MasAgro to iteratively adapt the technologies that are working locally. MasAgro currently has hubs across all the regions of Mexico, with more than 450 modules.

One example comes from Oaxaca, a state in southern Mexico known for its indigenous cultures. Oaxaca is the poorest state in Mexico; daily farmer income might be $2.50. In its mountainous areas, farmers farm on inclines so steep that they tie ropes around their waists while working. Many are subsistence farmers whose livelihood, and likely the family's food supply, depends on the success of their crops.

Imagine if you were to approach such a farmer with a handful of seeds, saying that the seeds would increase the farmer's crop or income. Because the loss of a single crop would mean devastation for the farmer's family, those new seeds are not a risk easily taken. However, the hub system allows a farmer to

DESIGN TOOL: CO-CREATION

Enlisting users to help you modify, enhance, or choose among a portfolio of concepts, rather than waiting until a concept is fully developed to present it to them, is called co-creation, in design thinking language. If you want your innovations to be meaningful, you need to invite into your process the people who will use them. In a world where we are used to being the "experts," yielding this role to our stakeholders may make us uncomfortable. But innovation is about learning, and stakeholders have the most to teach us. The sooner you put options in front of them to react to, the faster you'll get to a value-added solution.

visualize the new technology in action, grown under local conditions, rather than relying on abstract arguments about its scientific superiority.

Visualization, as we have seen in other stories, serves multiple important purposes. Early in the design thinking process, it is a tool to encourage discussion and dialogue. Later in the process, it expedites the testing of assumptions through prototyping and refinement. Eventually, it becomes a tool for making the vision a reality. The experimental plots and side-by-side modules are, in fact, three-dimensional visualizations that first allow a conversation to take place. The conversation helps both the farmers and the research workers learn how to adapt to the local environment. Their resulting experiments produce results that inform the next round of planting.

For example, farmers might choose to experiment with a different type of seed or with fertilization. In a dry region, they might experiment with drought-resistant varieties. Alternatively, they might engage in conservation agriculture and conserve soil by leaving behind crop residues to protect the soil from being blown away and to add moisture-retaining texture to the soil. If a farmer requires the crop residue to feed animals, an alternative that might meet both needs would be a seed that produces many leaves along with the maize.

Some results take longer than others to show, but when farmers can see the results on the experimental plots of land or can see what other farmers adopt on their own land (in the side-by-side modules or the extension areas), they are encouraged to follow suit. As Hunt explained, "It is often when they see with their own eyes the difference that a technology can make that their interest is then captured." With the stakes so high, providing results that farmers can see for themselves, tailored to local conditions, is critical.

What we learn from best practices in design thinking is that successful prototyping starts with the quickest and simplest prototype that you can design. A technician might start a relationship with a farmer by offering a small sample of seed, such as a five-kilogram bag that will grow just a few rows of crops. If interested, the farmer will start a discussion with the technician. Starting with a small experimental plot, the testing eventually builds up to a small farm. Next, farm by farm, the area of extension is expanded. Through successive iterations, co-creators can learn and refine their solutions. Each prototype, in this case each plot of land, allows for better performance the next time. The hubs serve to visually tell a story and to cut through communication barriers, allowing MasAgro and the farmers to combine the old and the new into best practices that serve local farmers and communities' unique needs.

Building on Traditional Systems with Modern Ways and Technology

MasAgro is looking not only to increase food productivity and sustainability but also to increase the farm income for these small farmers. One example of efforts to increase farm income builds on the traditional, indigenous system of farming in Latin America, called *milpa*, which combines three staples in a field. Maize is grown along with bean plants that climb on the maize stalks and pumpkins on the ground. MasAgro introduced fruit trees to the traditional mix. Hunt shared:

> When you combine maize, beans and pumpkin, you get a pretty rich diet. What we're doing is taking that very rich traditional system and respecting it, refining it, and improving the economic well-being of those still practicing it. We respect this system, we want to work with this system, farmers want to maintain their systems, but how can we leverage this system for a bigger benefit?

The traditional crops feed the family, while the fruit trees add to the market opportunity, increasing the farming income, particularly for small farm holders. In Hunt's view, this represents a historic opportunity:

> With NAFTA, the bigger farmers, with access to roads and credit, are turning to fruits and vegetables to serve the US and Canadian markets. This opens the opportunity to connect these residual, neglected, poor communities, not only to improve their technology but, more importantly, to link them to markets. That's the bigger perspective. It's an opportunity for the neglected to join the global economy. The opportunity is there, but that doesn't mean that they can access it. And to access it is not only having access to the market; it's having the right product of the right quality, et cetera. And that's where we come in.

As Carolina explained, this modification of the milpa system is an example of how the hubs allow for sharing and learning in both directions. The hubs also allow for successful local technologies, such as the milpa system itself, to be emphasized and scaled with help from MasAgro. In addition, Carolina explained that MasAgro offers continuity. Successful programs and projects that might have been lost with a change of government and policy are sustained through MasAgro's ongoing presence and influence. "MasAgro provides an umbrella to these local innovations," Carolina noted.

Another example of building on tradition is the naming of the seed varieties. Although accurate noting of the date that seeds should be planted is an important agronomic technique, it can be hard for farmers to remember new dates for different varieties. MasAgro made an agreement with seed sellers to name seed varieties in the Oaxaca region after saints, to make it easy for farmers to remember to plant that type of seed on the saint's day. Connecting to the area's deep-rooted religious and cultural traditions changes what might otherwise be a challenge or a chore into a meaningful action. These small gestures demonstrate an understanding of local culture and a willingness to help farmers in a manner that is respectful and sensitive to the local community.

Many of the thousands of farmers in the MasAgro program are also using technology to help them farm. Technology allows for data-driven farming and creates an opening for MasAgro's certified technicians to work with farmers across Mexico. More than twenty thousand farmers are registered in standardized electronic logbooks, which help to track data and improve farming. In addition, farmers receive agronomic climate information via the MasAgro mobile phone service, which uses GPS tracking in the phone. For example, in 2014 MasAgro started offering GreenSat, a program that allows wheat farmers to fine-tune the optimum amount of nitrogen for their crops with the help of data from satellite images. Hunt described how it works:

> We have a whiz machine, a handheld device that looks like a big water gun, called the GreenSeeker, which zaps the ground and gets a reading of what the fertilizer needs of a particular patch of ground are. This replaces taking a soil sample to a lab. But GreenSeekers require tender love and care, cost several hundred dollars, and require expert use. You zap and get a reading (and test and test the accuracy of the reading and refine the GreenSeeker), and zap and zap, and soon you have quite a comprehensive georeferenced soil fertility map.

> A great innovation, but how to get the information to farmers? One of our scientific whiz kids, with the freedom to think and innovate and test, came up with an app. Any farmer

can load the app on their cell phone, push it, and get a fertilizer recommendation for the patch of land the farmer is standing on.

As with all programs, MasAgro's intent is to closely monitor the results of this innovation and to adjust accordingly. As Hunt explained, "We continually test and ask and test and ask and test and ask, until we seem to be getting it right."

For example, MasAgro recently made a foray into social media. The original idea was to target policy makers and farm leaders to form a social network. After a few months, MasAgro noticed that the concept had virtually zero participation from the targeted groups. However, a rich network of extension staff was using the platform to exchange information. As a result, the social network changed direction, becoming a platform to share and exchange best farming practices. MasAgro experimented and learned.

Partners in the Value Chain

Beyond advising farmers, MasAgro looks at all factors in the agricultural journey, from seed selection and planting to the consumption of the final product, while also offering additional support for financial needs and market access. Through this holistic systems perspective, MasAgro endeavors to understand the needs of participants in the value chain, from those who crush the maize into flour to the restaurant chefs who use it to craft original menus.

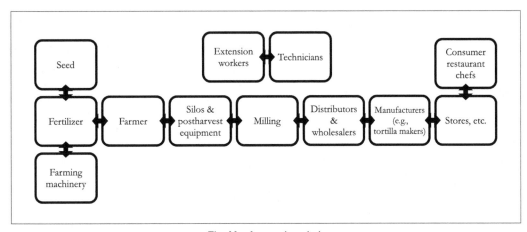

The MasAgro value chain.

MasAgro researchers in the Socioeconomic Studies group consistently review the value chain to see what the market is purchasing, what channels are being used, how the product is used, and where farmers might gain opportunities to participate. With extensive research, they help farmers select the right seed for the right market. Furthermore, they help with access to markets: MasAgro may aid a farmer in choosing a crop variety that results in a higher market value, or farmers may be directed to a market that values the farmer's existing crop and may pay more for it.

For example, MasAgro will test maize with tortilla manufacturers to better understand the desired qualities of maize in a tortilla. Armed with this information, MasAgro technicians can guide farmers to select seeds that will offer the traits desired. One farmer, for example, switched from a low-value maize to a higher-value colored maize that is desired by tortilla makers for special-occasion tortillas. Another example, from Oaxaca, was a switch to a native maize that is preferred by high-end chefs serving elite restaurants in the United States. A switch to a different variety or a different market, or both, can result in a 25 percent increase in income, which can then transform lives, with broad-ranging effects. Hunt noted, "Very often, an increase in family income leads to an increased investment in schooling for the children, in particular for girls, who may not otherwise attend school." This is one more example of the kind of positive yet unintended consequences we have seen in other stories.

Not only are farmers earning more income by adopting better farming techniques; they also are better able to engage in postharvest activities that lead to increased income, such as constructing metal silos to protect their crops from insects and rodents. Silos not only allow farmers to protect the household and market food supplies but also offer flexibility in timing so that growers can sell their crops when pricing is favorable and thereby increase their income. In addition, the introduction of silos may support local small businesses. MasAgro offers a training program in which locals learn how to make silos to sell to other local farmers.

Partnering to Learn and to Disseminate Information

A network of partnerships, implemented over time, is critical to MasAgro's success. Itself the result of a partnership, MasAgro partners with national, state, and local governments as well as with other international organizations and with local partners, which may be researchers, civic or church groups, farmers' associations, or universities. These relationships enable MasAgro to train technicians and extension workers who will learn from and disseminate local best practices. These partners reach out to local farmers with greater impact and accelerate the learning.

To develop local partners, MasAgro offers training at various levels of intensity. As we shared earlier, a local farmer who takes the lead in investigating a new technology will work with a trained MasAgro technician to refine that technology in light of the local needs. The farmer may then be trained to share the refined technology with others, creating a viral spread of the new approaches. Local farmers may also be trained to share specific information, such as facts about the agricultural calendar or techniques to keep in mind when planting crops. A second level of training is more extensive and may take up to a year. A third level of training is for elite technicians, who will then train other trainers.

Because the trained partners often have deep local roots and are familiar with the people, ways and traditions, and dialect of a region, they are well positioned to serve their local communities. Ultimately, they both serve and belong to the group. Trained partners, whether they are certified MasAgro technicians or extension staff, assist by connecting farmers with what they need, such as seed tailored to the region's climate, or specific machinery.

In its partners, MasAgro looks for best practices, whether local or international. As Hunt put it:

> One of the benefits of an international organization is that we have the benefit of that search for best practices on a global scale. We might find small machinery that is working in India or China and bring that into Mexico, or find a way that farmers are organizing in the Punjab and bring that to Mexico.

Here we see the idea of repertoire operating at an organizational rather than an individual level. In the same way that Dr. Melissa Casey at Monash Medical Centre was able to connect two disparate worlds because of her unique life experiences, MasAgro is able to reach across its global experience base to offer a portfolio of tailored local solutions. In fact, the hub system was actually developed in Ethiopia by MasAgro staff, who then went to Mexico to establish the hub system while tailoring it for the local environment. Currently, MasAgro is working with the Guatemalan government to create locally adapted innovation systems similar to but not exactly the same as those in Mexico.

Transforming Lives through Small Experiments

MasAgro focuses on three main indicators to evaluate progress: yield increase, income increase, and adoption rate. These indicators are chosen, refined, and agreed upon with top officials of the Mexican ministry of agriculture. MasAgro tracks and reports on these indicators on a quarterly and annual basis. In addition, the agriculture ministry has hired an independent group of Dutch academics to review the data.

The success metrics that MasAgro has achieved are compelling.

Success Metric	2011	2014
Participating farmers	4,000	228,495
Certified MasAgro technicians	32	150
Extension staff	100	2,300+
Hectares with MasAgro technologies in use	22,000	849,638
Partners (public and private organizations)	50	170
Demonstration plots (hectares)	40	1,350
Increase in income (in US dollars)	$4.3 million	$165 million
Number of MasAgro beneficiaries	16,000	915,000+

Ultimately, engagement in the hubs is appreciably higher, as indicated by the numbers of participating farmers, certified MasAgro technicians, extension staff, and partners. More hectares and demonstration plots of land are using MasAgro technologies. MasAgro beneficiaries have grown at an enviable rate. Hunt shared:

> We started by measuring our impact in terms of hectares or acres where at least one of our technologies was being implemented, but more and more we are measuring by the number of technologies that are being adopted in any particular patch of land.

Perhaps the impact of the program explains its 46 percent adoption index within three years, which, according to Bunmei, the external consulting firm that conducted the study, is unheard of. Comparative rates, the firm noted, would normally be in the range of 10 to 15 percent. Rates of adoption vary according to how easy it is to adopt an innovation or technology, the influence of early adopters, and the cost versus the benefit of adoption. The hub system propels the adoption of innovative technologies through training and local networks that support the practice of farming from end to end.

The project began in 2010, and although the results for 2011 were promising, the more dramatic increases occurred by 2014. In 2016, the Monterrey University of Technology and Higher Education named the MasAgro project one of the ten projects that are transforming Mexico. The innovation network created by its hub system is a powerful model for any organization seeking to catalyze the adoption of innovative technology.

Reflections on the Process

There is much to learn from the partnerships, co-creation, prototyping, and experimentation that shaped MasAgro. It takes a global village, working in cooperation with local communities, to solve complex problems and increase both productivity and long-term sustainability, protecting and nurturing both people and the planet. MasAgro is an innovation system that consistently seeks to enhance outcomes and impact. It blends scientific research and practice with local environmental concerns, traditions, and culture to present a compelling future. The MasAgro system allows farmers, including indigenous Mexican farmers in remote areas, to actually *see* a brighter future with their own eyes, rather than taking someone else's word for it.

Through its massive experimentation hubs, MasAgro has woven a system that allows an extensive network of partners to co-create with native farmers, learn what works, and disseminate best practices, whether these are local or international. With each partner and each hectare, MasAgro builds on its learning and success. As a result, it has improved both productivity and sustainability while advancing research and helping small farmers in remote or neglected regions develop the confidence to try the offered methods. MasAgro takes the local versus global conversation we started in chapter 9, in discussing the Community Transportation Association of America, to a new level. It offers a global repertoire of options while allowing solutions to be customized to an individual farmer's needs. The system is local and global simultaneously.

CHAPTER TWELVE

Integrating Design and Strategy
at Children's Health System of Texas

THE CHALLENGE TO THE GREATER GOOD

Too often, innovators create breakthrough solutions that organizations are incapable of successfully implementing. Even great ethnographic research that produces an understanding of stakeholder needs and generates appropriate solutions goes nowhere if an organization lacks the will, strategies, and capabilities to successfully execute new ideas. Design and strategy are not the same thing. Strategy reminds us who we serve and builds the capabilities to make it happen. Design tells us how to serve them, and the insights from design thinking inform the question of what capabilities to build. How do we tie design thinking that analyzes users' needs to the strategic process that steers organizations toward new futures and business models?

DESIGN THINKING'S CONTRIBUTION

Design thinking can do more than increase the potential of individual offerings and conversations to create value; it can drive fundamental changes in strategy. When Children's Health System of Texas identified the need for a new business strategy to address the worsening quality of life for children in North Texas, the hospital embarked on a multiyear customer-centered design thinking program that caused leadership to examine and rethink the fundamentals of their entire business model. Partnering with the Business Innovation Factory (BIF), Children's Health integrated design thinking with the hospital's strategic process to assess and build the capabilities to deliver a transformational new approach to health care that focused on facilitating family wellness rather than on providing individual medical care.

W hen the Children's Medical Center of Dallas became the Children's Health System of Texas, the name change was not about changing the mission. Launched by a group of volunteer nurses in 1913, the medical center was the first free "baby camp" in the Southwest, an open-air tent hospital dedicated to the care of babies from poor families. A hundred years later, the mission of Children's Health remained the same: "to make life better for children." As a teaching and research institution and the sixth-largest pediatric medical center in the United States, Children's Health had clear challenges: the Dallas children they served faced some of the most troubling health indicators in the United States, with nearly 30 percent living in poverty, as well as having lower life expectancies, higher rates of chronic conditions like asthma and diabetes, and spiraling obesity problems.

What the name change did represent was a complete rethinking of the way they would pursue their mission to improve the quality of life for children in Dallas: by combining design thinking with strategy to rethink the fundamentals of their business model.

This story starts, as so many of our stories do, with a seemingly straightforward problem that resisted straightforward solutions: the increasing frequency of emergency room visits for primary care needs that could have been treated more cost-effectively and conveniently outside of high-cost emergency rooms. Children's Health leadership had assumed that the problem was access; however, a network of sixteen ambulatory care centers placed throughout the community had failed to reverse the trend, and unreimbursed costs were escalating quickly.

CEO Chris Durovich reached two critical insights, one about patients and one about financials: (1) despite the high-quality medical care that Children's Health was providing, health outcomes for the children they served were *not* improving; and (2) as the funding model shifted from fee-for-service to population health, their business model was not sustainable. Chris believed that a different model was needed. He reached out with an invitation to a colleague he had known for years, Peter Roberts, an expert in population health with broad experience on both the insurer and patient sides of health care, to help Children's Health look beyond existing solutions.

Peter believed that the options represented by existing paths were inadequate and that Children's Health would need to invent new possibilities better suited to the community. To be able to effect sustainable change, Peter told Chris he would need three promises: strong support from the board and CEO, direct reporting to Chris, and the freedom to operate without asking permission—or obtaining consensus—at every step along the way. He got them all, joining the Children's Health executive staff as the president for population health and insurance services in September 2011. His first step was to develop a deeper understanding of the population Children's Health served and the communities in which the families lived. Peter was committed to placing the children and their families at the center of the design process.

Peter called on the help of Michael Samuelson, a nationally known expert in prevention and wellness. They started a door-to-door listening tour throughout the Dallas community to "meet the neighbors" and get to know the health care providers, social service agencies, school systems, faith-based community, and city government. Peter explained how this led them to design thinking:

> We spent time in the pediatric emergency room, talking to staff, to patients and families, and we kept seeing the same kids coming in week after week with asthma problems. Why? We realized that there must be a deeper story that we didn't understand. That caused us to start down the design thinking path.

With the help of John Kania, an expert in the Collective Impact approach, they formed the Health and Wellness Alliance for Children, a community-based organization of more than seventy-five organizations and agencies serving children. However, the Alliance was missing the active involvement and voice of the families themselves.

Enter a team of partners from the Business Innovation Factory, a nonprofit firm with a mission that complemented Children's Health's: to achieve transformational change in social systems, directed by the communities themselves. Founded by Saul Kaplan, a business manager and consultant with diverse experience across industries, BIF was a unique organization, combining traditional strategic know-how with leading-edge innovation methodologies to achieve an unusual mandate: creating a real-world laboratory to explore new business models and systems solutions to wicked problems in the areas of health care, education, and government. Saul believed that, by combining big thinking with small experiments and by helping leaders to incrementally improve their existing model in parallel with building a new one, breakthrough—and sustainable—new business models could be created. BIF's job, as Saul saw it, was to help leaders change their lens and imagine new possibilities, allowing them to escape the straitjacket of their existing business models. BIF's approach emphasized competency building because capabilities were, in BIF's view, the core building blocks that allowed organizations to deliver new outcomes.

Saul brought in a colleague, Eli MacLaren, to lead the Children's Health/BIF team. With more than a decade of experience in managing social ventures, Eli was a systems thinker and an early mover in social entrepreneurship, with a track record of success. Creating a new business model began, in the BIF process, with understanding the kind of new future that a client wanted to create, so that they could "backcast"—work from the future *backward* to assess what needs to change today. Exploratory research made that possible by producing insights that first defined the jobs that people wanted or needed done and then fostered the identification of opportunity spaces that defined the boundaries of the search for solutions.

In July 2012, Eli's team and Children's Health staff began work on a multiphased deep listening journey at Children's Health that brought design and strategy together, focusing first on understanding the kind of new future that they wanted to create and then unbundling and realigning their capabilities to get there.

Phase 1: Laying the Foundation

Phase 1 lasted four months and provided the foundational research to inspire new thinking about business model possibilities. During phase 1, the team focused on identifying insights to guide their design work, based on research into the lives of children and their families and the role played by health conditions. They then translated these insights into design principles and used these principles to highlight areas of opportunity to close the gap between the experience that stakeholders were having and the one that they wanted and needed to have.

WHAT IS A BUSINESS MODEL?

"Business model" is a term much used but often little understood, in either the business or the nonprofit worlds. It is much more than a description of a new product or service. A business model not only describes key activities; it lays out the *value proposition* behind an offering (how it creates value for a defined set of stakeholders) and the *capabilities* and *resources* needed by the organization to implement that value proposition. It also considers sustainability from a financial viewpoint. In other words, a business model lays out both how an organization *creates* value with a particular strategy and how it *sustains* that value as a result of doing so. Business models, in that view, are just as critical in the social sector as they are in the for-profit world.

To start, Eli spent two days in Dallas, interviewing staff and patients and getting a high-level sense of the situation. Using this information, a design brief was created, focusing on the question of how to inspire healthy communities with citizens at the center. The team knew that they wanted to focus their work on needs, motivations, behaviors, and value systems—the human factors.

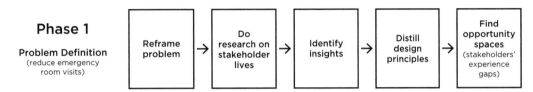

Flow of the process in phase 1.

This desire shaped the research agenda, which was multifaceted. The team began by looking at available statistics to determine who was repeatedly using the Children's Health emergency department for primary needs, despite the inconvenience and disruption for families of doing so. They discovered that locals were brought to the emergency room primarily by preexisting pulmonary conditions like asthma. Metabolic diseases like diabetes were a secondary area. Accordingly, the team's research program, and the work of the Health and Wellness Alliance, focused on children with chronic pulmonary conditions, largely from south and west Dallas. The team also wanted a variety of patients in the research sample—some with no conditions but struggling to maintain good health; some with chronic conditions and some without. The sample included nonemergency patients who faced similar socioeconomic conditions.

During the recruiting process, the design team identified families by relying on what BIF called "trusted agents," such as pastors, neighbors, and directors of YMCA branches. These collaborators would prove critical to successfully engaging the community at the outset, and then again in crafting solutions. The initial research involved thirty-two semistructured interviews and led to shadowing to get a deeper understanding of patients' lives and to gauge their "say-do" divide—the difference between their statements and their actions, or what people say versus what they do. The team used journaling, journey mapping, and collage making to increase patients' awareness of and ability to reflect on their own perceptions and experiences. They observed and interviewed stakeholders in different locations, including ambulatory care centers, grocery stores, playgrounds, and schools. They hosted conversations called "community whiteboards." The aim throughout the research was to identify the *experience gap*, the difference between the situation patients were experiencing and what they actually needed and wanted.

Findings: The Five Elements of Wellness

A set of high-level insights emerged:

1. If Children's Health wanted to improve health, it needed to focus on *families*, not just on kids.

2. What families wanted was a better *life*, not better health. If parents needed to feed their kids fast food to get to work on time, they would do so, placing health at a lower priority.

3. Families also wanted to feel *in control* of their health journey. Yet, in medical care, Peter noted, "we do things *to* people and *for* people, not *with* them."

4. Families listened to those they knew and trusted—teachers, pastors, YMCA staff, and other families who had been through similar experiences.

As the team dug deeper, they uncovered a set of insights about the key elements of wellness. These five elements critically influenced the health and well-being of children and their families. They included the following:

1. *Balanced outlook.* The research uncovered two differing outlooks that were fundamentally shaping family behaviors and decisions in Dallas. One was a *reactive*, short-term, "quick fix" attitude in which families, who were often dealing with poverty and resource constraints, struggled from one crisis to another. This outlook led to activities aimed at escaping reality, like watching TV, and a tendency toward actions based on convenience. Thinking in the short term, these reactive patients focused on treating symptoms rather than addressing the root cause of any problem. Because emergency room visits require less planning than making appointments at ambulatory care centers, emergency room care was the norm for reactive families. A *proactive* outlook, on the other hand, encouraged families to take a longer-term perspective and to focus more on preventative care.

2. *Personal power.* Here, again, the team identified two ends of a continuum. Families with a *protective* mindset limited their children's exposure to stress and to the people or environments in which threats developed. Though seemingly positive, this protective nurturing had a negative effect on a child's sense of self-efficacy and encouraged overreliance on parents. Families with an *exploratory* mindset, on the other hand, trusted their children to manage their own health, which increased children's sense of personal power and encouraged them to develop accountability for their own decisions.

3. *Sense of self.* A child's sense of self develops out of experiences and relationships. A child with a chronic condition like asthma can develop an *unstable* sense of self, often resulting from a lack of quality time spent with family because of continuous crises and hectic schedules. These children can come to see themselves as having something "wrong" with them and to allow their illness and its limitations to define them, leading to resignation and a vulnerability to negative influences. Children with a *stable* sense of self, in contrast, develop identities that are not tied to their condition. They are more likely to be motivated to see themselves as "normal" and less likely to let setbacks define their fate.

4. *System of support.* In this element, the continuum ranges from limited support to strong. *Limited support* networks can often force parents to leave children alone, which may allow children to behave in ways that impede their health, like eating junk food, or render them more susceptible to peer pressure and the adoption of unhealthy attitudes and behaviors. A *strong support* network, on the other hand, enhances children's development by exposing them to a broader network of positive (and sometimes negative) role models and encouraging them to make healthier choices. These families often have a closer relationship with the child's doctor, as well, treating the physician as a trusted advisor.

5. *Connected knowledge.* This final element of wellness was related to communication and the extent to which families are able to gather and process information about a child's health. Families characterized by *disconnected information flows* are prey to misconceptions and false beliefs and generally don't share information openly and effectively with caregivers. In families with *connected information flows*, children, parents, and caregivers reveal information freely and establish trust and consistency.

These five elements of wellness, the team believed, need to be in place to drive families toward healthy behaviors and outcomes.

The five wellness factors.

Translating Findings into Design Principles

From these elements, the team created a set of design principles, or criteria, to guide the development of solutions:

- *Personalize the experience.* Invite co-creation and give people choices rather than one-size-fits-all solutions.

- *Meet families where they are.* Pay attention to the reality of families' lives, and try to bridge the gap between what should, and what can, be done.

- *Honor children's role in their own development.* Encourage children to play a role in their own health, allowing them to test their autonomy and to feel accountable for their choices.

- *Facilitate an open and transparent dialogue.* Improve communication flows and build a common language.

- *Build both individual and collective knowledge.* Encourage a child's broader support network to be involved in achieving better health outcomes.

- *Foster sustained engagement.* Build habits and reinforce healthy behaviors that keep health in the foreground of attention, rather than only during crises or interactions with caregivers.

These design principles, in turn, pointed the team toward the identification of a set of opportunity spaces where team members believed successful solutions that met these criteria could be found.

Identifying Opportunity Spaces

Rather than defining specific solutions, the opportunity spaces identified promising areas in which to look for new concepts. BIF looked for three categories of opportunity: product or service, organizational structure, and systems and partnerships. A broad set of opportunity spaces was critical to the process, as Eli described:

> It is a challenge if your opportunity space becomes so narrow that it's only about a particular product or service. We go through exercises that think about opportunity spaces in three categories. First is product or service. The second is organizational structure—brands, roles, product extensions. The third is in terms of systems and partnerships, things that are external for the organization. One and two are going to get you point solutions. Three is where you're going to find systemic solutions. You need to have a set of solutions from categories one and two that support the core business. But it's the solutions that come from that third horizon that are transformational.

As in earlier steps, the intent still was to improve the wellness of children with asthma, in particular, and to identify concepts that channeled families away from the emergency room and into other sources of care. Getting clarity on specifically what a transformation looked like was key, and a preferred method for doing this involved the use of the "from-to" construct. For each opportunity space, the transition *from* an existing situation *to* a preferred one was specified.

Each opportunity space posed a different question:

1. *How might we facilitate a greater sense of control beyond the emergency department?* Because research suggested that many families used the emergency department when they felt a lack of control, the team's goal was to seek ideas that helped the family move *from* fear and helplessness *to* a sense of power and an ability to plan. The team suggested solutions that, for example, provided access to better information, decentralized care planning, and helped children articulate their feelings and experiences, while providing a safe environment for exploring limits.

2. *How might we create more convenient sources of care?* Because the emergency department was often a family's most convenient source of care, the team's second goal was to move families *from* decisions made on the basis of ease *to* co-creation between families and caregivers, which identified flexible options better suited to the reality of the family's circumstances. The suggested solutions in this area built trusted information sources within the community itself and improved the attractiveness of nonemergency care.

3. *How might we make health more tangible for children in order to engage them?* Because it is difficult to see the link between their health and the choices they make, children do not always understand or attend to the consequences of their behaviors. The team's goal was to nudge children and families *from* limited understanding of the impact of their actions *to* awareness and accountability. The suggested solutions included making healthy goals more meaningful to children, sharing those ideas widely across any child's support network, and providing frequent real-time feedback.

4. *How might we inspire, guide, and support first-generation change agents?* Because families cannot always be relied on to make and encourage good choices, it made sense to try to reach around them to work with the children themselves. The goal here was to move *from* a place where children feel isolated, uninformed, and unsupported *to* one where children are able to connect with others facing similar issues and to lead their families in the right direction. The team suggested solutions that would provide mentors and offer children opportunities to share their stories and get positive reinforcement for their achievements.

5. *How might we deliver care beyond the child?* Because families can play such a critical role in children's health, the goal here was to move *from* a place of ignoring their influence and the

whole context of a child's environment *to* one of acknowledging and treating root causes and building a family network that is a positive influence. The suggested solutions would help caregivers see the whole of a child's life, situate care within the family unit, and equip children with life skills to make healthier choices as they grow.

At this point, during phase 1, the BIF team had gathered data, identified insights, created a set of design principles, and ultimately identified a set of opportunity spaces, to conclude their foundational research. The opportunity spaces of phase 1 served as the foundation for the design brief for phase 2. Reflecting on the importance of phase 1, and the groundwork it laid for the work to come, Eli noted:

> The most important point of the first four months of work is to help the institution and community stakeholders in the Health and Wellness Alliance shift their lens and be willing to look at the problem differently. I think that most organizations can't currently see the experience gap because they're looking at it through their own lens. So, in their mind, their system is not being used correctly, and they are focused on how to get people to do that. But maybe the system is no longer relevant or no longer meeting customers' needs. How do we see that gap? Only when you shift your lens from the existing system to what people actually need. And then use that as the basis for new possibilities.

Phase 2: Business Model Development

Consistent with BIF's belief that it is important to look for both incremental and transformational change, phase 2 had multiple components. It focused first on identifying improvements to Children's Health's existing business model and then on creating a transformational new one. Core to both processes was a focus on identifying the capability gaps—recognizing what the organization could do today versus what it needed to do to give stakeholders the experience they truly wanted and needed.

Phase 2A: Improvements to the Existing Business Model

In this phase, the team focused on MyChildren's (as it was called at the time), the division that managed the ambulatory care centers at Children's Health. They began with a set of clear goals in mind, aimed at improving the ability of the existing business model to better meet the needs uncovered in phase 1. First, the team wanted to engage the staff to develop a common understanding of the key organizational capabilities that MyChildren's already had. The next priority was to identify the gaps between the existing experience that these capabilities were providing for children and their families and the criteria that the phase 1 research had revealed were needed to achieve the five elements of wellness. Finally, based on the identification of these experience gaps, specific methods for improvement could be defined within the opportunity spaces previously highlighted. The creation of a plan for the design of experiments to test the methods concluded phase 2A.

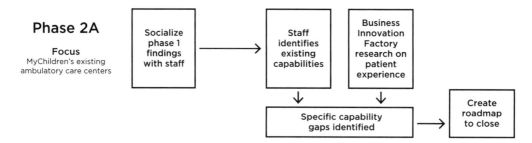

Flow of the process in phase 2A.

The first task in this phase was to help the staff at Children's Health truly understand and inaugurate a sense of ownership for the learnings in phase 1. The belief was that, by listening to the families tell the story of their own experiences, staff would be encouraged to move from a "place of judgment to a place of possibilities," as Eli described it. She continued:

> Rather than "this is how the system works and how they should be using it," we want to help staff shift their lens—get them out of their expert hat and into a beginner's mindset that is willing to look at the problem differently. When you create conditions where people can listen and dialogue, then you set things up for success.

The emotional shift, not the intellectual one, was most important, in Eli's view.

The next challenge was exploring the medical center's capabilities as an organization and how to integrate these with capabilities in the community. Children's Health staff were aware, BIF believed, of the say-do gap, of myths versus reality, but they hadn't been given permission to actually articulate where the lack of alignment might be and how to address the gaps. This was accomplished through a series of capability-mapping sessions with two different groups at Children's Health: those operating the ambulatory care centers at MyChildren's and a second group, the executives in the population health department, who oversaw a broader set of activities, including a health insurance company, care management, information technology, the Health and Wellness Alliance, virtual health, and faith-based and school-based programs. This work served two purposes. Eli explained:

> We wanted to understand the capabilities that the institution currently had so that we could use those in order to improve the existing practice, as well as be part of the new business model. We did capability mapping to understand where people were aligned and not aligned—could they articulate their business model and the capabilities they had today?

Another important role this stage played was to invite staff fully into the design process and to prepare them for the changes that would come, as Eli explained:

> People feel threatened by work they think is going to disrupt their job. You have to help them to see themselves in the future. One of the great things about capability mapping is that capabilities are made up of people, processes, and technologies. Once you map out what the key capability is, you can engage them in conversation about *How might we use this capability differently?* That helps them see a home for themselves. And use their stories, their insight, and their expertise so that they hear their voices reflected in the future state. You co-create so that they feel like they helped build this new model. There's an old adage that change is painful when done *to* you but powerful when done *by* you. If you can just tap into that, you're golden.

Because the team wanted people to surface where they actually were versus where they'd like to be, part of the workshop asked them to identify five or six myths and used the kind of visualization approach we have seen in so many stories in this book. They staged a "graphic jam": staff were asked to think visually about their organizations, the key things that they needed to be able to do in order to deliver on their core business model, and how these things were organized. Eli asked them to draw individual images and then posted the results for review, using the images to spur reflection on what was going on. Thinking about the resistance she often encountered to drawing, she observed:

> At Children's, they will often groan when I come into an executive team meeting, and say, "Please don't make us draw, Eli." And I can't draw to save my life. But you have to stop trying to use your language to understand. Draw me a picture, because your words are full of meaning that nobody else shares. So it's about trying to get at people's mental models and really tease out the differences, to understand how far apart people are.

Examining the differences between how staff from various functional silos viewed their capability set allowed work to be done across the Children's Health system. The involvement of community stakeholders also highlighted the lack of integration between the medical care systems and the community service agencies.

Ethnography in Phase 2

Meanwhile, Children's Health staff and the BIF team engaged in more ethnographic fieldwork to identify critical experience gaps—differences between the actual, present patient experience and the experience that families needed to help them take ownership of their personal wellness. The previous phase 1 research had focused broadly on families' lives; this phase 2 research focused more narrowly on their health care–related experiences. The team interviewed patients and their families before and after medical appointments, observed primary care practices in action, and shadowed patients through both well and sick care.

Emerging from this work was a clear strategic insight highlighting the current model's false assumptions: "It was apparent that the medical home model in use was designed based on the existence of a set of behaviors and mindsets that the population it serves rarely possess," Eli explained. Comparison of the assumptions underlying MyChildren's existing delivery design with their target stakeholders' actual positioning along the five elements of wellness illustrated the central dilemma. To work well, MyChildren's existing model assumed that patients and their families already occupied the "wellness" end of the continuum and had a balanced outlook, exploratory mindset, strong support network, stable sense of self, and connected knowledge. In reality, few families in the Dallas population enjoyed many of these elements. Their realities were more often a reactive outlook, an avoidance mindset, a weak support network, an unstable sense of self, and a disengaged information flow. This disconnect was a key factor contributing to the inappropriate use of emergency services that Children's Health was experiencing.

BIF also used another tool we have seen before in our stories, jobs-to-be-done analysis, to specify more clearly some of the critical functional, emotional, and spiritual tasks that needed to be accomplished to move families toward the wellness end of the continuum.

JOBS TO BE DONE

ELEMENT OF WELLNESS	REAL WORLD NEED	JOB TO BE DONE
PERSONAL POWER	Emotional	**Agency:** Permission Giving, Leveling Up
SENSE OF SELF	Spiritual	**Self Awareness:** Expanded Horizons, Story Sharing, Reflection
SYSTEM OF SUPPORT	Social	**Trusted Networks:** "Your Person," Confidant, Andragogy
BALANCED OUTLOOK	Functional	**Resourcefulness:** Map of the Territory, Security in Structure
CONNECTED KNOWLEDGE	Functional	**Interpretation:** Meaning Making, New Lens/Filters, Translate Experiences into Growth Opportunities

Jobs to be done to move families toward wellness.

The BIF team's research eventually identified twelve specific experience gaps, all relating to one of the five elements of wellness. For each gap, team members described the experience currently delivered by MyChildren's, compared it with aspirations for meeting the phase 1 wellness goals, and specified the capabilities needed to close the disparity. For instance, the presence of a strong (versus weak) support network was an aspect highlighted by phase 1 research, yet generally only parents were engaged in any child's medical process. A potential answer could be to develop a new Children's Health educational or social capability aimed at enlarging a child's health network. Within the support network concept, existing MyChildren's practices focused almost exclusively on the child, whereas research made clear that family health was a strong influence on children. Hence, targeting family health became another capability-building opportunity.

A second clear insight accounted for other factors influencing a family's use of medical care services: the nonmedical determinants of health had a much greater influence over a family's health and well-being than medical factors had. The Centers for Medicare and Medicaid Services has estimated that clinical care accounts for only 20 percent of the modifiable factors that influence health. Other critical factors include socioeconomic status, transportation, housing, and social or environmental stressors—essentially, anything in a family's environment that influences the health of various family members. For example, the nonmedical determinants of health, which were not being addressed by insurance companies or medical care providers, might include asthma triggers in substandard housing environments, which cause a child to have repeated asthma attacks and lead to frequent use of the emergency room.

The Growing Role of the Alliance

At Children's Health, the realization dawned that addressing this constellation of medical and nonmedical influences on health, which families faced each and every day, was a wicked problem that required a systems approach, collaboration between uncommon partners, and a bundle of interventions that were aligned and integrated. The Health and Wellness Alliance would play a critical role as the integrator, aligning and focusing individual community initiatives focused on children, under a common agenda, to achieve measurable impact in selected areas, such as childhood asthma.

WHAT IS AN UNCOMMON PARTNER?

An important cornerstone of BIF's philosophy is the value of actively seeking what they call "uncommon partners," collaborators who live in a different part of the ecosystem that surrounds your challenge. As BIF's Saul Kaplan described it: "Collaborators are everywhere . . . New ideas, perspectives, and the big value-creating opportunities are in the gray areas between the unusual suspects. It seems so obvious, yet we spend most of our time in our respective silos." He advises enabling "random collisions," because "magic happens in the interstitial space between us." We see this idea play out in the asthma example, where different communities were all working hard to address the issue, all doing "God's work," as Peter described it, but all with limited resources, capabilities, and reach. Architecting a committed and coordinated ecosystem that works together—pooling resources and building on each partner's differing capabilities, knowledge, and relationships—lets the magic begin.

The changing of the institution's name from Children's Medical Center of Dallas to Children's Health System of Texas was an important symbolic step in publicly recognizing that the role of the medical center in the community needed to change. Peter explained the rationale:

> We wanted to help people (staff) understand that the future payment system was going to move away from paying strictly for the actual costs of medical services to paying for health outcomes; they would move from paying for individuals to paying for populations and their health. If we're going to be responsible for population health and we know that nonmedical issues are even more important than medical ones, we knew that we had to look at ourselves differently, to see our responsibility as much broader than just medical care. That is why we changed our name.

Implementing the New Approach

Now that the team had identified the experience and capability gaps, they went to work with MyChildren's primary care practitioners to begin to implement the new approach in the existing business. This effort did not go as planned, and they did not achieve the results they had hoped for. As Peter explained:

> After a while, we realized that focusing on the physician was just not going to work. In retrospect, it was never going to work. Why it didn't work was quite logical, but we didn't see that at the time. First, the doctors were organized to deliver acute care services. That's what they got paid for delivering. Insurance reimbursed them for individuals. They didn't see their role from a systems perspective, from a family perspective. It was unrealistic of us to think those organizations would take responsibility for the health and wellness of a family. They had no time and no capacity to integrate their work with the social agencies who could, in fact, be a great help to pediatricians. We realized then that we couldn't drive the change from the perspective of primary care. We needed a separate integrator function.

The team concluded that if the medical homes could not be the integrator—they were too individual-patient focused and reactive, didn't see their role in the larger system, and didn't have the time or the capacity to work at that level—then the team would need to create a separate integrator function. No one stakeholder could take the lead by themselves. Peter noted:

> The key learning that I hadn't realized before was the need for an integrator function. These uncommon partners don't naturally work together unless there is an integrator. In our new model, the lowest-level integrators are the individual coaches and navigators; at midlevel, we have the Alliance; the highest level is changing policy—working with government and insurers.

Phase 2B: Business Model Generation

Phase 1 provided the foundational research to identify population needs; phase 2A examined My-Children's existing practice to identify experience gaps and the missing capabilities driving them, which needed to be addressed to accomplish Dallas families' well-being goals. Cumulatively, these activities highlighted the need for change at a broader systems level and pointed toward the need to design a transformational business model that was wellness (versus sickness) centered, citizen (versus physician) driven, prevention (versus intervention) focused, partnership based, and community supported. The new model, team members believed, needed to be rooted in a decentralized yet integrated system of support for both the health and the well-being of families, as defined and directed by families themselves, leveraging trusted sources within the community.

Critically important, a financially sustainable system of wellness also needed to be created. To accomplish this, the Health and Wellness Alliance and the BIF team focused the next stage of the process on a highly participatory design approach, aimed at engaging a diverse group of thinkers and consumers from the Alliance to help them explore what a revolutionary model might look like. Together, they would construct a new ecosystem.

Flow of the process in phase 2B.

Eli talked about why this approach was critical:

> I'm a big proponent of participatory design—designing with the population and not just
> for them. There is often this tall wall that institutions try and build between themselves
> and their users, and they overthink participatory design and make it more difficult than
> it needs to be. They wonder about concerns like who are the right people to engage and
> will they show up? That's used as the point of resistance for not doing it. But just go out
> and talk to somebody. I once read this tweet that said it doesn't take ten thousand hours
> to perfect the art of talking to a customer—just start a conversation with the person next
> to you.

Business model generation began with four different sessions aimed at mapping community resources and developing a deeper understanding of what Eli called "the mechanics that define trust and connectedness within communities." The team met with thirty-plus families across west and south Dallas, in diverse community settings, to identify the key institutions, resources, and people who might offer valuable local knowledge for designing the new business model.

Next, having been identified by the families themselves, these trusted sources were invited to a participatory design studio focused on a single question: How might we design a new system, one that connects convenient clinical care with self-managed well-being?

The session that addressed this question brought together hospital administrators, physicians, nurses, social workers, and staff from Dallas school districts, the Dallas Housing Authority, the YMCA, and various faith-based organizations. The BIF team shared their phase 1 learnings with the group, identified opportunity spaces, and provided a sense of the big questions facing the design task. Next, the individual attendees, working independently, identified the capabilities that each of their invited institutions might contribute toward addressing the health and life problems. They captured their ideas on sticky notes. Each attendee was then invited into a group conversation at one of five tables, where they shared their individual ideas with each other and clustered the ideas around common themes.

On the basis of their combined ideas, each table was asked to imagine a new end-to-end well-being experience, from the point at which children and their families entered the experience to the point at which they exited, with specific phases identified: awareness, entry, engagement, and extension. Each of the five tables had diverse participants working together—yet they all designed much the same model. Children's Health staff, with support from BIF, then built out a one-page value proposition that captured the new model they had created together, which they all committed to adopt.

Family Health and Well-Being Value Proposition

Customer Problem

Up to 80% of health outcomes are driven by non-medical factors, including environmental, behavioral, and social determinants of health.

Healthcare systems and insurance plans are reactive by economic design. The primary focus is high-cost treatment with minimal focus on low-cost education and prevention (medical self-responsibility, early detection, early intervention, health maintenance).

Medical and insurance services focus on individual patients with limited regard for the context of family – including general community circumstance, i.e., employment, crime, education, health literacy and economic stability.

Silo fragmentation within and between medical providers, insurance coverage and community services. The result is delay, confusion, contradiction and medical error.

Investment and Expenses

- *Innovation:* Design thinking and leadership staff
- *Navigators:* Care management and family coaching staff
- *Integrators:* Alliance - to leverage community partnerships
- *Services:* Value-based contracts with community agencies
- *Technology:* Workflow and interoperable data solutions

Our Solution

Provide families a framework that enables a greater level of self-direction with regard to addressing both medical and non-medical determinants of health and wellbeing.

Key Service Elements:
- Coaching of family-led action planning
- Navigation of resources available from healthcare providers and community agencies
- Coordination of care across all categories of health determinants

Success Measures

- Enrollment in CHST insurance services products
- Engagement in family well-being programs
- Measurable progress toward family goals
- A positive experience
- Improved well-being and positive health outcomes
- Appropriate medical utilization with lower cost of care

Our Unique Value Proposition

We believe enabling family well-being leads to individual health, which ultimately reduces the reactive dependence on acute episodic medical services.

Competitive Advantage

- Mission "make life better for children" enabled through family orientation
- Alliance capabilities to bring stakeholders to the table around children and families
- 4-year journey in deep listening and co-creation with families
- Understanding of - and a head start on - technological needs and value-based capabilities

Scaling Sequence

- Design workshops
- 24-family prototype
- StarKids
- ACO covered lives
- CHST employee population
- Medicaid/CHIP

Customer Segments

Covered lives where we have 1st or 2nd dollar risk - and their families:
- Medicaid managed care
- CHST employee & dependents
- Commercial agreements

Revenue Streams and Return on Investment

- Reduced spending on care for covered lives
- Increased plan enrollment due to differential service offerings
- Grants and gifts associated with community health and non-medical determinants
- Medicaid Section 1115 waiver funding
- CMS – Innovation Center funding or similar sources
- Increased market share for medical services

The Children's Health value proposition.

To capture how these system-level flows impacted the experience of individual children and their families, BIF visualized their experience journey. They elaborated on each of the four phases (awareness, entry, engagement, and extension) and included multiple steps, as well as the people and technol-

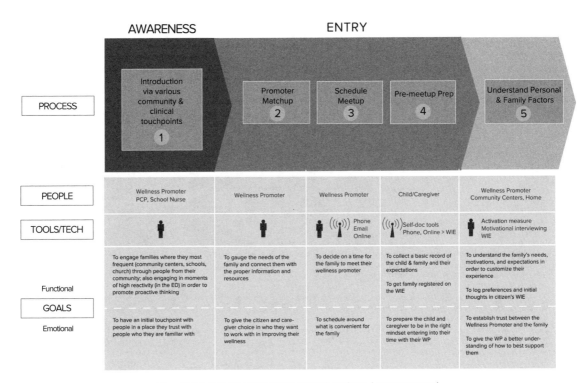

The Children's Health journey map (continued on next page).

ogy involved in that step. Both the functional and the emotional goals, or jobs to be done, were emphasized. As an individual came into the system to be matched with a wellness promoter through various community and clinical touch points, the wellness promoter scheduled meetings, assessed needs, set goals, and created wellness plans, together with the individual or family, and then finally reached out to a broader support network to motivate action and access resources. Finally, BIF brought experience to life by chronicling the story of particular patients and their families under different scenarios: wellness, sickness care, and chronic care management. A fourth scenario told the story of a first-generation change maker.

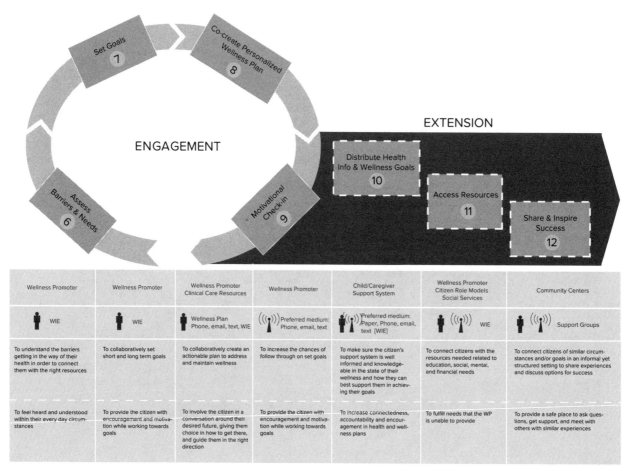

Wellness Promoter	Wellness Promoter	Wellness Promoter Clinical Care Resources	Wellness Promoter	Child/Caregiver Support System	Wellness Promoter Citizen Role Models Social Services	Community Centers
WIE	WIE	Wellness Plan Phone, email, text, WIE	Preferred medium: Phone, email, text	Preferred medium: Paper, Phone, email, text [WIE]	WIE	Support Groups
To understand the barriers getting in the way of their health in order to connect them with the right resources	To collaboratively set short and long term goals	To collaboratively create an actionable plan to address and maintain wellness	To increase the chances of follow through on set goals	To make sure the citizen's support system is well informed and knowledge-able in the state of their wellness and how they can best support them in achiev-ing their goals	To connect citizens with the resources needed related to education, social, mental, and financial needs	To connect citizens of similar circum-stances and/or goals in an informal yet structured setting to share experiences and discuss options for success
To feel heard and understood within their every day circum-stances	To provide the citizen with encouragement and motiva-tion while working towards goals	To involve the citizen in a conversation around their desired future, giving them choice in how to get there, and guide them in the right direction	To provide the citizen with encouragement and motiva-tion while working towards goals	To increase connectedness, accountability and encour-agement in health and well-ness plans	To fulfill needs that the WP is unable to provide	To provide a safe place to ask ques-tions, get support, and meet with others with similar experiences

The Children's Health journey map (continued).

Designing a Learning Launch

Children's Health and the Health and Wellness Alliance elected to move their ideas forward by conducting an experiment in a specific segment. They decided to begin with asthma, one of the most prevalent and utilization-intensive childhood diseases. Their aim was to define a common agenda and goals. Until then, few in the Alliance knew each other. Peter described their coming together:

We had no clue how we related to each other. So we put together the asthma equation, a visual model for asthma and the factors that were affecting these families and kids. When we put this together, people were stunned. We were all working on the same thing, but from different parts of the elephant. But none of us had ever looked at the whole elephant.

The early indicators from the asthma work provide strong support that Children's Health and their Alliance partners are moving in the right direction. By progressively linking families with clinical, social, community, public health, philanthropic, educational, environmental, and government programs, the statistic that started the whole project—emergency room visits—was halved for asthma over the four-year period. Outcomes went beyond utilization of medical care. While doing home visits, for instance, the Alliance realized that many houses had asthma triggers that needed to be cleaned up, sometimes by landlords, and though the Alliance had no formal authority, it was able to work with city health inspectors to change inspection codes. "But there is no silver bullet," Peter observed, "no simple solutions. We need multiple solutions that involve multiple stakeholders."

A critical piece of the puzzle was how to sustainably fund the new business model. Though payment models were shifting, fee-for-service remained the dominant mechanism. How could they fund a system that required payment for services that no longer needed to be delivered? Children's Health stood ready to make more investments, but it could not fund the entire system. Government-funded social agencies lacked the flexibility to shift priorities and reallocate funds in the short term. Community agencies lived on limited funding, year to year, in the form of grants and gifts. Relying on annual grants and philanthropy provided unreliable funding. Building a workable, sustainable economic model would require the same kind of creative thinking that developed the new business model in the first place.

Fortunately, as we have seen in other stories, individual repertoire helped the team to see new opportunities. Remember Dr. Melissa Casey's secret life as an Australian tax expert prior to heading the psychiatric clinic at Monash Medical Centre? In a similar way, Peter's decades of deep involvement in the insurance industry and understanding of funding led him to see what others might have missed: a chance to use the state of Texas's Medicaid program, which covered children and pregnant women, as a funding mechanism. By combining private and public sources of funding, Children's Health could use resources from its licensed insurance company (that resulted from enrollees' utilizing less expensive medical care), coupled with funding from the Texas Medicaid Section 1115 Waiver program, plus philanthropy and grants.

Such funding would give them stability for five years to experiment with the new approach to determine what kinds of outcomes they could produce. Children's Health's existing HMO would receive the state funding, and the prototype they were preparing to roll out would enroll twelve thousand to fifteen thousand children in their HMO. Peter explained how this would work:

> Texas state Medicaid contracts with private HMOs to act as insurance intermediaries, paying them a fixed premium per month per child to provide care. This intermediary acts almost like a bank: it holds the dollars and controls spending. It can reallocate resources for more preventative care. In this way, insurance companies can be catalysts for change.

Eventually, Peter hypothesized, the new preventative model will generate profits that can be reinvested.

The team also believed that measurement would be critical—first, to establish whether the changes did in fact increase family well-being, and then to examine the link between family well-being and a host of longer-term measures around health outcomes and care utilization. Plans were already in place for systematic evaluation of the prototype, incorporating the four levels of outcomes in the Kirkpatrick evaluation model: experience in the program, confidence in the ability to improve wellness, progress against the family action plan, and improvement in the family well-being quotient—a measure of family wellness that the team developed, based on the five key dimensions of wellness that the BIF research revealed during phase 1.

As they prepared to roll out their prototype, the team prepared a simple overview of the key elements to guide the process.

Reflections on the Process

The Children's Health story illustrates how design thinking can contribute to two core elements essential to successful strategic change: a deep, fact-based understanding of the current reality (of both stakeholders' needs and current organizational capabilities) and a new vision for the future (a more promising value proposition and the new capabilities needed to deliver it). Design thinking allowed Children's Health to ground their discussions of the ideal future in the real world of their patients' lives, rather than in the world as their clinicians wished it would be, "if only" patients used the system correctly. In doing so, it allowed them to devise a strategy capable of addressing all of their needs.

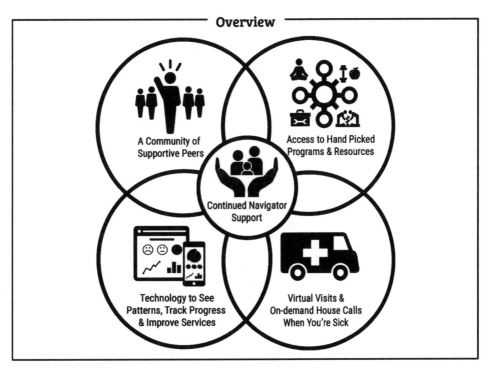

An overview of the new business model.

New strategies that offer dramatic increases in value creation for stakeholders and are executable within the constraints of today's reality emerge most readily from such an approach. They do this by creating a strategic conversation that is fundamentally concerned with the two gaps that really matter in creating new business models: (1) the gap between the experience that a customer is having today versus the experience the customer would prefer to have (BIF's experience gap), and (2) the gap between the outcomes that an organization is currently capable of delivering versus the capabilities needed to close the customer experience gap (BIF's capability gap).

This entire backcasting process rests on the quality of insights about what is missing for customers today. Here, design thinking's ethnographic approach in **What *is*** provides the tools for a deeper analysis of needs, as when it helped the MyChildren's team identify the five elements of wellness and translate them into design criteria. Design thinking's possibility-driven focus in **What *if*** allows the translation of these criteria into a set of solutions that are then tested against both stakeholder and organizational needs and constraints during **What *wows*** and **What *works***. When the attempts to transform the existing business model of MyChildren's ambulatory care approach failed, it was evidence of the power of the existing medical illness–centered model to resist change. This key learning freed Peter and his team from their attempts to continue to push (and likely fail) to reform the existing business model and set them instead on a new path to co-create a community-based system focused on wellness. It is design thinking's tools and process, expertly deployed, that make all of this possible (plus, of course, courageous leadership).

As someone who had been immersed in the world of health care reform for decades, Peter reflected on how the introduction of design thinking changed the hospital's innovation conversation. His takeaways centered on the experience of deep listening, the time it took, and power of structured conversation across the health care ecosystem:

> Really reaching an understanding of the families themselves and the community social agencies that surrounded them—that was very different than anything I've ever done before. And I realized that there were levels of listening that I'd never understood. It took a long time to understand and reflect on that. And I had never pursued an ongoing collaboration before with such a range of uncommon partners, one with such a sense of purpose, that was pulled together in that very structured and focused way—a group of people who had all been working hard to improve health for kids, but not working together. Doing "God's work" but with negligible impact and sustainability. Now we have a common agenda, shared measurements, and new funding opportunities. That is very different than anything I have ever experienced previously in the world of health care.

Eli, too, talked about the power of bringing design thinking and business model innovation together:

> People always ask us what the right business model is, the one that will solve their problems. But the thing is that there is no right business model. A business model is a

generative act. The whole notion of design thinking is that it gives us the power to work in really messy areas like this. Don't just shy away from messy kinds of problems—find a way to frame it that feels good and powerful.

Peter concurred:

Health care badly needs new business models. That's what I have learned on this journey. We have wicked problems. And we have a lot of programs, but what we need is whole new business models. We need to pool experiences and learn from each other. It is going to be an exciting next few years. We are going to make design thinking part of our DNA.

The collaborative strategy envisioned in the evolving Children's Health model brings with it the complex task of coordinating the network of partners and establishing priorities and capabilities. But it also brings a deeper pool of resources, understanding, and commitment on the part of the partners working together. They have a common (or should we say *uncommon*?) shared sense of why the existing health care model is neither successful nor sustainable, and they see a shared possibility that their collaboration can move toward a different, truly healthful future.

Yet, at some level, this seemingly complex task of marshaling support and consensus across such a diverse set of partners seems very simple to Peter:

If you've sat in different chairs, listened deeply, you start to understand what success looks like. Families want their kids to be able to play sports. Medical center folks want no crises in asthma control, no emergency room visits. Docs want families to follow the medical directives prescribed for their child. Insurers want reduced utilization—and data. The YMCA needs funding. Pastors want people to go to church. Social service agencies want stronger family ties. Each stakeholder needs to be rewarded. So my job is actually pretty easy: I just listen.

PART III

Moving into Action:
Bringing Design Thinking
to Your Organization

In the ten years that we have been teaching design thinking, we have worked with individuals from many backgrounds— elementary school teachers, MBA students, doctors and nurses, NASA scientists, business managers, accountants, and leaders from the government and nonprofit worlds. Many came with serious doubts about their ability to think creatively and lead innovation in their organizations. They believed that, without support from wonderful design experts like those we have met in our stories—like Kingwood consultant Colum Lowe at BEING, or Eli MacLaren at BIF, or CTAA's Peer Insight team—they could not introduce and practice design thinking in their organizations. But our experience working with people new to design tells a different story: we all have these abilities within us, waiting for an invitation to show up!

Remember Ken Skodacek at the FDA, Marliza Rivera at Whiteriver Indian Hospital, and Dr. Don Campbell at Monash? None of these inspiring innovation leaders had any formal training in design. What they had was a passion for exploration and learning, and the courage to try.

In part 2, each of the ten organizations we met chose a combination of tools to suit its purpose. Some emphasized exploration tools like journey mapping, personas, or jobs to be done. Others focused on testing tools like assumption surfacing and learning launches. Nearly all used visualization, ethnographic interviewing, and prototyping. They often gave differing attention to the four questions—some emphasized the exploration of stakeholder needs, asking **What *is*?** and **What *if*?**, while others focused on testing solutions, asking **What *wows*?** and **What *works*?**

The organizational paths they chose were equally varied. Some established innovation labs, ran workshops, and offered mentoring. Others worked with consultants, universities, or other outside partners. Nearly all offered some kind of training in design thinking—though their specific approaches were as varied as the partners they worked with.

The richness of this variety is both stimulating and intimidating. So many tools and methods, so little time. For the novice, and especially for the Georges among us, raised in an Innovation I world, the array of choices can seem bewildering. Where to even begin? What tools to use and questions to answer?

In answering this, we think back to Carolyn Jeskey's advice to her CTAA partners: keep it simple. Learning a new approach—especially one as different as design thinking seems—can be intimidating. Success requires support and structure. Fortunately, the support we need can come from the *process* itself.

In this section, our focus is on helping you to take learnings from the inspiring stories in part 2 and make design thinking work for you. In these final chapters, we will look at one more story of a group of innovators hard at work making their own small slice of the world a better place. This story, however, differs from the stories in part 2. In this story, we will tag along, step by step, on the journey of a group of dedicated educators, Joan Wells and her team at Gateway College and Career Academy (GCCA), as they work through their challenge, using a comprehensive design thinking method we have developed at Darden.

Our experience teaching people who are new to design tells us that using this kind of detailed end-to-end process to guide learners' initial design thinking efforts significantly aids in developing mastery. Structure and specificity reassures and motivates those practicing design thinking methods for the first time. It helps them see where they are headed and teaches them how to transition successfully between the exploration, idea generation, and testing phases.

As discussed in part 1, the design thinking method we use focuses on four simple questions: **What *is*?**, **What *if*?**, **What *wows*?**, and **What *works*?** In our design thinking tool kit, these questions are accompanied by fifteen specific steps that lead innovators through the process as they seek answers.

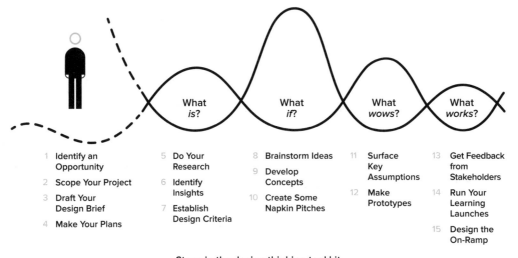

Steps in the design thinking tool kit.

Once innovators get comfortable with design thinking's methods, tools, and mindsets, they mix and match the steps, emphasizing some and skipping others, and pick and choose among the variety of tools offered. As design thinking becomes more natural and intuitive, they adapt our process to fit the needs of their specific projects. But, in the beginning, those learning design thinking benefit from a systematic approach. The four-question, fifteen-step methodology creates an educational environment in which the ambiguity of the innovation space feels (and is) more manageable. The process reassures team members that it is safe to convene new kinds of conversations.

In the next two chapters, we will follow the educators at GCCA as they tackle their very first design thinking challenge: how to reduce the dropout rate. The GCCA team utilized the four-question process in its entirety and captured each step in a set of templates provided in *The Designing for Growth Field Book*—and generously offered to share them with you. Their work is an excellent example of the design thinking process in motion.

Armed with nothing more than an online course to teach them how and a commitment to improving the experience of their students, they successfully introduced design thinking to GCCA. In chapters 13 and 14, they share not only the process and the works in progress they created along the way but also their emotional journey.

So let's meet Joan and her team.

CHAPTER THIRTEEN

The Four-Question Methodology in Action:
Laying the Foundation

In our four-question, fifteen-step design thinking methodology, almost half of the process is spent laying the foundation for innovation, before we even get to idea generation. For those with an Innovation I mindset, where brainstorming ideas (step 8 in our approach) comes first, this gradual on-ramp can be tough to accept. But the groundwork we lay in steps 1 through 7 is the reason why creative ideas show up when we are ready for them in step 8. To better understand how this works in practice, let's look at the process in action.

Gateway College and Career Academy in Riverside, California, is an early-college charter high school for students who have dropped out or fallen significantly behind in their credits toward high school graduation. A Gates Foundation–sponsored initiative, the Gateway program addresses a serious problem: every year, an estimated 1.3 million students in the United States drop out of high school. Lacking a high school diploma, these youth face well-documented prospects of low wages and limited opportunities. Gateway's mission is to offer a second chance to these students, to help them succeed academically, and to prepare them for a more promising future. The Gateway program, begun in 2004, is nationally known.

At GCCA, students attend school on a college campus and enter as a cohort to complete an intensive foundation term together, after which they enroll in high school and college classes, which are double-counted toward high school and community college degrees. In this story, an interdisciplinary team of educators at GCCA, led by Joan Wells, uses the design thinking process to identify a problem scope with creative potential; to engage a diverse set of students, faculty, and staff in the conversation; to curate critical insights; and to align the team behind an array of solutions, all with the goal of keeping at-risk students in school. In this chapter, we follow the GCCA team as they work through steps 1 to 7 of our fifteen-step process. These early steps lay the foundation for their idea generation and testing process (steps 8 to 15), which we examine in depth in chapter 14.

We first met Joan in a Coursera MOOC (massive online open course) that provides a high-level overview of design thinking that we have taught to almost two hundred thousand students, beginning in fall 2013. Intrigued by the potential of design thinking in the education sector, Joan joined us for the inaugural run of a more detailed, step-based course that Darden began offering in June 2014. She has worked closely with us ever since, becoming a skilled facilitator in the four-question methodology and acting as a senior mentor to students in our online offerings.

Back in 2013, design thinking was new to Joan and her colleagues at GCCA, but she was already committed to learner-centered strategies at Riverside College and had been part of the initial GCCA planning team. Joan joined GCCA's board in October 2013 and was asked to focus on output measures. As she learned more about the method, she realized that using design thinking to look for ways to address one of education's thorniest issues—reconnecting disengaged youth to high school diplomas—would be a natural fit.

Gateway programs throughout the country serve an extremely diverse student population, and the one in Riverside is no exception. Students there range in age from sixteen to twenty-one, with an average age at entry of seventeen. Reflecting the school's Southern California location, nearly two-thirds of students self-identify as Hispanic/Latino, 20 percent as white, and 9 percent as African American. Most enter GCCA significantly behind in high school credits and are well on their way to leaving school. Reasons for their disengagement vary, ranging from challenges associated with transitioning to high school and navigating adolescence (like bullying, gender identity, and pregnancy) to personal and family crises. Many disengage from their high school experience when they sense that others, including their teachers, don't believe in them. As described on the Gateway to College National Network website:

> Every Gateway to College student has a unique story about how they came to the program. Some students found themselves out of school and in need of another opportunity

to complete their degree and pursue a postsecondary credential. Others found that their traditional high school setting did not provide the holistic support they needed to be successful. All of our graduates share stories that are a testament to the power of hard work, perseverance, and support from caring adults.

In 2014, the GCCA program in Riverside celebrated its tenth anniversary while facing new challenges: a leadership transition from its founders; enrollment issues; changes in the California Education Code, which mandated greater on-campus seat times for students; and an expanded mission. In 2013, the school sought and received authorization as a charter school from the Riverside County Office of Education, which enabled the school to expand to multiple sites within the Riverside Community College District.

Lower-than-desired retention rates led to continuous pressure to find new students. This raised several questions for GCCA leadership. Had recruitment efforts inadvertently positioned the early-college high school as a less rigorous experience than it was designed to be? Was GCCA increasingly attracting the students who were furthest behind, and were some not ready to engage academically? Were they finding the students for whom the program had been designed, and were these students succeeding? All of these issues had implications for GCCA's mission, its program design, and its commitment to the community.

In March 2014, the new GCCA leadership team—interim director Miguel Contreras and dean of instruction Kathleen Bywater—joined forces with Joan Wells and Shelagh Camak, vice president of workforce and resource development. Each brought a passionate commitment to enhancing their learner-centered focus. Shelagh, with extensive experience in program and service design for nontraditional students, was the primary designer of Riverside's Gateway model. Together, the team focused first on the school's recruitment pipeline. As Joan explained:

> For this learner population, we can be very successful at bringing students in, but keeping them in is always a challenge. So the problem I was invited to help the team work with is one of recruitment: using our recruitment process to enable their success. We don't screen to select the best students or those facing the fewest challenges. We don't want to achieve success that way. Our model is to bring students in and then build a

holistic counseling structure around them . . . These are great, smart students, but they're dealing with a lot of stuff in life. We don't do students a favor if we bring them in and not support them. They have to do the work.

Initially, the project was expected to be primarily analytic, using the wealth of data already available to the team to illuminate the academy's "funnel" numbers: How were students coming in? Where and why were they falling out? What were the issues?

Design Thinking Enters the Picture

The GCCA team struggled as they worked to make sense of the sea of data on the subject. Initial measures didn't always make sense to the team. Data were collected and entered into systems by three external entities: California's community college system, the state's K–12 system, and the Gateway to College National Network. By design, each of these systems reflected different assumptions about structure, regulatory environment, and policy arena. As the team reviewed standard reports generated by these systems, they realized that they were dealing not only with multiple measures but also with different field, cohort, and outcome definitions. None of the systems truly captured the outreach and applicant experiences, nor did they meaningfully capture students' reasons for leaving or not engaging. It was difficult to decipher what was actually happening with students as they were recruited, enrolled, and progressed, or as they left the program. Even when reasons were coded, they weren't at a level that provided insights. And because of the changes in the California Education Code, it was not even clear that past program data would be a good predictor of the future.

As Joan learned more about Darden's four-question structured approach to design thinking, she found that its four questions and fifteen steps helped her to look through a new lens at the challenges that GCCA faced. She encouraged the GCCA team to consider using the new approach:

> As we worked, it became clear that we really needed to go back to the learners and look
> at who we are reaching, what's the message that they're getting out there, what's our
> message to the community college and to the various counselors at the high schools,
> so that we're actually bringing in students that not only have the skill set to begin the
> foundation term but also really understand the day-to-day commitments of attending

and turning in work. We needed to do some creative thinking and we knew that. While we definitely had a rich understanding of what the issues were that students faced, we needed to look for additional insights that we might not see because we're in the trenches. And we knew that we needed to experiment a lot, because the answers just are not there. It's not like we can go to a best practice and pull it off the shelf.

To Joan and the GCCA team, the issues seemed made for a design thinking approach. The team ordered *The Designing for Growth Field Book,* which laid out the fifteen steps and offered a series of templates to walk the learner through the process. Serendipitously, Joan received an e-mail announcing Darden's new in-depth online course. After consulting with Shelagh, Joan enrolled in the course. The team adopted a modified train-the-trainer model, using *The Designing for Growth Field Book* and Joan's course experience to supplement the team's project work. They decided to give the systematic process a try on their funnel challenge.

At the Beginning: Before the Four Questions

As many of our stories in part 2 demonstrated, one of the biggest contributions of design thinking is to hold us in the problem space long enough to develop the kind of deeper insights into the problem that foster more creative ideas later on. Joan knew this to be true, and before even beginning to address the first question of the **What *is*** stage, she and her team committed to a series of discussions aimed at ensuring that they had the right kind of problem for design thinking, a scope that would give them an actionable result, a clear, shared sense of what the project entailed and who should be involved, and a research plan to get them there.

Step 1: Identify an Opportunity

Not all problems lend themselves to design thinking. If you are sure that you understand the problem and have good data to solve it with, then use it! Save design thinking for Innovation II–type problems—those where you don't have good data, where you worry that you may be solving the wrong problem, or where multiple stakeholders can't seem to agree even on what the problem actually is, much less on solutions to it. Save design thinking for areas of high uncertainty—areas where real human beings aren't making the choices we'd like them to make and existing approaches and solutions aren't working. Remember that design thinking is not a one-size-fits-all solution; it is best for certain types of problems.

What we call "tame" problems lend themselves to traditional Innovation I approaches, in which we can agree on a definition of the issue, identify alternative existing solutions, and compare the proposed solutions for cause and effect to arrive at a best answer. Messy, wicked problems, however, often have a lot of data, but it's debatable whether the data are actually relevant and cause-and-effect relationships are difficult to predict. Usually, when you find yourself questioning your own definition of the issue, you're looking at a good choice for a design thinking approach.

Joan and her team worked through a list of questions in *The Designing for Growth Field Book* to help them assess whether the challenge was suited to a design thinking approach. The answers confirmed their initial thoughts. Their issue was clearly human centered—that is, a deep understanding of the learners and other key stakeholders, such as faculty and counselors, was essential to success. Though they had hunches about the nature of the problem, the team faced many unknowns and many interdependent aspects, and they felt the need to explore the problem itself more, another indicator of design thinking's relevance. The team also had substantial data—almost too much—but only a limited framework to guide their analysis and interpretation. Finally, a new leadership team was supportive of trying a different approach.

To begin the project and build understanding, Joan got permission from Darden to share a set of readings and a video of design thinking in practice at a Danish meals-on-wheels program, available for free on the Design@Darden website, which she thought would resonate with the team. By May, the data project had officially transitioned into a design thinking project using the four-question, fifteen-step methodology. GCCA's dean of students, Robin Acosta, joined Joan, Shelagh, Miguel, and Kathleen on the team.

Kathleen found the start-up of the process exhilarating: "I was very high when we very first started. I was excited. I was learning so much!" Joan, as team facilitator of the design process, felt similar excitement, but also anxiety:

> As the project started, I thought we were on a path to something, but there was a question—is this the right path? Can we do it? We're exploring terrain that nobody else has

figured out either, as we try to find the better solution for these learners. The school was already staffed with very competent professionals, so it wasn't that anyone was doing anything wrong. The question was "What else are we missing?"

Question	Design thinking is appropriate if:	Linear analytic methods may be better if:
Is the problem human-centered?	*Deep understanding of the learners and other humans (HS counselors, parents, GCCA personnel, etc.) is necessary and possible.*	
How clearly do we understand the problem itself?	*We have some knowledge, instincts and hunches. We need to explore and reach agreement on appropriate action.*	
What's the level of uncertainty?	*There are many unknowns as well as significant program model changes.*	*We need to bring in data on past pipeline experience but due to model change these may not predict the future.*
What's the degree of complexity?	*There are many connecting and interdependent facets to pipeline. It is hard to know where to start, so we've selected a focus on the beginning of the pipeline (to completion).*	*Quantitative analytic methods, though necessary, have not been sufficient in solving similar problems.*
What data is already available to you?	*There is a wealth of unanalyzed data but a limited framework to guide analysis and interpretation.*	*We have data, but still need to validate it and adopt a framework(s) for analysis.*
What's your level of curiosity and influence?	*Leadership is highly interested in exploring and willing to assist. Leadership includes director, academic and support services deans, and CC VP overseeing Gateway day to day.*	*We will have to follow some routine and mandated processes. However, as a Charter School, we might be able to adopt significant variations to improve outcomes.*

Step 1: Questions to identify an opportunity.

This kind of anxiety is not unusual at the start of a design thinking project. We are stepping into the unknown, and all but the most intrepid Geoffreys among us tend to experience a mix of excitement and concern. Years ago, as we started to teach the design thinking approach, we felt the same way. Time, however, has taught us to trust the process (as Dr. Don Campbell at Monash Medical Centre reminded us earlier).

Shelagh and Joan were mindful of the new leadership and the potential that the design thinking process might hold:

> One of our goals was to break the team out of the trenches—help them get to that thirty-thousand-foot view—to move a bit away from the accountability culture that you have in K–12, to more of an inquiry and assessment culture.

Convinced that design thinking was right for them, the GCCA team moved to step 2, scoping their project.

Step 2: Scope Your Project

The next challenge the team faced was how to frame the specific opportunity they wanted to pursue. They were looking for something that seemed actionable and that would generate interest among the stakeholders they needed to engage to tackle the issue.

This step is critical, even for teams that believe they already have the perfect scope identified. In step 2, the conversation gets the diversity of team members' views out into the open and begins the essential work of aligning them around a shared view of their stakeholders' reality, which we have seen as critical to success in many of the stories in part 2. Communication problems get in the way of innovation when everyone assumes that others experience the situation in the same way. Even if we all speak the same formal language, every noun and verb has a different connotation, forming a different image in each human's brain. The more perspectives are spelled out, and the more visualizations a team produces, the more the team members can be confident that they are talking about the same thing.

On June 5, 2014, the expanded GCCA team met to discuss step 2, determining the scope of their project, which they had initially framed as "helping disengaged learners connect to GCCA diplomas and successful college experiences." They invited Jill Marks, the founding director of the school, who was now serving as the Gateway to College National Network's California regional coordinator, to join them in the scoping exercise, as they experimented with broadening and narrowing the challenge. In the conversation that ensued, each team member brought personal perspectives to the definition of GCCA's recruitment/retention problem. Reflecting her new position, Jill brought the network perspective and consistently urged the team to consider a broader definition of the opportunity, while others identified specific barriers that would narrow their study, such as transportation and family issues. It was a long afternoon, as Joan explained:

> We actually spent much more time than we expected on how to scope our idea. We went back and forth quite a bit. We would sometimes branch into, "Well, maybe we need to focus better on the messaging to the high school counselors?" When you start talking about the recruitment funnel, it gets kind of mixed in with marketing and that superficial kind of marketing. So we did do a couple of go-rounds where it's just a messaging thing. We also know that our school is both to serve learners but also to disseminate information and change policy. So we moved up into broader issues like the role of the community. Then we pulled back down to our learners and issues like "What is actually the word on the street among the learners?"

At one point, the team focused on the issue of student readiness: were students just not ready academically to start the foundation term? Students begin GCCA with a foundation term experience, which is a cohort-based semester with an intense curriculum in math and English to prepare them for college courses. They also enroll in a GCCA college-level guidance course to work on life, study, and time management skills. A few who are academically prepared may pick up an additional college course during this first term. After successful completion of the foundation term, students continue advancing through a guidance curriculum and enroll primarily in college courses with other community college students.

The team considered whether students were not turning in work or not attending class because they couldn't do this work. Eventually, faculty members at the table convinced everyone that this was not the real issue. Students were able to do the work, but other aspects, like barriers to attendance that students faced, hindered their performance.

Guided by the template in *The Designing for Growth Field Book*, these far-ranging conversations about scope helped the team to explore student problems more deeply, as they struggled to identify the particular problem or opportunity that they wanted to focus on.

Scoping Template

What is a broader area of opportunity around this?

Are there other areas of opportunity to help students achieve economic self-sufficiency?

What is a broader area of opportunity around this?

Are there other areas of opportunity to enhance students' sense of self-worth?

Ask yourself
What's one reason this matters?

Economic self-sufficiency

START HERE
Current area of opportunity:

How do we help disengaged learners connect to GCCA diplomas and successful college experiences?

Ask yourself
What's another reason this matters?

Self-worth, efficacy

Ask yourself
What's one barrier that gets in the way?

Attendance

Ask yourself
What's another barrier that gets in the way?

Underprepared academically

What is a narrower area of opportunity focused on this?

How do we help learners prepare to attend on a daily basis?

What is a narrower area of opportunity focused on this?

How can we begin to address skills deficiencies before Day 1?

Step 2: Scope template.

By the end of the day, the team was exhausted and overwhelmed by the myriad possibilities for framing GCCA's challenge. Team members decided to take a break and come back fresh the next morning. In hindsight, Joan believes that the time for overnight reflection made a big difference:

> With an overnight to reflect, we came back the next day and decided to focus on the opportunity to push the counseling curriculum further into our recruitment pipeline. It was probably that overnight, but we had a kind of "aha" moment and said, "Why don't we just focus on what we can do with the group that's coming in the door, that we will register at the end of July? Focus on what we can do to fix that part of the process and learn from that." We settled on learning what we could from the students in that particular incoming class and improving their success.

The decision to narrow their scope—to focus specifically on the incoming foundation cohort—allowed the team to move into action and gave them permission to think small. Team members didn't need to start with the whole recruitment and enrollment cycle if they weren't ready to go there. Their decision to look at just a slice of the process allowed them to do something quick for the next cohort of incoming students and learn from that.

The scoping process accomplished much more than just setting a focus for the project, Joan believed:

> Scoping, for me, was just this really rich conversation—it was a real breakthrough for us. We really wrestled with issues and came together as a group. It was supposed to take an hour or two and it took us across two days. But we needed those two days, and that conversation was an important one for the organization. It also became, for me, part of an ethnographic interviewing process: I was learning how my teammates viewed the problem, what they were frustrated with, what they thought the most common challenges to students were. And that's where this new team kind of gelled—we became a leadership team.

Here we can see how the design thinking process accomplished several of the goals that we talked about in parts 1 and 2. It helped the team continue to push their definition of the problem and to search for a scope for their efforts that would both encourage their creativity and allow them to work within the boundaries of the time and resources they had. At the same time, the discussion engaged the team, allowing each member to fully share their own perspectives and views. Most teams, when they stay with this kind of open-ended exploration of the problem space, eventually find themselves beginning to align, as the GCCA team did. If this alignment doesn't occur, we suggest that the team may need to pursue a more experimental approach, moving to step 3 with several alternative framings of the problem.

Step 3: Draft Your Design Brief

In our design thinking methodology, the design brief is a short write-up that clarifies the project's intent, underlines the questions a team wants to explore and the stakeholders to explore them with, and postulates what success might look like (though not yet how to get there). Like virtually everything else in design thinking, the design brief is actually a work in progress, and it can—and likely will—change as you work through the creative process and your understanding of the issue evolves. Indeed, you might consider the design brief a tool for managing risk throughout that evolution, because it prevents you from veering off on interesting tangents. As teams map unfamiliar terrain, reframing problems into possibilities and imagining alternative futures, checking in with the design brief keeps the team headed in the right direction, focusing on the desired outcomes and how to get there.

Just because—or especially because—you are working in the uncertain environment of Innovation II, your management of the project needn't be similarly chaotic. Just the opposite, in fact. Many key elements of the design process are uncontrollable, so it is all the more important to drive ambiguity out of the management of those elements. Literally, the design brief gets everyone on the same page, ensuring clarity, control, and transparency in the management of the project. The design brief, in short, is the North Star of the project, providing a con-

HOW MUCH DEBATE IS ENOUGH?

One of the judgment calls in design thinking is when to allow debate and when to put it aside. An important goal early in the process is to surface the diversity of team members' perspectives on the problem. This will naturally encourage a certain level of debate among competing definitions of the problem, which is good.

What we want to avoid at this point is debates about different *solutions*. Debates about the definition of the problem tend to broaden the discussion and open up new perspectives. Debates about solutions, on the other hand, tend to narrow the discussion. In addition, we want to encourage listening to understand each other's perspective rather than to demonstrate the superiority of our own position.

Still, at some point, the team will need to move on. If debates remain unresolved and alignment isn't happening, we suggest moving to the next step: trying to design a plan that will allow you to gather data to explore the different areas of opportunity. In the design thinking process, we want to avoid getting stuck in nonproductive debates. Move on, learn more, and then revisit.

stant answer to the question "Where are we headed?" It should be brief yet complete and should be revisited at every key milestone during any design thinking project.

After the extensive conversations in step 2 around the scope of the project, Joan found it easy to draft a design brief, and she circulated it to the team the next day.

Design Brief	
Project Description	*Despite current practice, students still have trouble understanding and overcoming barriers.* *Our hypothesis is that we can reduce attrition and promote success through our recruitment process—in an open access enrollment context?* *Preliminary research indicates that attendance and academic habits (productivity) limit success.* *Can we do something in the recruitment process to address these two barriers to success?*
Scope	*Initial focus on the incoming class of 2014* *Focus on what action can be taken in the recruitment phase (prior to 1 week boot camp) to prepare students to attend, engage and complete assignments*
Constraints	*Open access mandated* *Counselors are on 11 month contracts* *Faculty are on 10 month contracts*
Target Users	*Learners* *GCCA Counselors* *Parents*
Exploration Questions	*Explore the human dimensions of our recruitment-acceptance-enrollment process.* *What are the primary drivers of attrition in the first 30 days?* *What barriers to attendance and completing assignments limit student progress?* *What barriers to attendance & homework completion can be addressed between the lottery date and Day 1?*
Expected Outcomes	*Lower attrition rates* *Improved academic success*
Success Metrics	*Pipeline metrics, TBD* *At 30 day point, end of term, start of second term*

Step 3: The design brief template.

Step 4: Make Your Plans

Design brief in hand, it is now time to plan your assault on the details of information gathering. You'll want to consider three primary aspects of planning: a people plan, a research plan, and a project plan.

Though we have called the design brief the North Star of the process, the people and research plans may be even more critical at this stage than the design brief itself. You can always alter aspects of your design brief quickly at your keyboard, but it takes time and resources to go back and locate new stakeholders to interview or observe at a later stage in the process, if you missed them in the first round. So think carefully about these elements. When you're making the people plan, consider everyone whose cooperation you need in some form—customers, colleagues, partners, frontline workers, administrators, and anyone whose input might help you discover new insights around your area of opportunity or problem. Their comments will give you the input you need to create the research plan and to begin to consider what tools you'll use in your project plan.

On June 12, the GCCA team met and drafted their project, people, and research plans. In their people plan, they identified five key stakeholder groups, each with its own point of view, who had substantial influence on the process:

- **New students**, who faced significant hardships and who, the team hypothesized, might not fully understand the commitment needed to succeed and might not trust educators. They were likely anxious about entering the program, fitting in, and performing academically.

- **The parents of students**, who the team thought probably shared students' concerns

- **GCCA counselors**, who were generally caring and supportive, but overworked and frustrated at the lack of commitment from some students

- **GCCA faculty**—again caring and committed—who believed that students must learn to be accountable and were disheartened when students failed to keep up

- **Community college faculty**, who shared the characteristics and views of GCCA faculty generally but who also believed that everyone should be treated as a college student, receiving no special treatment

Stakeholder/User #1 Name: *Rising Foundation Students*	Stakeholder/User #2 Name: *Parents*	Stakeholder/User #3 Name: *GCCA Counselors*
What is their current point of view? How will their behavior or actions need to be different in order to address my challenge?	**What is their current point of view? How will their behavior or actions need to be different in order to address my challenge?**	**What is their current point of view? How will their behavior or actions need to be different in order to address my challenge?**
Point of View	**Point of View**	**Point of View**
Need to do deep research. Ideas from team dialog include: May not understand the commitments required to succeed. May not trust educational actors after previous experiences. May be anxious about a new school and about college. May be anxious about fitting in with other students. May be anxious about balancing other commitments. Some face significant hardships that must be addressed through social services.	*May not understand the commitments required for their student to succeed. May not trust educational actors after previous experiences. May be anxious about their student enrolling at a new school. May not have knowledge about college. May be anxious about their fitting in with other students. May be anxious about their balancing other commitments, including those the family depends upon.*	*Caring & supportive but frustrated. Feel that the commitment is explained to students repeatedly. Overworked. Disheartened when students leave or fail to progress. Proud of those who succeed.*
Behavioral change		**Behavioral change**
Seek assistance. Learn how to manage barriers. Build support network. Plan for contingencies. Attend. Complete readings & assignments.	**Behavioral change** *Be supportive. Understand and reinforce the commitment and behaviors. Help their student manage barriers and other commitments. In some cases, learn to manage parental commitments without being a barrier to student.*	*Find/design ways to communicate the GCCA experience so that students understand.*

Step 4: The people plan.

Stakeholder/User #1 Name: *Rising Foundation Students*	Stakeholder/User #2 Name: *Parents*	Stakeholder/User #3 Name: *GCCA Counselors*
What am I curious about related to this stakeholder? *What is the student perspective at this point in their journey? What are the peer and parental influences helping or hindering?* *Why do some challenged students succeed while others similarly or less challenged stop out?* *How can we help students manage their barriers to success?* • *Knowledge* • *Skills* • *Dispositions*	**What am I curious about related to this stakeholder?** *What is the parent perspective at this point in their student's journey?* *Are parents 'available' to be supportive? If not, is there another adult that can play this role?* *How can we help parents manage the barriers to their student's success?* • *Knowledge* • *Skills* • *Dispositions*	**What am I curious about related to this stakeholder?** *What are counselor perspectives? What approaches have been tried? What do counselors feel are barriers we are not addressing?* *What other approaches might be tried to address this problem?* *What other resources exist at the college or in the community to assist?*
How can I develop empathy for this stakeholder? *Secondary research: Exit interviews or counselor's notes on exit; counselor notes on successful students re barriers and their management.* *Interviews with students (Rising Foundation; currently enrolled students; alumni; and leavers if possible)* *Analysis Tools:* *Job to be Done Tool* *Journey Map*	**How can I develop empathy for this stakeholder?** *Secondary research: Counselor notes, if any.* *Interviews with parents* *Analysis Tools:* *Job to be Done Tool*	**How can I develop empathy for this stakeholder?** *Secondary research: Value chain & Pipeline to understand role and activity* *Analysis Tools:* *Job to be Done Tool* *Value Chain*

Step 4: The people plan (continued).

The team thought about the new behaviors that might be required of each stakeholder for eventual project success, what they needed to learn about each group, and how to build empathy with each.

As team members prepared their research plan, they first focused on already available secondary data and the existing literature. They considered how to find and connect with critical stakeholders in a more human-centered, less statistical approach. They knew that individual stories about actual students and their needs, and even people's offhand comments or actions, often revealed unarticulated needs and desires. They had an almost overwhelming amount of secondary data to work with: various reports from the Gateway to College National Network and substantial literature on achievement gaps. But they were looking for insight on a deeply human scale.

As they created their ethnographic plan for primary data gathering, they were forced to make compromises on some of their ideals. Because it was summer, for example, they had little chance to speak with GCCA faculty and counselors. Fortunately, several team members had counseling backgrounds. As they planned interviews with students, they also reluctantly gave up the idea of doing one-on-one interviews or interviewing students who had exited the program, because of timing issues and regulatory constraints. Joan regretted this loss:

> I really wish we were able to do the one-on-one ethnographic interviews with the students, particularly those that we lose. We don't know what's driving them leaving school—attendance is just kind of the bucket we put them in because we don't get to know them well enough. Maybe it's the family, or a transportation issue? Not being able to get in and really do the ethnographic interviews is a reality, but it's frustrating.

Despite these compromises, the team believed that they could learn a lot by meeting with existing students in groups, and they decided to schedule the meetings as "pizza lunches" to encourage attendance.

WHEN IS GREAT THE ENEMY OF GOOD?

As the GCCA team's experience reflects, the design of research almost always involves compromise. We frequently see people hesitating to do *any* ethnographic research because they can't do *perfect* ethnographic research. Think back to Eli MacLaren's advice in the Children's Health System story: just get out there and talk to somebody. Any conversation is a move toward goodness.

Who/what will we study?	Where will we find the people or information?	What questions/ issues will we explore?	Number of observations, interviews, or inputs	When will the research happen?	Who on the research team is responsible?
Literature, previous studies	GtCNN, research reports	What can we learn from the literature and other aggregate reports?		Ongoing 6/16 to 6/20	Jill/GtCNN Joan Core Team
Pipeline data (secondary research)	GCCA database	Explore/identify points in pipeline. Where students tend to fall out.	2013-14 cohorts	ASAP	Miguel with assistance from ?
Students (secondary research)	Counselor notes	Explore reasons for exit. Explore reasons recorded for why students struggle with attendance & productivity.	2013-14 cohorts	ASAP	Robin with assistance from ?
Students	Interviews	Explore unarticulated needs that lead to or, if addressed, might mitigate barriers to attendance/ productivity.		June 26	Interviewer: Shelagh Notes: Joan
Parents	Interviews				
Counselors	Interviews	What happens? What reasons or barriers for poor attendance/ productivity? Perceived gaps? Ideas for innovation.		June 26	Interviewer: Notes: Joan
GCCA faculty	Interviews				
RCC faculty	Interviews				

Step 4: The research plan.

The project plan can be the most challenging to devise, because it asks you to consider which tools from the design thinking tool kit to customize for your own journey through the four questions. Throughout the stories in part 2, we saw many of these tools in use; among the core tools are ethnographic interviews, jobs-to-be-done analysis, journey mapping, direct observation, and personas. The GCCA team decided to emphasize a combination of ethnographic interviewing and journey mapping. Though they loved the idea of creating personas, they felt it was important to keep their first pass at the method simple and decided to save this additional step for later.

Now the team was ready to move into action and explore **What *is*?**

What *is*? Overview

The first four steps in our design thinking methodology have aimed at ensuring that would-be design thinkers engage in the process with an appropriate challenge to tackle (step 1), an understanding of the many levels and facets of that challenge (step 2), an aligned view of the project's targeted stakeholders and what success might look like (step 3), and a set of thoughtfully completed planning documents to guide them (step 4). Having completed these steps, the GCCA team was ready to spend time in the **What *is*** stage, exploring their challenge in depth without trying to generate solutions. Innovative solutions, they believed, would arise from deep insights into the lives of the students they wanted to support. They were not yet looking for answers; they were looking for insight into the students' current reality.

Step 5: Do Your Research

Human-centered design is built on a foundation of empathy. Our goal is to develop a deep understanding of our stakeholders and their lives, to see them as real-life human beings. Without deep insights about the current reality of stakeholders, our imagination starves.

From June 19 to June 26, the GCCA team conducted ethnographic research with representative faculty, counselors, and students. An extended pizza lunch with students was a big success. The open lunch was scheduled on a day when about thirty-five students were on campus for a guidance class or other reasons. Students were invited to the lunch and were told a bit about the project. Almost all students who were invited came, and candor was not a problem. They came in small groups and kept coming over the course of the two-hour lunch. The session started with a group of eight students and grew as more students joined. Some students stayed the whole time. Shelagh, an experienced facilitator and ethnographic interviewer, expertly brought out their experiences. She led the conversations, and Joan took careful notes.

They also decided to give students the option of creating a storyboard. Most chose to just talk, but in one session a young man sat very quietly in the front, drawing. By the end of the session, his storyboard told his personal tale. The storyboard described his insecurity about school and his doubts about his capabilities. He'd missed the first day of class when he started at GCCA, and the teacher called to see why he wasn't there, prompting him to come the second day. When his first English and math assignments were returned, and he saw that he had done well, he had an epiphany: "I'm worthy. I can do it."

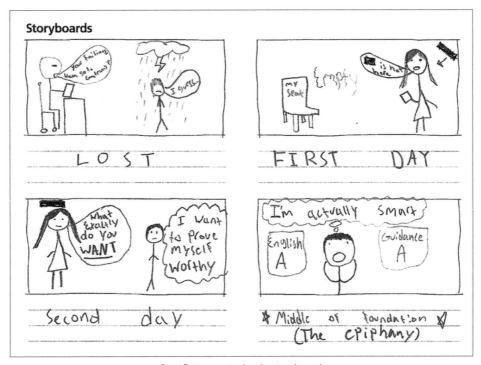

One Gateway student's storyboard.

The team found all of this ethnographic data invaluable. For some team members, it was a high point of the study. Joan explained, "I felt really great because, when we interviewed the students, I came to know them in a different way." For others, it was a mix of highs and lows—anxiety beforehand, enthusiasm after. As Robin explained:

> For step 5, my first instinct was I was anxious, because I wanted the students to show
> up, but I was also excited to hear what they had to say, because I always know what they
> have to say is always the best part of it. So it was also a high for me when I saw that it was
> a breakthrough for the team.

As the team invited the students into the conversation, the conversation broadened to include new perspectives they brought.

Step 6: Identify Insights

Now we reach what we consider to be one of the most important steps in the entire methodology. For many, identifying insights is probably the single most challenging aspect of the design thinking process. Superficial insights lead to obvious ideas, and without the discovery of new and deep insights, the remaining design thinking steps are unlikely to produce intriguing results.

As you do your research into all your stakeholder groups—your colleagues, customers, suppliers, clients, partners, anyone who can affect your project—you can't expect any of these stakeholders to hand you a significant insight. You are often searching for things that they themselves do not fully understand and can't articulate.

You can organize the search for insights in various ways, but all involve people working in teams. The "Gallery Walk" approach we often use involves putting the data on full-size posters and inviting an assembled group of collaborators to browse. Posters capture what you learned during your research and can be very low fidelity. The Gallery Walk is also a convenient method for inviting other stakeholders into the design conversation and reaching out to people who are not on the research team.

One challenge of doing innovation work is that, over time, any team begins to see the world in new ways, but then they must attempt to communicate ideas to others who have not been part of the process. Engaging important stakeholders in the search for insights helps to ameliorate this problem and paves the way to alignment around new opportunities. But teams can also summarize the data in a dossier for members to review either before or during an insight session.

In early July, the GCCA team began their search for insights. Joan compiled the notes, from both secondary and ethnographic research, into a packet for team members. They spent a day reviewing it. The team met on July 8 to look for insights and create design criteria. Because the team was small, Joan suggested that they simply read through the packets individually and write down what each person thought stood out. She also created a mini gallery with posters of some of the information.

The session lasted a full day. In the morning, the team reviewed what they had done and read the packet of information that Joan had prepared. The team co-created a student journey, noting any ideas they found interesting or surprising, to help create on a whiteboard a journey map of a typical student experience. Thinking aloud about the level of anxiety students faced at each point, the team had their prime "aha" moment when they collectively realized that students faced high anxiety *well before* the first class. They all realized that this anxiety could best be addressed when the students registered, rather than waiting until the first day of school. The journey map helped them understand when anxiety peaked and illustrated the leverage points when counselors' intervention really mattered.

As team members devoted time to summarizing, they also discovered they were, as a team, solidifying their alignment about the current situation and the opportunities for innovation, as seen in many of our part 2 stories. At this stage, the design thinking process helps team members do the important work of curating—drilling down in a sea of different data points to determine what really matters.

By the end of the day, the team reached consensus on a set of insights:

- **Students really valued assistance in managing practical barriers**. "Just coach me how to get to campus" or "Coach me how to deal with all the social service issues" were typical requests. Some students were in the juvenile justice system. Others were in foster care. Some were homeless. They were really seeking services.

- **There were strong student voices on managing the various emotional barriers** that individual students brought to school with them. Many students observed that, through their GCCA experience, they found the belief that they could actually succeed, even excel; they recognized their own value and intelligence. (Remember the storyboard?) Nearly as important, they observed that GCCA faculty, counselors, and peers believed that they could succeed.

- **Students did not want GCCA to be a continuation of high school**. GCCA students enrolled because they sought the college experience that the academy promised, which the team knew was a core challenge. "Make this a college," they urged. "Build our college culture." "I'm here for college; don't waste my time." "Help me understand the expectations and opportunities."

Surprisingly, a significant cohort demanded that the academy hold their fellow students accountable. The strong personal accountability message surprised the counseling team. It appeared to reflect social perceptions and students' personal emotions regarding their own accomplishments and how others might perceive their diploma. They were succeeding because of their hard work and managing barriers with the assistance of others (counselors, teachers, parents, and GCCA peers). They observed that some unsuccessful students might be too young or not yet mature enough to understand. Other students worried about peers that they knew wanted to succeed but didn't turn in the work, even after working on it. While they wanted to be compassionate, students did not believe that relaxing GCCA's expectations was the answer. They were at GCCA for college, and others needed to be, too.

Step 7: Establish Design Criteria

The results of insight identification in step 6 is not a set of solutions. Instead, it is a succinct expression of the job those solutions must do, in the form of design criteria to be created in step 7. The criteria capture the conclusions from the **What *is*** stage and provide the yardstick by which possible solutions will be evaluated. The design criteria do not tell you what to do or how to do it; instead, they describe the attributes of an ideal solution.

For each insight found in step 6, the GCCA team considered the statement "If anything were possible, our ideal solution would . . ." and filled in the rest of the sentence on the basis of that insight. Like many other teams in our experience, they found it easy to translate their insights into criteria. Their ideal solution would:

- leverage existing resources and events,
- help students manage "practical" problems that inhibited attendance and academic success,
- ease first-time students' anxieties,
- build the college culture,
- communicate GCCA's expectations clearly,
- be compatible with existing technology platforms and policy, and
- be deployed before the start of the new term on August 28.

The design criteria are the bridge between **What _is_** and **What _if_**. After weeks of work, the GCCA team was finally prepared to generate solutions. It was time to enter the **What _if_** stage and create some ideas to work with.

CHAPTER FOURTEEN

The Four-Question Methodology in Action:
Ideas to Experiments

In chapter 13, the Gateway team laid the foundation for successful human-centered innovation by selecting an appropriate challenge that was well suited to design thinking, carefully planning the project, and conducting ethnographic research into the lives of the students they wanted to better serve. Armed with fresh insights and a solid set of design criteria created as they progressed through the first seven steps of the process, they were prepared to move into the idea generation and testing process.

What *if?* Overview

As we move into idea generation (finally!), we focus on brainstorming (step 8) and concept development (step 9). Separating brainstorming from concept development allows us to build more complex, multilayered solutions to the messy problems faced in the social sector. As we heard repeatedly in the stories in part 2, there are few silver bullets. Instead, we must look to construct portfolios of solutions and then let our stakeholders tell us which ones work best for them.

In brainstorming, we focus on divergence, trying to generate as many and as varied ideas as possible. In concept development, we will look for ways to select the best of those ideas and synthesize them into packages of solutions that, together, achieve an impact that no single solution could. Think of the brainstorming results as being like the individual pieces of the Lego blocks you played with when you were young. Emptying them all on the floor was fun and made a dramatic statement, but it didn't produce much that you could play with; it was only when you combined them in different ways to make a rocket or a pirate ship that things got interesting.

Steps 8 and 9: Brainstorm Ideas and Develop Concepts

Brainstorming has been around for a long time. Too often, however, good ideas are lost as a result of some common but ill-conceived approaches to it. We observe problems like the "boss effect," where everyone waits for the most highly paid person in the room to pronounce a solution, or the shout-out problem, where loud voices overwhelm the conversation and contributions from introverts are minimized. Human dynamics often block full creative engagement and are hard to avoid or overcome, so you will need to work to mitigate communication issues in whatever brainstorming process you use. Approaches that incorporate silent, individual idea generation (on paper) followed by public sharing, insisting that everyone present get involved, minimize these impediments. Good brainstorming requires encouraging the right mindset, that of the creator, not the critic (the critical mindset gets a chance later, in the **What wows** stage). Like the Gallery Walk in step 6, it is also a great opportunity to invite a broader set of collaborators into the conversation.

But, so often, the surprising out-of-the-box solution you'd hoped for doesn't show up in brainstorming. Take heart. The outputs of brainstorming are usually too raw and incomplete to be exciting in and of themselves. In concept development, we take the most innovative ideas from brainstorming and thoughtfully combine them to generate creative bundles of solutions, which we call concepts. Concept development involves choosing the best ideas from brainstorming and assembling them into detailed solutions. It is analogous to a movie director editing the best takes into something creative yet coherent, dropping shots and scenes in the process. We want to construct multiple concepts so that we can offer multiple choices to our key stakeholders. Whereas insight identification and brainstorming are best done by a diverse group that includes people outside the innovation team, concept development usually is best done by the dedicated core team.

But sometimes the ideas and concepts just show up, with little need to resort to the structured processes for steps 8 and 9 that we describe in *The Designing for Growth Field Book*. That is what happened at Gateway College and Career Academy. Joan Wells and her team rolled easily from the discussion of design criteria to the identification of solutions in a single day, on July 8. They started to list ideas on a whiteboard. As Joan described it, "All of a sudden, everybody's minds clicked, and we had six or seven different points on the board that we thought were worthy."

The team did not feel the need to use formal brainstorming and concept development tools. The ideas just started to flow. Immediately after that session, the leadership team laid out a framework identifying what a solution needed to include and started working on the five concepts they had created. In one productive day they identified insights, developed design criteria, and generated ideas ready to be summarized and explored.

Step 10: Create Some Napkin Pitches

The napkin pitch provides a simple format for summarizing, communicating, and comparing new concepts. It provides a consistent template, so that side-by-side comparisons can be made across multiple concepts. The term *napkin pitch* derives from the notion that a good idea can, and should, be communicated simply—as on the back of a napkin. The napkin pitch enforces simplicity and helps avoid the temptation to stack the deck in favor of one option before others (especially key stakeholders) have an opportunity to validate your thinking. Equally important, it puts concepts into a distilled form that lets stakeholders focus on the essential elements.

You will never have enough time, energy, and money to explore all the concepts you've identified. Consequently, the need to make tough choices among high-potential projects is inevitable. Some will need to be set aside, at least for now. One powerful concept in design thinking is that we explore multiple options while letting users validate them.

By July 15, the GCCA team had finalized five napkin pitches. One napkin-pitch concept was titled "Welcome Meetings: One-on-One Counseling/Coaching Sessions." It was designed to build the counseling connection earlier in the enrollment process. The benefit was early communication with students and the reinforcement of program expectations in a personal, face-to-face counseling relationship that would ease first-time students' anxieties. This concept would shift the timing of existing counseling sessions to the beginning rather than the end of August. Instituting these welcome meetings would require the development of standard content to meet the design criteria identified in step 7. Crucially, welcome meetings would rely on the willingness of the counseling faculty, who not only would have new content to communicate but also would need to adjust their summer schedules. The rationale behind the idea was that better-prepared students would have less attrition and enhanced academic success, facilitating a better balance of new, transitioning, and continuing students in the school's enrollment.

Napkin Pitch	
Concept Name: *Welcome Meetings: Early One-on-One Counseling/Coaching Sessions*	
The Big Idea *Build GCCA's counseling connection sooner in the enrollment process.* *Engage students in an individual coaching and planning session immediately following registration day (July 29).* *Clearly communicate program expectations and opportunities and help students begin to manage practical problems and anxieties likely to impact attendance and engagement.* *Begin to address attendance and academic "habit" challenges earlier than in the past so that students are ready and able to engage on the first day of the foundation experience.*	**Needs/Benefits** *Students will benefit if we:* *Begin to build the personal counseling or coaching connection that will serve each student throughout his/her GCCA experience.* *Early student planning and preparation will improve attendance and academic engagement.* *Early student-counselor connections will ease some first-time student anxieties.* *Early communication and reinforcement of program expectation*
Execution *This concept shifts the current GCCA one-on-one counseling sessions to the beginning rather than end of August. Therefore, it leverages current practice and expertise.* *Develop standard content for counselor-student interactions that incorporate the following design criteria: Communicate Expectations & Opportunities; Help Students Manage "Practical" Problems of Attendance & Engagement; Ease First Time Student Anxieties.* *Schedule appointments with students on registration day (July 29). Appointments will take place between July 30 and August 14.* *Personnel: GCCA Counselors* *Materials & Resources to be located & validated, gathered, or developed: Handbooks, Student and Social Services directories, websites, etc.* *Partners: RCC Student Services, Community Social Service Providers, etc.*	**Business Rationale** *Earlier counseling sessions will better prepare students to attend, engage and complete assignments.* *Reduce attrition and improve student success.* *Improved retention will improve the program reputation as well as the school budget.* *Improved retention and student success will permit building a more balanced school enrollment mix of new, transitioning and continuing students.*

The napkin pitch for Welcome Meetings.

Another concept was called "Remind.com." Named after an existing educational text messaging app, this concept involved the use of text messages to remind students of steps to get ready for school. These messages could include preparation/planning reminders, check-ins, campus news and tips, and even reminders to enjoy the rest of the summer. The goal was to reinforce the connection with entering students. The team hoped to connect with students early and build relationships before the beginning of school. Such regular contact, they hypothesized, would reduce student anxiety prior to the first day of class by letting them know what to expect and would help students begin to organize and prepare for the start of school.

With these and other concepts in hand, the GCCA team was now prepared to test their ideas in the **What *wows*** stage.

What *wows*? Overview

In design thinking's front end, we held the organization's requirements and constraints at bay while we drilled down on stakeholder essentials. We were concerned that we might filter stakeholder needs through powerful organizational dimensions and never get to breakthrough thinking. But now, as we prepare for testing, we need to bring the organization's requirements back in. A return to the design brief and criteria should remind you of the strategic organizational goals you wanted to accomplish on this innovation journey.

We transition from idea generation into testing by first examining which of the portfolio of concepts we have created might reach what we call the "wow zone"—the intersection of what stakeholders want and what the organization can sustainably offer. As we prepare to enter the land of experimentation, we first surface the critical assumptions behind why we believe that our concepts should be successful for both the stakeholder and the organization. We then create visual prototypes that allow us to test our critical assumptions in a way that feels real to those from whom we seek feedback.

In the wow zone, we are seeking the intersection of three critical requirements: what the stakeholder wants, what the organization can deliver, and a sustainable economic model for the future. In business, the need for a sustainable future would entail the search for a profitable business model. In the nonprofit world, we still need a sustainable financial model underpinning our delivery of the concept. The only difference is whether we are trying to create a surplus for stockholders or to wisely use a set of resources, whether from donors or government.

We treat our concepts as hypotheses in **What wows** and test them with small experiments in **What works**. But the design hypothesis that we are going to test is not the same as a scientific hypothesis. Scientific hypotheses are about securing better explanations for things that exist but that we can't yet see or understand. We have nothing to test in a design hypothesis because the concept being tested is still a figment of our imagination. The only direct method for testing a design hypothesis would be to build it first—and that is precisely what we are trying to avoid! What we need to do, instead, is test our underlying assumptions about why the idea is good, rather than the idea itself. Let's see what the process looks like in action.

Step 11: Surface Key Assumptions

As we have already said, all new concepts are hypotheses—well-informed guesses about what stakeholders want and value and what our organization can deliver. Projects regularly fail because reality turns out differently than we assumed it would. Consequently, design thinking tries to minimize failure by figuring out the assumptions behind our napkin pitches and testing them. By surfacing and testing key assumptions, we seek to discover which ideas are based on questionable premises before throwing money and resources at them.

Think about the importance of trying to actively nullify a hypothesis. Dedicated researchers pay particular attention to why any hypothesis may not be true. That's what we're after in this step. Though it's tough to seek flaws in our own brilliance, we must do so. We always hope our napkin pitches are good ideas, but quickly and efficiently weeding out bad ones is key. Venture capitalists may invest in ten projects, hoping that all will succeed, but know from experience that only two are likely to. Since they can't know in advance which two it will be, figuring out *when* to stop investing in the other eight is just as important as—maybe more important than—backing the two winners. If you want to fail fast and cheap (that often-repeated Silicon Valley motto), then exposing and disconfirming false assumptions may be the most valuable activity of all.

Sometimes, you have good existing data and can conduct thought experiments (similar to traditional analysis). We always start here, because these experiments are the least expensive, least intrusive kind. If we don't have relevant data already in hand to test our assumptions, we need to go out and get it through field experiments. Starting with low-fidelity prototypes, we go into the field again to interact with a few real stakeholders and simulate reality by having conversations with them. The most accurate kind of experiments are live, 4-D experiments conducted in the real world by offering higher-fidelity prototypes. We call these experiments "learning launches."

To assess **What *wows*,** the GCCA team reviewed their napkin pitches and identified the assumptions underlying each one—what would need to be true to make each a good idea. They sorted them into assumptions about why each pitch created value for the students, how each pitch would be implemented in practice, and how each could be scaled and sustained.

For each assumption, they considered how best to test it. They could:

· conduct a thought experiment using data they already had in hand;
· conduct a simulation by beginning a dialogue with the key stakeholders involved, using a storyboard or other kind of prototype; or
· test it via a live experience.

Thought Experiment	2D & 3D Simulation Experiment (one-on-one)	Live (4D) Experiment (one-on-one)
· *Learn through analysis of existing data* · *Typical time frame: one or two days* · *No exposure to third parties required*	· *Learn through dialogue with stakeholders using storyboards or prototypes* · *Typical time frame: one or two weeks* · *May require us to expose our intentions to selected stakeholders*	· *Test via a live experience of the offering (e.g., a 30-day live trial)* · *Typical time frame: 30 to 90 days* · *Requires us to expose our offering to many stakeholders*

Experiments to test assumptions.

For the "Welcome Meetings" concept, the assumptions included that students would value one-on-one meetings and would experience reduced anxiety and improved performance as a result of such meetings.

Concept Name: *Welcome Meetings (Early One-on-One Counseling Sessions)*	
VALUE TEST Stakeholders want it Stakeholders will pay for it Partners want it	*Students overcome or manage barriers to school attendance and engagement emanating from some trauma or underlying condition (ranging from family, peer or school dysfunction to poverty, homelessness or poor health to specific life-changing events). (Thought Experiment, 4D)* *Students, particularly those who might become early leavers, will value early access to counseling services and will sign up and show up for their scheduled Welcome Meeting. (Thought Experiment, 4D)* *New standard counseling protocols will improve student understanding of attendance and engagement expectations. (Thought Experiment, 4D)* *Early August sessions will result in better student planning and preparation. (Thought Experiment, 4D)* *Pre-experiencing attendance by planning to attend (Plans A to C) will improve students' commitment and ability to attend. (Thought Experiment, 4D)* *Earlier sessions and follow-up will ease first-time student anxieties. (Thought Experiment, 4D)* *Early August sessions will reinforce students' connection with GCCA. (Thought Experiment, 4D)*
EXECUTION TEST We can produce the experience technically We can serve stakeholders We can operate the process as it grows	*Counselors are available to shift session timing to early August. (Thought Experiment, 4D)* *Counselors will value and adopt new protocols. (Thought Experiment, 4D)* *Counselors are available to follow up with students (in mid to late August). (Thought Experiment, 4D)* *Early August sessions will result in better school planning and preparation to respond to specific needs of the fall 2014 cohort. (Thought Experiment, 4D)* *With more advance knowledge of student barriers, GCCA and its partners can more effectively coach students to develop and implement their plans to attend. (Thought Experiment, 4D)* *Student services and social service partners will be available to effectively respond and assist with identified student needs. (Thought Experiment, 4D)*
SCALE TEST *Addressable stakeholder group is big enough* *We can serve additional stakeholders affordably* *Revenues exceed costs at scale*	*One-on-one counseling can be scaled as enrollment grows and the school expands to 2 sites. (Thought Experiment)* *Learners can be recruited to access this service (now mandatory). (Thought Experiment, 4D)* Note: Enrolled students are required to participate in these sessions. Welcome Meeting appointments will be set during the registration day experience on July 29.
SUSTAINABILITY TEST We can sustain the venture over time Opportunity costs are few Advantage increases as we grow the venture	*Early August is better than late August for these sessions. Identifying problems, assisting with strategies, and establishing relationships early in the student experience will improve attendance and engagement outcomes. (Thought Experiment, 4D)* *There are few opportunity costs to shifting the timing of the Welcome Meetings. (Thought Experiment, 4D)* *Improved retention will grow enrollment and improve the mix of first-time, transitioning and continuing students within the school. (Thought Experiment, 4D)*

The key assumptions, with the experiment type for testing.

As the team deliberated which approach—thought experiment, simulation, or live test—would be best to test each assumption about welcome meetings, one execution assumption stood out: that counseling faculty would make themselves available to students during what was normally vacation and prep time. In the past, counselors had not met students until the first week of school and would then cobble everything together. The new concept required that counselors meet with students as they registered and then to continue to meet as students needed throughout the semester.

On the leadership team, director Miguel Contreras was from counseling ranks, and Robin Acosta, the dean of students, was GCCA's lead counselor. When the team tested their assumptions with thought experiments, their experience and rapport with other counselors suggested that GCCA counselors would be willing to make such a commitment. But the team believed that this key assumption needed more than a thought experiment; it needed to be tested directly with counselors.

Step 12: *Make Prototypes*

Throughout the stories in part 2, we saw the importance of creating visual representations of ideas, which we call prototypes. When many of us hear the word prototype, we think of fully featured, almost-ready-for-prime-time versions. Design thinking prototypes start off much more crude, with details and specificity mattering only if they create a preview of the experience in stakeholders' minds. These kinds of prototypes are, as Michael Schrage described them, playgrounds, not dress rehearsals. The prototyping goal in design thinking is not perfection; it is bringing concepts to life for potential users. Where architects create blueprints and models, designers generally use visual or narrative approaches: images and stories. Prototypes can even include role-playing and skits. The reason that we surface assumptions before we prototype is because, early on, we want to test the most critical assumptions first. These prototypes do not need to capture a concept in its entirety; they only need to represent individual elements so that each can be tested separately.

While it is easy to prototype a new toothbrush, prototyping in the social sector usually means designing experiences, which requires not physical objects but storyboards, user scenarios, experience journeys, animations, and concept illustrations.

Prototyping elicits more accurate feedback by creating a more vivid experience of any new future. Psychologists report that helping people "pre-experience" something novel is an effective proxy for the real thing and significantly improves the accuracy of human behavioral forecasting. Indeed, evidence emerging from neuropsychological research suggests that imagining a specific future activates the same neurological pathways as experiencing the actual event does.

Whether in the form of storyboards, journey maps, user scenarios, or business concept illustrations, low-fidelity and often two-dimensional prototypes offer specific tools to make new ideas tangible and allow us to solicit more accurate feedback during **What *wows*** and **What *works***. In the most successful innovation projects, designers prototype early and often, leaving "emptiness"—room for others to contribute—in their early iterations. A prototype that leaves room for input invites stakeholders to complete it and helps them become invested in the idea. Prototypes that appear perfect may encourage users to say what they think we want to hear, and the last thing we want to encourage is the false positive as we sort out the nonstarters from the good ideas (remember the venture capitalists and the critical importance of figuring out which eight projects to stop investing in). It is the false positives that raise the costs—and risks—of innovation.

Prototyping can sound intimidating, but it needn't be. Just figure out the story you want to tell and visualize the concept in pictures, using as few words as possible. Always visualize multiple options. Create choices for the stakeholder. This can be as simple as asking users to check the option they like best. In one of our favorite examples, a health care clinic prototyped potential office layouts by hanging bedsheets from the ceiling to act as walls and using cardboard boxes as sinks and desks. Asking doctors and nurses to move around the space while performing their normal activities, designers shifted the sheets and boxes so that the medical staff could pre-experience different options and determine which layout best suggested efficiency.

Back at GCCA, the team's prototypes came together quickly. At the July 16 meeting, counselors began crafting prototypes. GCCA already had experience with Remind.com and Edmodo (which is similar to NovoEd or Facebook but is designed with stronger privacy for teachers and students). Both were already in use by some faculty, so the team did not need to prototype these platforms. They only needed to craft common messages and add an assignment for the incoming cohorts. For Remind.com, they developed a message, and for Edmodo, they created an assignment that students would bring to their first one-on-one meeting with a counselor after registration day, which would also be tweaked to be a more welcoming experience. After the July 16 meeting, the extended counseling team continued to share prototypes of messages during planning meetings and via e-mail to iteratively settle on the series of Remind.com messages and a first Edmodo assignment. Members also tweaked their first counseling meeting protocols and prepared to meet with students immediately after registration.

Having created journey map prototypes, and armed with their assumptions to be tested, GCCA team members were ready to step outside of themselves and seek input. They were ready to consider **What *works***.

What *works*? Overview

In the **What *works*** stage, we take our ideas to real stakeholders, first in one-on-one conversations and then in field experiments. The challenges in **What *works*** are designing experiments and then listening to feedback nondefensively. Team members who struggle with the first two design questions, the fuzzy front end of idea generation, are often more comfortable in the **What *works*** stage because it requires different expertise. Whereas Geoffreys generally love **What *is*** and **What *if*** Georges tend to excel at **What *wows*** and **What *works***. An ideal team will include both sets of skills, as we talked about in chapter 2.

Because designers are generally taught in studio settings, where critiquing is key, they learn to detach their egos from their creations and to hear criticism nondefensively, as part of their training. The opposite is true for most of us. When we ask teams to seek feedback and present learning launches, one major principle is that they *not* defend their choices. What matters, instead, is whether the teams understand others' criticisms. As long as team members understand the assessment, they have the choice to accept it and change or to decide that any disparaging analysis is not important and ignore it. First, however, their job is to listen carefully.

For many, especially Geoffreys, design thinking gets difficult in **What *works***. In many ways, design thinking is about emotion, empathy, human-centeredness, and understanding what someone else is thinking or feeling—areas where Geoffreys flourish. But the experimental phase is about focusing on data. It is OK to "fall in love" with our stakeholders but not our solutions. Here, we are conducting tests on our hypotheses, and we need to think like scientists.

Step 13: Get Feedback from Stakeholders

Prototype in hand, you now return to your key stakeholders to seek their feedback. Seek, and hear—especially the bad news. If your prototype is crude, they will fill the "emptiness" with ideas on how to improve it. Again, observe their reactions at least as much as you listen to their words, and truly invite them to co-create with you a better product, concept, creation, or experience.

Remember, your primary reason for assumption testing is to learn. Let them teach you. Take photos of whatever your stakeholders wrote on your storyboard prototype; capture when they laughed, when they sighed, and when they threw up their hands. If they crushed your concept for reasons that can't be fixed in the next iteration, throw in the towel (but inventory that napkin pitch!). Then, go back with your iterated prototype (less crude, adapted to their feedback) and co-create with your stakeholders again. You might continue for three or four rounds until they are as invested in the napkin-pitch concept as you are.

As the GCCA team moved closer to testing, getting feedback from students was not possible because the summer term had ended and students were no longer on campus. On July 16, Robin met with the rest of the counseling staff to seek their input and, in particular, to test the assumption that counselors would be willing to implement the early-advising approach. Robin experienced a mix of anxiety and excitement at this step:

> I was so anxious. I must have looked like I needed medication when I was asking the counselors to take that on and change their days off, knowing what I was asking. But it was also a high point because it's exciting to try something new and to implement something.

As the design team had hoped, the counselors were on board with the concepts the team had developed and were willing to sacrifice vacation time for testing.

Step 14: Run Your Learning Launches

Having run an initial set of thought and simulation experiments, you are now ready to conduct experiments to determine whether your napkin pitches will fly in the real world. You know who your partners will be, you've got a solid grasp on the users' needs, and your prototypes have become more sophisticated. But the future is still uncertain. We call experiments conducted in the real world "learning launches." Though similar to a pilot or a rollout, they are not the same. Forming a bridge between one-on-one stakeholder co-creation sessions in step 13 and the ramp-up in step 15, a learning launch is about moving into the real world and how much more you can still learn.

Remember that say-do gap? Until this point, you haven't asked any stakeholders to truly put skin in the game. No money, no resources except a bit of time. The launch, however, needs to feel real to a number of stakeholders and to everyone on your team. The true test of any new concept includes stakeholders demonstrating their enthusiasm through their actual behavior, ideally over a period of time. Do they value it? Do they use it the way they said they would?

But now, before you move into step 14, go back and compare the design brief and criteria to your now-developed concept to verify that it addresses what you wanted to accomplish, that it meets the "Our ideal solution would…" requirements, that the constraints are addressed, and that you have some way of measuring success. You may love the idea—and we hope you do—but does it do what you set out to do?

Designing the launch itself is straightforward. First, you need a working prototype that focuses on the key assumption you're testing and goes beyond the low-fidelity models you created in step 12. Then you need to set tight boundaries and plan for the launch to end. Set concrete limits on variables such as length of time, number of stakeholders, features, and geography. Though you want to work in fast feedback cycles, you should expect surprises when your napkin-pitch idea meets reality. Consequently, processes for handling dissent, resolving conflicts constructively, and adapting on the fly are great assets.

You will do a series of learning launches as you iterate your offering to match the new learning that the launches are producing. Each launch, based on what you learned in the prior one, narrows the search and focuses the desired outcome until you've addressed the metrics you set in your design brief. Ultimately, learning launches result in decisions. If you decide to move ahead with additional development, the learning launch should tell you how. Continue your learning launches until all issues and assumptions have been addressed (and, you hope, solved) and you're ready to move into implementation.

The GCCA team felt ready to move their ideas into reality. Around that time, the leadership team (Miguel, Robin, and Kathleen) headed to the Gateway Network's annual conference in Boston. This event gave them time together, and they seized on it to plan their learning launch. They realized that they didn't need to select just one napkin pitch; they could combine four of the five into an integrated solution. As Robin explained, "When it all came together, we realized, 'Wait a minute. We don't have four or five counselor pitches; we actually could integrate them into one.'"

The team hunkered down and brought everything together and created a Welcome Month, fostering a new, nearly monthlong welcoming phase within the GCCA recruitment process prior to the first day of school. Upon their return to campus, the GCCA leadership team launched the concept almost immediately, simply because the semester was starting. As Joan described it:

> We did a quick thought experiment: How would this look? What might we do? Key assumptions had already been tested with the counseling staff: Were counselors available? Would the technology work? So we went live because the students were coming in the door.

Learning from the Learning Launches

Initial feedback from the learning launch was encouraging. GCCA surveyed the students in classroom assessments during the first week of school. Students were asked, for example, how much contact each student had with his or her counselor prior to day one. With almost the full class responding, 38 percent had been in contact with a counselor four or more times—a higher percentage than in the past. Another item asked about the effectiveness of the welcome meetings. Nearly 60 percent of students responded that their counselor contacts were effective in helping them plan to manage attendance barriers. Seventy-nine percent responded that the Welcome Month undertakings helped them feel less anxious about school, and 82 percent reported that counseling and activities helped build their awareness of program expectations. Notice that the queries directed at students did not ask whether they *liked* the Welcome Month or wanted it continued. Instead, they tested for the specific outcomes around attendance, anxiety reduction, and increased awareness of program expectations.

Both counseling staff anecdotes and students' responses indicated that students did indeed understand both GCCA's and other students' expectations better than in the past. The team used GCCA enrollment reports to monitor retention and attendance and discovered that the new student cohort had much better September attendance in weeks two and three than past cohorts had demonstrated. By mid-October, 92 percent of the cohort was still enrolled, reflecting an improvement over the 88 percent fall 2013 retention rate reported by the Gates Foundation, which sponsored the Gateway program. The changes appeared to be producing positive differences.

As the team met in January 2015 to review progress, a few next steps were already on their agenda. One was to create a second learning launch for the spring term. This task proved more challenging than expected because circumstances in January differed markedly from those in August. January students did not have as much time to think about the challenging program as the fall beginners did.

They often enrolled with the feeling that GCCA was their "last chance," but without much thought as to the commitment required to succeed. Counselors, too, faced different situations. They were busier in December and January than in the summer and could not provide similar availability.

These challenges felt like a serious setback to some members of the team. Miguel experienced this period as one of his worst moments in the design process, thinking to himself that, after all their work, they were going to have to start over. Robin felt the same way: "I remember the realization that we couldn't replicate the fall. It was a real low for me." Kathleen echoed their sentiment: "I felt low as we started to plan the second learning launch, because it became really apparent that we couldn't just replicate the first one. And I remember feeling 'Was it all for nothing?'"

Yet the team persevered, adapted and invented ideas to deal with the new challenges and launched a successful spring term. "We launched, and I was back to feeling positive," Kathleen noted. Miguel experienced the same effect:

> Once we launched in January, I felt positive again. And now, having gone through it once more and doing the third learning launch, it feels so much easier. Yeah, we will tweak things, but we know that we have a goal that we want to accomplish and I think it's kind of baked into our process now. Now it's "We need to get together and figure out welcome week." It's just a whole different feeling.

One remaining important goal was to better understand differences among students. To do this, Joan turned to the persona tool:

> We know we have many different types of students, many different needs, many different backgrounds. That's our next phase for the recruitment project. When you bring our students into the room, the diversity of reasons that they're behind, and their needs, are just incredible. We have students that are just incredibly shy and they are bullied. We have students that were engaged in problem behavior and now they're getting back on track. Throughout our whole process, not only recruitment but student-support services messaging, the speakers that they bring in, or the extracurriculars that they do, it will be influenced by understanding the various personas that are represented in our student body. I think that would be a huge cultural shift for us to move to that level.

To accomplish this, a new group, separate from the original GCCA design team, was set up, with Joan again acting as chair. Robin also joined the new team. The new team first went back to the online learning world to view the segments on Darden's advanced discovery tools. They also used the instructional materials for the tools included in *The Designing for Growth Field Book*. They then reviewed the original ethnographic data gathered the previous summer, along with other relevant GCCA reports. The group wanted to move quickly to experiment with the persona tool, listing dimensions of potential difference among the students that they thought might be useful.

Two personas emerged quickly: Family Ties Miguel and Artist in Residence Robin. Others followed as the team continued to reflect on the students' motivating, and sometimes competing, interests and commitments. Eventually, the team developed seven personas, on the basis of their observations of behaviors. Team members then asked and answered a question about the jobs to be done: What did each want the GCCA experience to help them do? The group also discussed the journey of each persona to and through GCCA.

Artist in Residence:
Robin

Bio

One can recognize Robin as an artist in residence within a blink of an eye – upon first impression. her art is part of her identity and evident in her style, manner and conversation. She is a creative person with a real passion for her art.

Robin didn't fit in her large school environment as well as she would have liked. She was bullied and struggled with identity questions. She was overwhelmed by her own high expectations and the expectations of others. She was often reticent in class and sometimes willing to take an F rather than speak or fully engage in group assignments.

Robin thrives in GCCA's small school environment. She values her college student identity. The culture is welcoming. There are other students like her. While she may still speak infrequently in class, she is comfortable sharing her art and artistic life outside of school. She demonstrates strong academic skills and plans to continue in college.

Robin looks to GCCA to help her learn to manage her anxieties. She worries about her transition to RCC classroom experiences and seeks strategies to ease back into RCC's large school environment. She can be disappointed when college experiences don't live up to her expectations. She sometimes has to be reminded that some assignments must be completed as assigned – even when she doesn't see their relevance or her artistic vision points elsewhere.

Behaviors

All personas are gender neutral. The following observed behaviors, characteristics, & motivations led the team to identify Artist in Residence as a GCCA learner persona.

- *Learner may be reticent or shy in class. They might take an F rather than talk.*
- *Learner talks freely about their art; may even perform or share talents outside GCCA.*
- *Learner's art is clearly part of learner's identity.*
- *Learner thrives within a small school setting.*
- *Learner demonstrates strong academic skills.*

Needs/Goals/Job to be Done

- *"My art is central to who I am."*
- *"I identify as a college student and want a college experience, not an alternative high school experience."*
- *Learner seeks strategies to manage anxieties.*
- *Learner seeks strategies to ease the transition from GCCA's small school environment to RCC's large school and college classroom environments and beyond.*
- *"I need a program of study and schedule designed to meet my learning needs and goals."*

Example of a student persona developed by the team.

When the group sensed that they had identified a comprehensive set of personas, they sought feedback from other key stakeholders. All responded that the personas seemed to mirror what they had seen and helped them to better understand the students. Joan explained:

> We learned a great deal from the deep dive into our ethnographic research. We believe it revealed real differences within our learner population. We have years of survey and student data. Though extremely valuable, our summary statistics do not bring home our learners' needs, goals, or jobs to be done as well as have the personas. They talk to us and, clearly, are more than the sum of their barriers, needs, or goals. They give new meaning to our collective commitment to be learner centered.

GCCA made significant changes as a result of this new work. They removed "at-risk" from the school's mission statement, feeling that it not only adversely labeled their students but also mislabeled them, for reasons Joan explained:

> We now understand that "at-risk" doesn't meaningfully apply. The seven personas represent learners seeking programs and services to accomplish education and career goals. At the same time, they seek assistance in managing and completing jobs to be done that may limit access or engagement within traditional educational contexts. We are chartered to help them connect to resources, navigate their journeys, and succeed.

Step 15: Design the On-Ramp

The final step in the process, designing the on-ramp, often constitutes its own mini design project. Having worked to create a value-enhancing idea, we are now no longer recruiting users to help test concepts but are creating mechanisms for would-be clients to find *us*. Getting the idea in front of a large group of potential prospects is the ultimate goal of designing the on-ramp. Of course, if the team members have done good stakeholder assessment throughout the earlier steps, they have laid the groundwork, and, in the case of a small, focused target group like GCCA's, awareness and understanding of the new concept may already exist. In this step, innovators seek a strategy to make users aware of how the new concept meets their needs, to convince them to try it out and, hopefully, to have them become advocates for it with others just like themselves.

Ironically, today, when seemingly everyone has access to so much information, when communication channels are everywhere, bringing a new idea to the world may be harder than ever. The clutter of ideas is so immense that, like shampoo shoppers in a grocery store aisle, even many who want to test a new concept can get overwhelmed by the number of possibilities and therefore return to their old, "safe" solutions. Solving the on-ramp issue, in effect, is a new design challenge. It often requires as much creativity as the creation of the concept itself.

For the GCCA team, which had spent two semesters learning how to best serve the school's incoming students—and with a commitment to continued learning—step 15 was not critical. They had already ramped up the services in real life. Most projects, however, serve larger client bases than students in a single community and therefore need to develop a plan for taking their now fully developed idea into the real world.

Reflections on the Process

Looking back over what the GCCA team had learned on their design thinking journey, Joan offered some reflections on the benefits of the process for the team. She first focused on the benefits of the structure it provided and its emphasis on the end user:

> The design thinking framework helped us tremendously. It gave us a process and a framework that was systematic. I think there's always a tendency to run off and solve the problem before thinking about it. As we started the project, it was really in recognition that, by default, not by intent, the school had moved towards an attitude of "Let's just bring them in and try to hang on to whoever we bring in," with an almost fill-the-seats mentality. And we wanted to wrestle some of that back. We are a group of people who are totally focused on the learner, but as we were doing our day-to-day, almost bureaucratic enrollment stuff, it was being lost. So design thinking really helped us refocus on the learners that we were engaging and ask the questions of what value we are providing even at that very beginning stage.

A second benefit, in her view, was the power of small bets and quick experiments:

> The team recognized that they didn't have to do lengthy studies to figure out what to do, that the value was in learning what we could as we were working. We didn't want to go live

necessarily as quickly as we did, but students were coming. We might as well, we thought. *If we keep doing what we were doing in the past, we're going to lose them anyway.* And we weren't causing any major ripples in anybody's world by just focusing on our students.

Finally, Joan noted design thinking's impact on the leadership team itself:

The design experience gives management a common vocabulary to communicate with employees and team members. The language of the new leadership team has changed. They talk about resetting their lens. It's a reset in recognition that even though this group of educators is really learner centered anyway, there are times you have to ask, "Hey, wait a minute, have we lost that learner lens?" It is focusing on the learner and what learners need. And then there's also the back and forth between the tools and the process steps. The process provides a framework to follow as we work through various problems.

And, as Miguel reflected on the process, he saw it evolve:

Maybe we jumped in a little quickly as we felt that time crunch. It was fast, and maybe we didn't do the process as thoroughly as we could have, but the things that came out of it were really good. I think the second time around we learned and we got different people involved, invited more voices from the staff. That was a really good learning experience, and I think that's going to show as we see the ownership of the process start to transition. I'm hoping to see the evidence of this positive experience bleeding over into other problems, other problem-solving efforts.

Shelagh Camak, the senior administrator who had requested the work, reported the team's reflection on its project journey and later iterations: "We are in a really good exciting place. It is a good tactic for all of us to really learn the process and understand it much, much better . . . We are all learning it together."

Joan shared some final thoughts:

GCCA has grown beyond a replication site. Our horizon has shifted from realizing an effective Gateway to College option for the communities served by Riverside City College to embracing GCCA's potential as a "skunkworks" organization. With the knowledge and expertise gained from over twelve years of experience, GCCA seeks to design innovative solutions for the learners it enrolls. Its understanding and empathy for these learners, as well as its commitment to action research, including design thinking, will enable GCCA to pursue a trajectory that works for students and informs its college and community partners as each seeks to meet the needs of our students.

CHAPTER FIFTEEN
Building Organizational Capabilities

We began this book by noting how a cucumber might derail social sector innovation efforts, even those we need the most. As we conclude, there seems little doubt that bringing creativity to any organization is difficult, but especially so in the social sector. Even Steve Jobs might have been stymied by cucumber problems if he'd started out buried in a governmental bureaucracy or had to overcome inertia in a hospital or school system. No one knows, or perhaps can even anticipate, what will stall the innovation process when there are vocal and diverse stakeholders, competing definitions of the problem, entrenched politics, and risk aversion at play—or even simply a Washington Post reporter adding color to an article.

Design thinking works to identify and address these issues as it emphasizes understanding all key stakeholders' deepest motivations and iterating through potential solutions to satisfy them. But moving solutions into action is rarely easy. No one can force a manager to expend resources or compel an organizational board desperate for dollars to fund a new idea. Since no one can identify every barrier to building a new future, the process we've outlined aims at understanding this reality and anticipating and addressing possible issues. We hope that you don't face your own cucumber problem, but probably you will—and we hope that our stories help you, like the Lab@OPM, to succeed in spite of them.

In part 1 of this book, we expressed our belief that design thinking helps deal with these realities by catalyzing conversations for change across difference. In part 2, we looked in depth at a variety of organizations using design thinking to address challenges to the greater good. In part 3, we explored one suggested process for structuring these conversations. In this last chapter, we first examine the big-picture takeaways from our design stories and then look at how organizations can better support these efforts.

In chapter 1, we made a promise: that design thinking could help innovators convene conversations that truly engage diverse stakeholders to build higher-order solutions collaboratively—*because* of their differences as well as despite them. This chapter looks at how the practices and outcomes in our stories come together to achieve this. We conclude by suggesting some actions at the personal level that will foster your ability to make an impact.

How Does Design Thinking Help?

As we look back at the big picture of design thinking's contributions, we see it accelerating innovation efforts in a variety of ways. Let's look at each in turn:

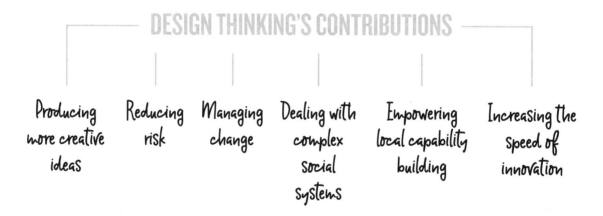

DESIGN THINKING'S CONTRIBUTIONS

Producing more creative ideas   Reducing risk   Managing change   Dealing with complex social systems   Empowering local capability building   Increasing the speed of innovation

Producing More Creative Ideas

How has design thinking helped our innovators improve the creativity of their ultimate solutions? First, design thinking encouraged enhanced creativity by keeping teams in the question long enough to reframe the boundaries of their challenges. Staying with **What *is*** before asking **What *if*?** encouraged Children's Health System of Texas to take a deeper dive into the lives of patients and families, leading to the realization that a larger focus on community-centered wellness (rather than building local clinics) held the key to reducing inappropriate emergency room usage. It also triggered a reexamination of the assumptions behind their medical care model—assumptions that turned out to be erroneous. Living in the problem space helped the US Transportation Security Administration recognize that they needed to ensure that innocent travelers remained calm in order to make malevolent intent more visible and to improve security. For the Texas Coastal Bend group, working with the Community Transportation Association of America led them to a new question: Could they transport *future trainees* instead of workers?

Second, design thinking enhanced creativity by using data from stakeholder ethnography to formulate design criteria that guided idea generation. Deep immersion in stakeholders' worlds, rather than imposing experts' views, led to crucial insights. When the doctors at Monash Medical Centre did the difficult work of uncovering Tom's actual treatment experience in outpatient psychiatric care and looked at it from *his* perspective, it changed the nature of the solutions they sought. What was missing, the clinicians realized, was a sense of *care* for Tom's long-term problems, and this need became the prime criteria for designing the new future that became Monash's Agile clinics. At the Whiteriver Indian Hospital, Marliza Rivera stepped away from her own comfort with technology (and what cognitive scientists would call an "egocentric empathy" bias) to acknowledge that her beloved kiosk idea, inspired by urban Baltimore's Johns Hopkins Hospital, was unlikely to be workable for those she served—primarily tribal elders intimidated by technology. Since an electronic kiosk might make the situation worse for her primarily elderly clients, her story illustrates the downside of focusing solely on a "best practice" approach to innovation.

Third, design thinking, through its emphasis on broad stakeholder engagement and co-creation, tapped into diverse perspectives to find higher-order solutions, first by assembling a diverse team and then by providing a conversational framework to help team members leverage their differences. CTAA insisted on diverse teams at each location, sensing that these varied individuals, many of whom had never met, would educate each other in ways that would produce higher-order, more systemic solutions and might form bonds that would equip them to work together on future problems, not just the present ones. Design-led conversations at the US Food and Drug Administration encouraged diverse stakeholders to come together to pursue important outcomes, like emergency preparedness, from a more systemic perspective. This collaboration, in turn, allowed them to surface and address root causes of the lack of preparedness. In that process, even the FDA itself discovered that regulation, its raison d'être, was not always the best solution. During these conversations across difference, design thinking avoids reaching for early, often mediocre compromises, seeking instead solutions that resolve unwanted trade-offs.

Reducing Risk

How does design thinking help innovators reduce the risk of undertaking innovation? Here again, design thinking's contributions are multipronged. First, it allows the formulation of better ideas for the reasons stated above: it encourages deeper exploration of the problem space, and it promotes user-driven ideation that leverages team diversity to identify higher-order solutions and keeps idea creation based in the reality of user needs. Starting off with better ingoing ideas goes a long way toward reducing the risk of failure. In fighting our own tendency to project our worldview onto those we are designing for, design's ethnography tools help us find solutions that users find acceptable.

Then, the testing process during **What *wows*** and **What *works*** adds an additional dimension that minimizes risk. Given the uncertainty of the innovation environment, no matter how good our exploratory work is, we can expect to be wrong. Despite our efforts to better understand stakeholders' jobs to be done and their experiential journeys, some of our solutions will still miss the mark. Successful venture capitalists expect the businesses they back to fail far more frequently than they succeed. Thus, for them, knowing when to *stop* investing can be as critical a skill as knowing when to start. The same is true for innovators. Consequently, helping to improve hypothesis-testing skills is critical. Here, design thinking tools minimize common decision-making errors.

For more than fifty years, cognitive scientists have explored a set of well-recognized flaws in decision makers' hypothesis-testing abilities. These flaws include overoptimism (the planning fallacy), inability to see disconfirming data (hypothesis confirmation bias), attachment to early solutions (endowment effect), and a preference for the easily imagined (availability bias). Design thinking's hypothesis-driven approach mitigates the impact of these biases by stipulating that innovators develop multiple concepts, create prototypes, surface unarticulated assumptions, and actively seek disconfirming data.

Identifying potentially promising but flawed solutions and developing the ability to design and execute cheap, fast experiments is critical to reducing innovation risk. Even expert scientists at the FDA can be ineffective testers when their emotions and personal beliefs interfere with their neutrality, as Suzanne Schwartz, their director of emergency preparedness, pointed out. Marliza's experiments at Whiteriver reduced risk by helping her to pivot from kiosk to paper to fast track as she learned quickly and cheaply what didn't work or wasn't legally permissible. At the Kingwood Trust, Katie Gaudion created prototypes—and *expected* some of them to be destroyed. Even beyond testing the quality of the ideas, Dr. Don Campbell discovered at Monash that learning launches of the long-stay app were not just testing ideas; they were building trust and ownership among the staff, reducing risk even further by increasing the likelihood of successful implementation.

Managing Change

How has design thinking helped innovators improve their abilities to manage the changes involved in carrying new concepts into successful action? Don's observations about the unanticipated benefits of learning launches for staff ownership of ideas suggest one direction. Ultimately, innovation requires that a particular set of human beings behave in new ways. Without encouraging different choices as part of implementation, our investment in creative idea generation and rigorous testing is useless. Since change theorists argue that behavioral change is intensely personal and subjective, this dovetails with design thinking's human-centered focus. It is not just users that we strive to understand; it is the entire set of stakeholders who are part of transforming new concepts into reality.

One popular theory of how change occurs illustrates vividly how design thinking's approach supports critical elements of change. It argues that behavioral alterations are a function of four factors: the dissatisfaction with the status quo, the clarity and resonance of the new future, and the existence of a pathway to get there, all balanced against any perceived loss associated with the change.

Level of dissatisfaction with the status quo

Clarity of the new future

Pathway

Loss

Design thinking methodologies encourage change and increase the likelihood of successful implementation by influencing each factor in that formula. Exploration of the problem during **What is** builds engagement that leads to alignment around the nature of the problems needing to be addressed, and that naturally deepens dissatisfaction with the status quo. Ethnography that identifies pain points and unmet needs helps develop empathy and builds change agents' resolve to make life better for those they serve.

Christine Miller at Monash reminded us of this when she recounted the impact Tom's journey map had on the staff at Monash: "It was shocking . . . We needed to feel the blockages and struggles." In Dallas, at Children's Health, Eli MacLaren worked to shift the mindset of clinical staff from one of evaluation (patients weren't using the system correctly) to one of empathy, or from a "place of judgment to a place of possibilities," as she described it.

But design thinking doesn't stop there. It works on the second factor: building greater clarity around what the new future looks like, as well. Based on that deeper empathy and understanding, design thinking helps everyone involved envision new possibilities for addressing challenges with clear and compelling concepts during **What if**. In Dallas, the Business Innovation Factory insisted on formulating a specific "from-to" construct for each of the opportunity spaces at Children's Health, to provide the detail that successful change requires. And by moving beyond complaining about current reality, design thinking confers an additional benefit: it gives people who are stuck in the problem space the motivation and hope that there can be a new and better future. Remember former high school principal Michael Donnelly's comment on the way the Kerry charrette process helped them think in a new way: "We'd been analyzing and defining the problem for years. This conversation was about *solving* the problem. It meant that there *could be* a solution. Maybe our problems weren't just an inevitable part of society evolving that we had to accept."

During **What wows**, prototyping and co-creation require that we flesh out salient details of any new future in even greater detail, adding further clarity. And in **What works**, experiments involving actual stakeholders further enhance the tangibility and vividness of the new future. MasAgro's practice of encouraging the physical planting of rows of old and new crops side by side provided the ultimate prototype in making the promise of modern farming techniques tangible to skeptical farmers.

Design thinking's emphasis on the particular also addresses the third factor: providing pathways to the future. It insists that we address the means as well as the ends—what resources will be needed?

THE FAMILY 100 PROJECT

New Zealand's Family 100 Project provides an example of the power of narrative to build empathy and, along with it, the kind of dissatisfaction with the status quo that motivates change. The project followed poverty-level families for a year to understand the issues behind being poor in New Zealand. ThinkPlace, a design consultancy, worked with the Auckland City Mission to distill the massive amount of data into the compelling story of a single mother, Charlotte, trying to hold a job, care for her children, and find food, medicine, and housing while utilizing Auckland's transit system. Few could fail to be moved by Charlotte's struggle in seeking the basics for her family, and a set of Auckland politicians were even motivated into personal action. "I didn't realize how time consuming and expensive it is to be poor," one deputy prime minister acknowledged, as he sought greater involvement from his staff, through volunteering in soup kitchens and shelters, to better empathize with their clients.

What training? What measures should we be paying attention to? What are the way stations along the path? Recall that the Institute without Boundaries left the Kerry community not just with potential solutions; it also included detailed timelines of the different specific activities needed along the way. BIF worked with Children's Health not only to create a new business model but also to design new metrics to measure wellness. And the local networks facilitated by the design processes at the FDA, CTAA, and Children's Health actually increased the resources available to achieve the new future by pooling the capabilities of the different players in the ecosystem.

Finally, the sense of loss that so often accompanies behavioral change—the loss of control when new solutions ask partners to assume more responsibility, or the lost sense of competence arising from the demand for new skills, or even, perhaps, just nostalgia for the comfort of the "good old days"—are outweighed by achieving greater clarity on the gains associated with change. At Monash, learning launches built trust and ownership that combated loss. Seeing the crops planted side by side reduced farmers' fears of accepting MasAgro's advice. No one said it better than Eli, regarding her work aiding the shift from medical-centered treatment of illness to community-centered encouragement of wellness at Children's Health:

> People feel threatened by work they think is going to disrupt their job. You have to help them to see themselves in the future . . . use their stories, their insight, and their expertise so that they hear their voices reflected in the future state. You co-create so that they feel like they helped build this new model. There's an old adage that change is painful when done *to* you but powerful when done *by* you. If you can just tap into that, you're golden.

Dealing with Complex Social Systems

In the background of our discussions, there is a shift even more fundamental than the one from Innovation I to Innovation II—one that we believe is driving the changing paradigm of how innovation happens. It is the shift from a *mechanistic* view of organizations and the larger systems they operate in to one that sees them as *complex social systems*. Traditionally, we have treated organizations and their ecosystem as though they were machines, inert *things* that could be controlled and managed and that made decisions based on logic and evaluation of consequences—the "rational actor" model. Now, we increasingly see them, instead, as collections of human beings who are motivated by differing logics and perspectives, whose reactions are sometimes based on emotions and politics and bureaucracy rather than careful, comprehensive decision making that "optimizes" the choice, as the rational actor allegedly does. Recent research illustrates clearly that the complex reality of social systems is not consistent with the convenient "rational actor" assumptions. These complex human social systems are inherently unmanageable and often chaotic. We can shape and influence their operations, but that requires different tools than customary approaches to strategy and policy traditionally offered.

How does design thinking help innovators deal with the complexity in modern social systems? It challenges the underlying premise of a rational actor approach by focusing on innovation as a *social* process, intimately tied to human emotions and reliant on inexact methodologies in which humans collaborate and solutions *emerge* over time. In doing so, it better reflects the actual reality of organizational life in the social sector. In this way, it gives us, as we argued in chapter 1, a social technology better matched to the reality of achieving innovation and change in the social sector. Let's look at how it does this, in more detail:

- In design thinking, the traditional notion of a single "optimal" solution, selected from among a set of alternatives identified in advance, is rejected. That premise is replaced in design thinking by a search for multiple possible solutions, with the most promising ideas emerging *during* the process, shaped by conversation among the players involved. In complex social systems, it is almost impossible to "optimize" in the usual sense—we lack both the alignment around objectives and the data to assess cause and effect. In the design conversations during the Kerry charrette, for instance, there was no "right" answer. Four areas of opportunity, identified by the community, sparked the conversation and continuously morphed throughout subsequent discussions as thinking diverged and converged during brainstorming by students, staff, experts, and community leaders. In fact, the emergence of solutions throughout the process, with their diversity and their continuous evolution and change, forms one of the characteristic themes in our research. We see it in nearly every story.

- Network effects play a much more critical role in complex social systems. Access to their powerful network is a key reason why the Ignite Accelerator program at the US Department of Health and Human Services accelerates innovation. Marliza was able to pivot quickly away from her second paper-based concept without doing any actual experimentation, after learning—through the IDEA Lab staff connections with HHS legal experts—that the Emergency Medical Treatment and Labor Act prohibits screening of patients on entrance to the emergency room. CTAA's ambitions are as much to construct local networks in the areas served as they are to solve the currently presenting problems. The same is true in Dallas, as Children's Health works to construct the kind of ecosystem that makes community-based wellness, rather than medical-centered treatment, even possible. Perhaps Ken Skodacek said it most clearly when he talked about the FDA's need to work across organizations: "When the FDA controls all aspects of the process, then maybe you don't have to bring in other stakeholders. But in many cases, a government agency is at the crossroads of an issue—we don't have complete control over it." This is true not just for government agencies. We see it in health care, in education, in charitable foundations. Increasingly, it is the network that matters. And design thinking has a unique ability to bring members of an ecosystem into productive conversation with each other.

- Efficiency, the dominant criteria in stable, simple systems, must be balanced against the need for resilience and adaptability in complex, unstable systems. Design thinking's patience with seeming inefficiency can thus be a positive rather than a negative. At Kingwood, when Katie used a mirroring technique to better understand what the world looks like from Pete's perspective, taking the time to experience ripping pieces off the sofa and leaning her ear against the wall with him, she uncovered insights that "efficient" methodologies like focus groups would probably not reveal. In our stories, the conversations *meander*. The inclusion of disparate voices takes time and patience. It is often chaotic. But out of that chaos we see better solutions emerge. From a short-term perspective, it may have looked initially more "efficient" for the FDA to mandate what issues would be addressed at the respiratory device meeting, but they would have missed perhaps the most essential learning of all: that training, not regulation, was the driving factor in preparedness.

One key feature in many of our stories is the avoidance of top-down standardization (always a favorite when efficiency is the goal) in favor of locally determined, customized solutions and processes. Standardization, again, may seem efficient in the short run, but in a complex world, adaptability favors solutions grounded in local conditions. Innovation is often driven by attending to the needs of a smaller subset, and then adapting that to a larger group. It also favors an emphasis on identifying design criteria—the qualities of desired solutions in general—rather than on the specific solutions themselves. Design criteria have more inherent resilience; that is, they are useful in telling you how to pivot when an initial solution fails. TSA's investment in their research into traveler experiences did not become obsolete when an unanticipated agency mandate shut down the creation of the Sapient-designed website. The information they learned was equally useful in the switch to the development of a mobile phone app.

Diversity plays an increasingly critical role here, too. Simple, stable systems favor homogeneity and usually see diversity of input as a nuisance. In complex social systems, heterogeneity is more valuable because it increases the range of both current information and the breadth of solutions generated. The introduction of new voices helps an organization see more opportunities—ones not necessarily path-dependent on previous choices. That understanding also produces the possibility for more intelligent and adaptable coordination. However, diversity must be of the right kind—it must be "requisite" diversity, in the language of systems theory.

Empowering Local Capability Building

Local, rather than global, decision making is likely to be most successful in complex social systems. This is because local intelligence is necessary and local action truly matters. Though the larger system is itself complex and difficult to predict, its subunits are less so, system theorists argue. These subunits tend to operate on what researchers call "replicator dynamics." As in a fractal pattern (in which each subunit is a smaller-scale picture of the whole), simple central guidelines—established globally but applied locally—are often the most promising method for bringing order and accomplishing change. These rules generally specify processes or the larger purpose, leaving decisions about the specific content of problems and their solutions to frontline staff. Considering design thinking as a set of "simple rules" allows us to coordinate and encourage innovation in complex social systems. Think of IwB's simple rules for charrettes, such as that no one can say no on day one.

Throughout our discussions—on producing better solutions, on minimizing risk and managing change within complex social systems—the power of the local has been a strong theme. This has taken the form not only of local intelligence on any particular issue but also of the creation of local networks capable of coordination and joint action. How has design thinking helped innovators build these networks of capabilities that allow for ongoing innovation? The answer is that it has democratized design in a way that brings new voices into the conversation to identify and solve their own problems, while fostering sharing across units.

In doing this, it addresses one of the key challenges in governance: the tension between centralization and decentralization. Centralization offers economies of scale as well as the ability to share best practices across units, but it often comes accompanied by the emphasis on standardization that we talked about earlier. Decentralization, on the other hand, offers responsiveness to local conditions and builds engagement to catalyze change but can make coordination and learning across units difficult to achieve. Design thinking, we have argued, can help us get at the best of both worlds.

CTAA uses design thinking as their mechanism for standardization and centralized control, but they focus on controlling the quality of the process, not the prescription of local outcomes. By combining the use of design thinking with the formation of diverse community teams who share their learnings with others, they seek the best of both worlds. MasAgro goes even a step further toward a powerful resolution of the central/local tension, building on the concept of repertoire at an institutional level. Think back to the stories we recounted in which an individual's unique repertoire—Dr. Melissa Casey's combination of experience as a tax specialist and psychiatrist at Monash, or Peter Roberts's work in both health care delivery and insurance at Children's Health—made a difference. At MasAgro, we see the benefits of an organization's repertoire. Because of its global operations, MasAgro is able to reach across its enormous cache of worldwide farming knowledge to create a broad menu of choices, and then work with community thought leaders to select the ones most appropriate to whatever locale they are currently working in. Farmers in Oaxaca, Mexico, have access to a global knowledge base while retaining the power to select the specific information that works best for them. Their successes, failures, and modifications, in turn, feed learning back into the larger system.

Finally, theorists assert that paying deep attention to actual human experience—working to understand it and convey it to others—is fundamental to producing successful innovation in complex social systems. Design thinking can play an important role in this, as New Zealand ThinkPlace partner Leslie Tergas points out:

> These complex systems are usually understood from a quantitative perspective, and what this fails to provide is meaning. We then end up with policies and other interventions that don't make sense for people, and a big gap between the intent of the policy and what actually happens. This is actually no wonder, if the design of such social complex systems has not been preceded by sense-making of the human experience in the system. What we are doing with work like Family 100 is starting to shine a light on the fact that there is a deep and reliable practice for uncovering the complexity of human experience, modeling what is happening, and then having the ability to use that in design and decision making about the future. Without this sense making and modeling of the human experience, policy makers and designers are making decisions in the dark, quite literally.

We see Leslie's words reflected in the power of some of the deeply personal stories we have heard in part 2, such as the story of Pete's enjoyment of ripping the sofa at Kingwood or of Tom lacking care at Monash, despite his seventy different interactions with staff. Hearing these stories changes us as it changed the innovators in those organizations. Their authenticity commands our attention; it makes what they tell us matter to us, not just them.

Increasing the Speed of Innovation

Ultimately, successful change of any kind relies on a sense of momentum. In the absence of momentum, as progress slows, even enthusiastic innovators run out of energy. How does the design thinking method outlined here help increase the speed of the innovation process itself?

To begin with, the process contains an inherent bias or inclination for action. By engaging the requisite voices, letting them shape the problem definition, and curating a set of design criteria that drills down to what really matters, we create committed people likely to seize the opportunity to act, to make small bets fast. Others, who are disengaged and/or confused, operating from a sense of compliance, will instead drag their heels and wait for direction from above. Alignment helps teams of innovators overcome workplace politics and collaborate, thus reducing the frictions that slow them down.

Curated conversations help innovators to focus on specifying essential design criteria—what is truly important—and to avoid being distracted by irrelevant data. Curated prototyping eliminates the need for debates and, instead, allows stakeholders to shape and select from a set of options.

Engagement, alignment, and curation lead to speed. Inertia, compliance, internal politics, and confusion slow us down. It's that simple. Looking at this self-sustaining cycle takes us back to Jim Collins's famous flywheel in *Good to Great*, with its accelerating momentum. In the short run, design thinking's early ethnography may, in fact, take more time than gathering people in a conference room and asking them to brainstorm from their personal perspectives. Placing small bets to start and iterating ever improved offerings may take more time than quickly scaling a half-baked solution. But, if positive impact on problems that matter is the goal, early hours invested in a design thinking process are, in the long run, both more effective and more efficient. They are time well spent.

How Can Organizations Pave the Way to Innovation II?

Having looked at the contributions of design thinking, let's turn to our second goal—helping organizations build a widely dispersed capability for innovation. Hopefully, we have made a compelling case for the timeliness of a transition from Innovation I to Innovation II. How do we facilitate that shift? As we close this last chapter, then, we offer a few final thoughts about specific actions, at both organizational and personal levels, that leaders can take to further the progress of design thinking. What can we learn from our stories about the role that their organizations played in helping our innovators succeed?

As we discussed in chapter 1, we saw no one-size-fits-all path across our stories. What we did see, however, was a clear departure from the traditional idea that change has to start at the top. Instead, we saw entrepreneurial activism at a grassroots level. People at all levels of the organization—from senior leaders like Peter Roberts at Children's Health to Marliza Rivera at the front line in Whiteriver—took innovation into their own hands and made a real difference in the lives of the people they cared about.

Recognizing that cultural change is difficult, we believe that small design thinking projects done under the organizational radar can be key to nudging organizations toward design thinking. Often, major change comes about because small teams try something new. When they have successful results, those metrics or testimonials become ammunition that eases acceptance of the next design thinking project in the organization. Having some examples of successful design-driven innovation may help even the most buttoned-down George better understand Geoffrey's seemingly wild thinking, and encourage the kind of small experiments that can break through the paralysis created by a "prove it" mentality.

These innovators aren't waiting for permission from above. And even if they get it, it is no guarantee of real change. Although most senior leaders talk about the need for creativity and innovation today, the cultural change needed to create the context in which Innovation II thrives will continue to be difficult, even for them. Many times we've seen senior leaders' decrees be given lip service by staff while, below the organization's surface, nothing really changes. Change is never easy—certainly not the kind of soul-searching changes that the shift from Innovation I to Innovation II requires.

For change to happen, it usually needs to move both from the top down and from a grassroots level up. This sounds more complicated than it is. We believe that under-the-radar projects from the front lines of organizations, over time and after successes, provide the tangible examples and outcomes that pull an organization toward utilizing design thinking on an organizational level. From the other end, senior management needs to understand how and why the physics of innovation—its natural laws—are different (as venture capitalists do) and must put in place a supportive infrastructure to help employees feel safe to explore new ways of thinking and behaving. This is done not by mandating or conscripting but by issuing an invitation. In the following sections, we discuss what we've learned from our stories about how management can build an infrastructure inviting employees to think and act creatively.

Actions for Impact at the Organizational Level

Think in Terms of Constructing and Managing a Portfolio of Concepts

This is the mindset of venture capitalists. So many of the bifurcations we draw in the innovation space—disruptive versus incremental, strategic versus tactical, long term versus short term—can hinder the development of innovation by casting the choices we make as either/or. The question: Do we focus on big-picture transformational shifts in business models, on wicked problems, or do we hunker down and focus on improving tomorrow's experience for a particular set of stakeholders? These false dichotomies become self-fulfilling hypotheses: either things change only in bits and the system is never reformed or, in the expectation of system-level change and the search for only "big ideas," nothing happens today.

To avoid these extremes, we advocate constructing a portfolio of concepts that manage risk and opportunity by arraying ideas along the kind of impact/difficulty grid we saw in the FDA discussions. In this way, we can lay out an ambitious long-term direction while also recognizing opportunities that are more modest and near-term. IwB's commitment to coupling big concepts with phased milestones in the Kerry story is a good example of what this looks like in practice.

Design thinking works to keep the big-picture desire always in focus while practitioners experiment and iterate with the small bets that can, over time, move the organization toward the larger goal. We don't want to eliminate this kind of friction from our innovation processes. There will always be a tension between incrementalism and possibilities. They seem to be opposites, but they need to work together. We need to specify "What if anything were possible?" and then be willing to act incrementally and opportunistically to get there. Small bets and intermediate milestones are—ideally—in service to a longer-term possibility, as the Kerry story demonstrates. This kind of desirable tension comes from moving into action, as Luigi of IwB reminded us, and it keeps us grounded in today's realities while still pursuing an ambitiously different future.

Provide a Structured Process Methodology and Offer the Opportunity to Learn It Well

Design experts, schooled in the methodology and frequently comfortable with ambiguity by nature, rarely rely on a structured process, preferring instead to think in terms of general categories of activities like exploration, ideation, and testing. In our years of working with novice designers, however, we have found these categories to be insufficient in equipping them to actually integrate design thinking into their day-to-day practices. Instead, we see too many return from design school boot camps with enthusiasm and inspiration, only to fall immediately back into business as usual. Especially in the case of risk-averse managers, who are often fearful of failure to begin with and are raised in large bureaucratic organizations, we find that a more structured, end-to-end methodology of the kind we discussed in chapters 13 and 14 makes a significant difference in their ability to actually incorporate design thinking's process and tools into decision making.

Closely related to this need for structure is the need for rigorous training. Given many people's unfamiliarity with design tools, the often challenging level of ambiguity and discomfort involved in putting those tools to work, and the often countercultural value system underlying the process, a significant amount of unlearning of orthodoxies and relearning of new approaches is needed. As with most practices, classroom learning alone is insufficient, and hands-on work with real projects is essential to the development of competence. Yet, in our work, we routinely hear stories of organizations with excellent reputations for employee training expecting graduates of one-day seminars to actually practice design thinking on their own live problems.

Recall Josef Scarantino's concern, in the wake of United Cerebral Palsy's failed Innovation Labs, that design thinking could become a buzzword with little meaning, without support and training to ensure its legitimacy. We share his concern. A hackathon here and there provides a fun introduction to new design thinking tools. It does not provide the foundation needed to do quality work on real problems affecting real stakeholders. In fact, it may damage the ambition to make design thinking more than the latest fad to breeze through management circles.

Another important form of support in our stories was the availability of coaching and facilitation, which both built confidence (especially among novices to the method) and increased the quality of output. In many projects, either a consulting firm (like Peer Insight with CTAA, BIF with Children's Health, BEING with Kingwood, or Sapient and IDEO with TSA), an academic partner (like IwB with County Kerry, or the Royal College of Art's Helen Hamlyn Centre for Design with Kingwood), or internal design experts (like the Lab@OPM with the FDA, or the mentors at HHS) were available to support novice designers as they learned the design thinking methodology. Importantly, these supporting individuals did not do the work for the team; they did the work *with* team members.

Activities like face-to-face interaction with customers, deep immersion in their perspectives, the creation of prototypes, and the design and execution of experiments are not common activities for people who are new to design in business or the social sector. The easier and less scary we make these activities, the more we'll hear "Yes" to our invitations to join a design thinking opportunity.

In the transition from Innovation I to Innovation II, we have noted, one of the most attractive features of the design thinking methodology is its focus on starting small. "Small" can take the form of modest projects or research plans, and even a single in-depth interview with a key stakeholder can hold important insights for innovation. Providing employees with the opportunity to explore small steps or to convene a few local conversations with outside stakeholders is a good starting invitation.

These initiatives don't necessarily need a big budget; when democratizing innovation is our goal, financial resources are often *not* the most important contributor to design thinking success. HHS, remember, *decreased* the size of its grant to winners of its Ignite Accelerator project. And we see scrappy design champions across industry and government bootstrapping their way to significant impact with little internal funding. What these bootstrappers *do* have is competency in design methods, confidence in their ability to work with them, time to spend on the project, access to their stakeholders, and the freedom to place small bets in the real world. The challenge of building a strategic capability where everybody designs is that many would-be design thinkers lack training, confidence, time, support, and enough autonomy to conduct experiments. Some even lack access to the stakeholders they want to serve. Senior leadership plays an important role in providing these pathways to innovation.

But many of the students we work with, whether online in our Coursera courses or face-to-face in our classrooms, have never met a designer, much less had one available to teach and coach them in these new methodologies and tools. Maybe you are one of these. If so, what can you do? We have some final advice to share, organized along the four questions.

Actions for Impact at a Personal Level

When Asking What is?

Invest in inspiration. Fresh new ideas don't arise by themselves. They are coaxed out of hiding by deep insights about the people for whom we seek to create better value. Take the time and energy to invest in ethnography to generate new and deep insights.

Engage new voices. Personal experiences make humans the successes we are, but they also ensure we see things the way we have always seen them. Voices with different perspectives jolt us from programmed responses. From the start, look for new influences to bring into the conversation, including those voices that you don't like, don't agree with, or think have nothing to add.

Beware solutions masquerading as problems. Nothing discourages engagement more effectively than someone pushing his or her own solution under the guise of co-creation. It is easy to cleverly word an answer in the form of a question, opportunity, or problem. Don't. The people whose help and ideas you need will see through the charade and you'll lose them—and worse, you'll miss out on more creative ideas, which never get the chance to show up.

Follow your stakeholders, not your tools. New Zealand ThinkPlace partner Jim Scully warned us against "turning design thinking into a religion." That is essential advice. Even beloved design tools as powerful as journey mapping can blind us to the perspectives of stakeholders, rather than illuminating them. We were struck by this reality as we listened to a recent description of ethnographic work that focused on family violence. Researchers had probed tenaciously for the details of the journey experienced by the women they interviewed. Trouble was, the women themselves had not felt like they were on a journey—they felt they were trapped in a web. And so these researchers put their journey mapping interview guides aside and immersed themselves in the perspective that made sense to the women they were studying. Being willing to "drop your tools," as our Darden colleague Lynn Isabella describes it, when they aren't a fit for the job at hand, is critical.

Go local. When in doubt (and in this uncertain world, you *should* be in doubt), go to the source. Find the locals who are actually doing the work, and seek their observations. Invite them to define the problem, rather than specifying problem definitions and solutions for them. Better yet, give them the infrastructure support to do the work themselves.

Be willing to wallow. Be willing to hold off on solutions and stay in the question **What *is*?** Be willing to feel overwhelmed by your data, and then be patient with yourself as you look for patterns. Few things are harder for action-oriented people. This process can seem inefficient and frustrating, but if solving messy human problems were easy, you wouldn't be reading this book.

Drill down to what matters most. Make the hard choices about what to pay attention to. A quote from Antoine de Saint-Exupéry, of *The Little Prince* fame, says it best: "Perfection is achieved not when nothing else can be added but when nothing else can be taken away." Creating a long list of design criteria is easy; narrowing it down to the essentials that matter is hard. But that is where the payoffs of focus, alignment, and engagement come in.

When Asking What *if*?

Work the tensions between seemingly opposing goals. At its best, design thinking identifies the trade-offs that stakeholders are forced to accept and comes up with higher-order solutions that turn trade-offs into opportunities. So don't accept compromises too early. Reach for the new possibilities that puncture trade-offs. Maybe later you will find that an ideal solution isn't possible, but if you start out believing this, your chances of getting somewhere truly new are zero.

Stop searching for the silver bullet. What is the difference between the possibility-driven search that breaks trade-offs and a nonexistent silver bullet? Mostly hard work. The search for a silver bullet seeks the perfect answer to complex problems, and we easily become discouraged when it doesn't become evident. Simple solutions that work for messy problems rarely show up. More complicated ones evolve during concept development.

Look for analogies, connections, and new combinations. Find different angles to look at the challenge and different ways of connecting ideas into bigger-picture, more systemic possibilities for change. Look for inspiration outside of your box. "Great artists steal," as the saying goes. Get to work on that (but give credit when you succeed).

Think of constraints as triggers, not stop signs. Overcoming barriers that others have accepted is often the route to creative solutions. It's fun to create new ideas, and so we focus on the importance of creative *answers*, but creatively *end-running constraints* to bring a new idea into reality is often more important.

Remember that small is beautiful. In a world where we are constantly exhorted to think big and strategically, to try to be "disruptive" in our approach, don't be afraid to head the other direction. The journey to best can start with better.

When Asking What *wows*?

Make it visual, visceral, or tangible. Build rough prototypes so that others can see, identify with, and build on your ideas. Put a spark in their brains so that they can co-create better solutions with you.

Actively seek bad news. We rarely overcome obstacles we haven't noticed. Once we enter testing, the sooner we acknowledge problems with new ideas, the sooner we can iterate to solve them, or the more quickly we can reduce risk in innovation by shelving weak concepts. Hearing that your baby is ugly—or even calling it ugly yourself—is hard, but necessary.

Focus on do-or-die assumptions. Testing takes time and energy, so deal with crucial assumptions first. These are usually related to value—and be sure to include value to all of the stakeholders whose support you need, not just users. You may save yourself the wasted effort of dealing with assumptions that don't matter anyway.

When Asking What works?

Harness the power of emptiness. Hold workshops instead of meetings—everyone wants to be part of a work in process—and let your stakeholders tell you what features your idea needs or doesn't need. Don't let your prototype look or feel as refined or polished as a dress rehearsal.

Worry about engaging, not convincing. Though it's difficult for most of us to avoid, stop trying to sell or defend your choices. Let your stakeholders fill the blank spaces with their ideas and insights. Tell your story—then let others reshape it. Maybe you've arrived at a great idea, but without others believing they had a part in the idea, it likely won't succeed. Take stakeholders to the water, but let them decide how much, and when, to drink. Help people find themselves in the new future. We'll repeat Eli's great advice one more time: buy-in comes when people see themselves in your offering.

Managing the Tensions

Our journey into design thinking has led us to believe that succeeding at it is ultimately about managing a set of tensions. We would like to see them go away, but giving these tensions thoughtful attention every day is more the reality of the life of a committed design thinker.

Here are our favorite strategies for your consideration. We are sure you will develop some of your own!

Stay in the question AND **have a bias for action**. Staying in the question isn't an excuse for endless theorizing that gets you stuck in the problem; having a bias for action doesn't mean rushing to solutions. Our approach to understanding the problem during **What *is*** is action based; our approach to understanding **What *works*** is based on thoughtful experimental design.

Love both the George AND **the Geoffrey in yourself and others**. Both have an important role to play in innovation. We need both dreamers and skeptics, so work as hard to develop empathy for the colleagues who drive you crazy as you do for the stakeholders you serve.

Have a plan AND **feel free to toss it out**. Plan the project and a pathway to it, but remember to be flexible as new information arises. This whole journey is about learning—but in a disciplined way. There are no "right" answers, just steps that advance, or don't advance, the efforts to meet your stakeholders' needs.

Immerse AND **detach**. The best ideas come to those prepared to wallow in the **What *is*?** question and to immerse themselves in the functional and emotional needs of their key stakeholders at the front end of the design process. But when we enter testing, we must be careful not to let our own emotions blind us to the reality of our solutions' ability to meet those stakeholders' needs, instead of the needs of our own ego. When we fall in love with our own ideas, our investment in personal ego can easily trump our investment in meeting client needs. Success in testing is about finding our inner scientist—a steely-eyed investigator of the truth, detached from any ego investment in the idea.

Give tools AND **rules**. We need rules for how we talk, and tools to see what solutions may be possible. We don't need rules to tell people what to do, or conversations that run amok, without structure or coherence.

Pay attention to the big picture AND **the little picture**. Peter Senge reminds us that we should consider the whole system—the big picture—to change the world. But, as Luigi Ferrara of IwB cautions, we also need to pay attention to the details. This moving back and forth between the abstract and the particulars is one of design's great strengths. Take advantage of it.

Where Do We Go from Here?

Or, as our Monash colleagues put it, "What *next*?"

By drawing attention to this fifth question, Monash underlines the point that change is the only constant and that the organization that settles into the status quo in this era of powerful uncertainties faces risks from inaction that may well be more significant than the risks of taking action. The old axiom "If it ain't broke, don't fix it" might have worked well in stable times, but today it endangers an organization that can't create new ideas or get them off the back burner because of internal politics or overworked staff. With futurists noting that the explosive growth in artificial intelligence has made the old "smart" into the new "stupid," many are arguing that mankind needs a stronger commitment to being human than ever before—to embrace humility, empathy, and human communication. The ability to explore deeply, empathize continually, ideate rapidly, prototype simply, and iterate constantly is what matters. These actions lie at the heart of design thinking and its contribution.

As we began this journey together, we argued that design thinking is following a path blazed decades ago by the quality movement—that design thinking could play the role in the innovation movement that Total Quality Management played in quality. Quality was eventually integrated into the fabric of organizations and simply became their way of doing business; quality became everyone's job. With the deeply wicked problems facing us today, particularly in the social sector, our future depends on making innovation the same kind of core competency, on combining the best of George's analytical thinking with the best of Geoffrey's creative ideas, to create the kinds of conversations that catalyze change, that democratize innovation, that invite everyone to be part of the process.

In talking about what he learned as a community organizer in Chicago, Barack Obama commented, "Change only happens when ordinary people get involved, get engaged, and come together to demand it . . . Show up. Dive in. Stay at it."

NOTES

CHAPTER THREE

44 **circles of influence and control** Stephen Covey, *The 7 Habits of Highly Effective People* (New York: Simon & Schuster, 1989).

53 **"I think . . . to solve!"** Laura Prestia, "An Alum's Perspective on the Ignite Accelerator," HHS IDEA Lab blog, October 7, 2015, http://www.hhs.gov/idealab/2015/10/07/alums-perspective-ignite-accelerator.

55 **"Ignite gave . . . promote innovation."** Prestia, "An Alum's Perspective." The final pitch is at HHS Idea Lab, "Illuminating the Technology Transfer Path: HHS Ignite Demo Day (04/23/2015)" (video), YouTube.com, published June 12, 2015, https://www.youtube.com/watch?v=-D1Vo5Y8Gn4.

58 **creative confidence is defined** Ben Grossman-Kahn, "Defining Creative Confidence," OpenIDEO, September 18, 2013, https://challenges.openideo.com/challenge/creative-confidence/inspiration/defining-creative-confidence.

CHAPTER FOUR

62   **"One of the most urgent . . . support."** John Donvan and Caren Zucker, "Five Tips for Candidates Who Want to Talk About Autism—Responsibly," *Washington Post*, February 11, 2016, https://www.washingtonpost.com/opinions/here-is-the-conversation-candidates-should-be-having-about-autism/2016/02/11/19d208b0-cb49-11e5-a7b2-5a2f824b02c9_story.html.

62   **"there were probably . . . priority."** Dame Stephanie Shirley with Richard Askwith, *Let IT Go: The Story of the Entrepreneur Turned Ardent Philanthropist* (Luton: Andrews UK, 2012).

CHAPTER TEN

184   **"When we criticize . . . thorough."** Ashley Halsey III, "TSA Struggles with Balancing Speed and Security at Airport Checkpoints," *Washington Post*, May 12, 2016, https://www.washingtonpost.com/local/trafficandcommuting/tsa-struggles-with-balancing-speed-and-security-at-airport-checkpoints/2016/05/12/615ccdbe-1860-11e6-924d-838753295f9a_story.html.

185   **"Two million . . . working together."** Kip Hawley, "Welcome," *The TSA Blog*, January 30, 2008, http://blog.tsa.gov/2008/01/welcome.html.

186   **"The transformational . . . and passengers."** IDEO, "TSA Checkpoint Evolution for Transportation Security Administration: Improving Airport Security through Human-Centered Design," accessed August 18, 2016, https://www.ideo.com/work/tsa-checkpoint-evolution.

197   **"We continue . . . top priority."** Ben Mutzabaugh, "TSA Takes to Facebook Messenger to Answer Fliers' Questions," *USA Today*, July 7, 2016, http://www.usatoday.com/story/travel/flights/todayinthesky/2016/07/07/tsa-takes-facebook-messenger-answer-fliers-questions/86762580.

198   **"It also . . . its image"; on Instagram** Lori Aratani, "An Unlikely Star of Instagram: Airport Security," *Washington Post*, November 28, 2016, A3.

199   **"The crunch . . . five-year low."** Jennifer Scholtes, "TSA Airport Lines: Chronicle of a Mess Foretold," *Politico*, May 27, 2016, http://www.politico.com/story/2016/05/tsa-airport-long-lines-223666.

CHAPTER THIRTEEN

252 **"Every Gateway . . . caring adults."** Gateway to College National Network, "Who We Serve," accessed February 20, 2017, http://www.gatewaytocollege.org/who-we-serve.html.

CHAPTER FOURTEEN

283 **playgrounds, not dress rehearsals** Michael Schrage, *Serious Play: How the World's Best Companies Simulate to Innovate* (Boston, MA: Harvard Business School Press, 2000), 169–71.

CHAPTER FIFTEEN

299 **One popular theory of how change occurs** Richard Beckhard (originally published in *Sloan Management Review*, 1975), citing David Gleicher; quoted in Steven H. Cady, Robert "Jake" Jacobs, Ron Koller, and John Spalding, "The Change Formula: Myth, Legend, or Lore?" *OD Practitioner* 46, no. 3 (2014), 32–39.

302 **Recent research illustrates clearly** David Colander and Roland Kupers, *Complexity and the Art of Public Policy: Solving Society's Problems from the Bottom Up* (Princeton, NJ: Princeton University Press, 2014).

316 **mankind needs a stronger commitment** Edward D. Hess and Katherine Ludwig, *Humility Is the New Smart: Rethinking Human Excellence in the Smart Machine Age* (Oakland, CA: Berrett-Koehler, 2017).

INDEX